CHOCKS AWAY!

CHOCKS AWAY!

ROGER A. FREEMAN

CASSELL&CO

Special edition for PAST TIMES

Cassell & Co
Wellington House, 125 Strand
London WC2R OBB

First published by Arms and Armour 1989 as
Experiences of War: The British Airman
This edition 2000

ISBN 0-304-35631-X

9 8 7 6 5 4 3 2 1

Designed and edited by DAG Publications Ltd
Printed and bound in Great Britain by
Cox & Wyman, Reading

PAST TIMES

Contents

Acknowledgements

A full list of the contributors whose names appear adjacent to their quotations in the narrative is to be found at the end of this book. To meet the aim of this work, ranks are omitted and it is hoped that this is not seen as disrespect, for some contributors rose to high rank. The book exists solely through the interest and willingness of these contributors' co-operation, to whom I tender my sincere thanks.

Acknowledgement is also made to Michael Bowyer, David Brook, Frank Cheesman, Alan East, Eric Munday, Dave Osborne, Merle Olmsted, John Rabbetts, Nat Young; to Ian Mactaggart and George Pennick for photographic expertise, to Bruce Robertson for editorial guidance, and Jean Freeman for preparing the manuscript.

Roger A. Freeman, 1989

Introduction

The forties were a very different world – a cliché, yes; but certainly that time *was* different in many important respects. Then, British youth were more disciplined, respectful and patriotic than their counterparts half a century on. Their experience was parochial and knowledge of other nations restricted to school geography lessons. No package holidays then to sunny climes, for foreign journeying was limited by expense and difficulties of travel. The working man spent his holidays at the 'seaside' if he could afford even that luxury. Most were paid literally by the hour, which meant no wages for holiday weeks, and short weekly pay at Christmas or when Bank Holidays occurred. Pre-war life was simpler and expectations modest. No television, washing-machines, refrigerator or vacuum cleaner, advances then only within the financial reach of the better or well off.

A semi-detached house, small car and white collar job might evaluate one to 'middle class' standing, but not to the aforementioned luxuries that would one day be deemed as essentials of domestic comfort. The divisions of class were also much more pronounced, largely allied to income. A factory worker would have rented terraced accommodation in the town; perhaps two up, two down, with a sewered lavatory in the backyard. A farm labourer might enjoy a large garden, but he often lived without benefit of electricity and piped water, which had still to reach many outlying rural areas; a flush lavatory was rare in those localities. In short, the industrial and agricultural developments that gradually elevated the ordinary person to the comparative affluence of the 1980s were at an early stage. What people did not have, they did not know. Life was generally harder; daily working hours longer and Saturday morning part of the working week, domestic chores harder, with less time for leisure.

Although there was more of a 'them' and 'us' atmosphere in the British society of 1939, national patriotism was not bounded by class. The menace of Nazi Germany was met with the same determination to support King and Country in a humble cottage as in a stately mansion. A conditioning in the glories of Empire was chiefly responsible for the common belief that Britain was still the greatest nation, whose values and traditions placed it head and shoulder above the rest. So when war was declared and something had to be done about Hitler there already existed an intrinsic sense of duty. For the majority it was unthinkable not to fight for one's country. Even the slaughter on the Western Front, not yet a quarter of a century removed, could have a dampening effect on patriotism. Perhaps fathers who had experienced the bitter taste of trench warfare were not enthused to encourage sons, but most did not dissuade. The tyranny and the threat to democracy of the Nazi regime, as projected by newspaper and radio, was accepted. The citizen was ready to become a warrior once more.

In the conflict of arms known as the Second World War, military aviation has been authoritatively assessed as making a decisive contribution to the Allied victory. The United Kingdom's participation in what was commonly called the air war was on a considerable scale relative to its total war effort, almost a half of armed forces expenditure. Of this only 10 per cent was invested in the Royal Navy's largely seaborne Fleet Air Arm, while the lion's share went to the Royal Air Force, the world's first fully autonomous military flying service.

The RAF had been formed on 1 April 1918 by amalgamating the Army's Royal Flying Corps with the Navy's Royal Naval Air Service. Aviation technology, then in its infancy, led to the military value of the aeroplane being questioned by the majority of conventional force commanders and strategists. Overall, in the first decade following the Great War, the RAF was adjudged a useful adjunct to the Army and Navy, particularly handy in far-flung corners of the Empire for 'showing the Flag' and policing the natives. To those who wore its blue uniform it was a pretty nice service to be in - and great fun if you were a flier. Air power remained largely a word in the vocabulary of theorists.

The slaughter of the Great War had left a heavy scar on national attitudes. Few families did not have a member who knew the horror of the ground fighting, while every village War Memorial bore witness to the scale of the sacrifice. Another conflict of that nature was to be avoided, and, while the general outlook was not pacifist, there was a turning away from the military at many levels. It was supposed that the German population, their economy in chaos, were likewise imbued with a 'never again' outlook. Even when the National Socialists offered to restore German pride, the leaders of most other European nations did not at first see this as a threat to peace. And when they did, appeasement appears to have been the favoured ploy to buy time.

In Germany the revived military were quick to embrace technology as a means of ensuring better equipment and ordnance, not least in the air. The tool of trade of an air force was the aeroplane and with the encouragement of the Nazi hierarchy the drive to develop aircraft more advanced than those of other European neighbours was pressed with vigour. Belatedly the British and the French moved to re-equip and expand their air forces, but not with the required expediency; there was still a belief that the gathering storm would pass by. As a result, the German Luftwaffe's equipment was in many respects superior to that of the RAF when war was declared on 3 September 1939. The Luftwaffe was also better trained for its task - primarily, tactical support of the ground forces. It would take the RAF months in some respects and years in others to achieve parity. The RAF, both leaders and men, believed they were more than a match for the enemy air force and, after costly experience, this eventually proved to be the case. Because of technical and tactical weaknesses, that success was achieved with heavy loss of lives. In retrospect there appears to have been a degree of tardiness in some areas in pushing the development of new aircraft, engines, armament and equipment, for technology should have been recognized as being of major importance in achieving the superiority that would lead to victory. This is not to underestimate the difficulties of making up for years of neglect.

What then of the ordinary men and women who made up the Royal Air Force and who often did not recognize their own part in any grand strategic plan or tactical move, but carried out the orders of Command, performed their duties, and lived or died? On the pages that follow I have set out to record the experiences of some of those who survived and through their words to evoke an expression of service life during the most extensive clash of arms in history. In recounting these events, attitudes, motivations, fears, hopes and many other aspects of individual expression are revealed, helping to convey something of the feel and flavour of RAF life in those days. Only the war with Nazi Germany and its European allies is covered in this work; the RAF in the Far East is to be the subject of a later volume.

Roger A. Freeman

Sprogs

JOINING UP

'I don't want to join the Air Force
I don't want to go to war
I'd rather hang around
Piccadilly Underground
And live upon the earnings of a high-born lady. . . .'

This well-known ditty rang out in many a Royal Air Force Mess during the war years, but it did not reflect the truth. Young men did want to join the Air Force, thousands of them. Aircrew were only drawn from volunteers and there were always more men who wanted to fly than the force could absorb. The disappointed usually opted for ground duties with the hope that one day their desire to become aircrew could be realized. Not that there was a dearth of recruits for non-flying duties. The RAF was also the first choice of the majority of conscripts.

Most young men who wanted to 'do their bit' and had family traditions of the Army and Navy were understandably drawn to those services. For many others who were reasonably well educated, in particular the ex-grammar-school boys, the RAF seemed to offer more interesting prospects, a developing form of warfare dependent on the latest technology and more fitting to the intelligent. And the RAF did require a good standard of education for the majority of duties in almost every operational branch of the service. Fred Lomas has no doubts about its popularity among his school friends:

'From my secondary school over half the boys who reached military age during the war went into the RAF. There seemed much more glamour attached to flying than there was to the work of the other services. We had our own Air Training Corps squadron at the school and if you joined you were pretty sure to be accepted for the RAF when you volunteered at 18. The appeal also lay in the more personal *esprit de corps* of flying units where it was you, or you and a few other chaps, alone in one aircraft. This was something conveyed by those who had joined up at the beginning of the war and who often came back to the school when on leave. I also estimate that of those from my school who went into the RAF and flew, about 80 per cent became casualties.'

The 'adventure of flying' angle is well represented by the desire of Jim Betteridge:

'I joined because I fancied myself as Biggles. Those stories inspired a lot of young fellows to want to fly. They certainly made me air-minded and in turn had inspired me to join the Air Defence Cadet Corps, forerunner of the Air Training Corps, and Air League in 1938. The latter was an organization set up to promote British aviation when it became apparent that we were lagging behind that of other nations during the mid-thirties.'

There were, however, many and varied individual reasons for joining the 'Raf'. Not a few young men saw it as an escape from a low standard of living and poor accommodation. Eddie Wheeler:

'By 18 I had outgrown my fold-up bed located in the tiny kitchen at home, and this became more problematic as time went on – bouts of cramp became more prevalent. It was at the cinema one evening that I saw George Formby in *Something in the Air* and immediately I felt convinced that my salvation could be in joining the RAF – if only to get a bed large enough to accommodate me without doubling my knees with ensuing cramp!'

For some a choice of uniform was important. It hung on one item of clothing for Alfred Jenner:

'When war looked highly likely, if not inevitable, the patriotic thing to do was join the Territorials or a reserve organization: so I joined the RAFVR (RAF Volunteer Reserve). My choice was based on the fact that the RAF was the only one of the three services where the lower ranks wore ties. I was called the day after war was declared and spent the next few weeks at Padgate in what was known as "square bashing". Not only were there no ties but no uniforms available for my intake. Instead we drilled in the civilian clothes in which we arrived. Unfortunately, in my case this included a pair of plus-fours which were then a fashion for the well decked out young man about the provincial town. The drill sergeant thought otherwise, particularly as the elastic which was supposed to retain each leg of the garment neatly beneath the knee proved too weak for the job. One or other was frequently flapping around an ankle when we marked time or drilled at the double. His remarks became more pointed and coarse as the days went by and it was with great relief that uniforms were at last received. These turned out to be old-style twenties uniforms with a high button tunic – and no tie!'

Others who were attracted by the uniform also saw the RAF as more accommodating to their way of life. Bill Japp:

'I think I volunteered for aircrew for a host of wrong reasons. A new airfield, Edzell, had been opened in 1940 near my home and my parents became friendly with the station commander. Then, at 17 I was given the occasional flight in an Anson or Dominie and was much influenced by what I observed around the station. I liked the uniform and fancied the idea of silken wings on my breast. Then too, it appeared to offer an easier way of service; bacon and eggs for breakfast, clean sheets on your bed, more gentlemanly conduct. There was no deep reasoning behind the decision to volunteer; no fire in my belly to fly as some fellows I met claimed to have.'

Patriotism was the principal spur to volunteering for military service, although such action was sometimes encouraged by the looming presence of conscription when one might not be able to join the service of one's choice. It was known that the army claimed most conscripts, and for many young men influenced by fathers and relations who had survived the horrors of infantry trench warfare in 1914-18, the prospect was undesirable. Particularly so during the 1939-40 'phoney war' period when the stalemate of static warfare appeared to be about to repeat itself. The army was also considered the dumping ground for ignoramuses and the uncouth element of society. If you aspired to better company the RAF appeared a safer bet. This, perhaps false, but widely shared belief, sometimes found endorsement through personal experience; as in the case of John Sampson:

'I was 17 years of age and in the Home Guard. One evening in the summer of 1940 we were being taught the rudiments of bayonet fighting by a sergeant in the Coldstream Guards. We had to rush across an open piece of ground with an ancient American Springfield rifle and stick the bayonet into a sack filled with straw, shouting as loud as we could during the process. I thought I had done quite well until the sergeant bawled at me, "Don't stand there like a pregnant nun." In that instant I decided the army was not for me and volunteered for aircrew duty with the RAF.'

The desire to fly remained the principal aim of volunteers throughout hostilities, with pilot being the most sought after position. On average, of every fifteen men who applied for pilot training only one was accepted. And only 60 per cent of volunteers passed muster at aircrew selection boards. Some individuals went to great lengths to be accepted. Bob Thompson was one:

'At the beginning of the war I was working in Birmingham and decided to give up my job and fly with the RAF come what may. I went to the local recruiting office and in due course got a letter telling me to report to Padgate for an aircrew selection board. There I was confronted with a group of senior RAF officers all decked out in their best and rather intimidating. The first question asked me was: "Why do you want to take up this dangerous occupation?" Well, I wasn't very good at the King and Country lark and was absolutely floored. I didn't know what to say. The interview floundered on and at the end they said they didn't think I was suitable for flying duties but they could find me a ground place. I said, "No thank you, I've set my heart on flying." I went away absolutely desolate, the bottom had fallen out of my world. After a few days I thought I'd have another go. So I went over to Sunderland to an aunt and asked if I could give her address if I went to the local recruiting office. She agreed and so I applied and received notice of another interview, this time at Cardington. Here again I was confronted with an intimidating row of officers. However, their questions took a different line. They opened with: "You're a healthy looking fellow, how do you keep so fit?" There couldn't have been a better question for I was able to say sailing, rugger and all the sports in which the type of blokes they were looking for would indulge. I was accepted.'

Even when they liked the look of you there was still the stiff medical to get through. A sturdy young man was demolished on learning he had a minor eyesight or hearing defect that immediately took him out of the running. In a few tests one's performance during the medical could be enhanced; as in George Irving's case:

'Enlisted for flying duties as a navigator, I was instructed to attend an interview and medical at Padgate on 2 November 1940. During the interview I stressed that I would make a much better pilot than navigator and although at the age of 28 I was on the maximum age limit for acceptance for training as a pilot, they agreed to give me the opportunity subject to passing the medical. The medical was very thorough, one of the tests was blowing into a little tube to hold a mercury level on the hundred scale mark and to maintain the pressure for at least fifty seconds. Being very determined not to fail I held on until I almost blacked out. The doctor was obviously impressed because he said I held the record to date by holding for 95 seconds.'

There was another feature of all Selection Board medicals which, although simple, gave many a problem. Jim Eley:

'As was usual, I was required to give a urine sample. When I couldn't, the official said, "I expect you were like all the others and "went" before you came in." I was given a drink of water and made to stand barefoot on a cold stone slab until I could "go".'

A bar to volunteering for military service was employment in a reserved occupation. In most cases this did not apply to aircrew acceptance which brought some men into the ranks of the RAF who had previously held other ambitions. John Osborne:

'I was a sergeant in the Home Guard and fancied army service. I was dead keen to get into the Reconnaissance Corps – armoured cars and light tanks – which had just been formed when I became old enough to volunteer in 1942. So I went along to the Recruiting Office and signed up, only to have my boss call me aside a few days later to tell me he had heard from the army but was holding my reserved occupation for 12 months – we were making alkathene parts for radars. Well, I wasn't very pleased. So, knowing he could not reserve me if I volunteered and was accepted for aircrew. I took the afternoon off and did just that.'

For non-aircrew, even acceptance into the RAF and partial training did not ensure continued service in a blue uniform. In the last two years of hostilities many hundreds of recently conscripted RAF personnel were transferred to the other services for various reasons. Jim Eley:

'While taking a 12-week Morse course at Blackpool, we were told that those who obtained the required speed would be transferred to the navy which was short of trained wireless operators. Wanting to keep one foot on dry land, I purposely failed the test. However, my time in the RAF was short-lived because soon after completing training I was told I was being transferred to the army who were in dire need of W/T operators. At the Huyton transit camp I met blokes who had been with me on the original course and had been sent to the navy. Apparently the army's need became greater than the navy's so they were transferred again. In the course of nine months they had worn three different uniforms!'

On the other hand the RAF received several trained fitters and riggers from the Fleet Air Arm as the navy had too many. The RAF also recruited army personnel as aircrew for army co-operation units. Rex Croger was an artillery officer who made the transfer following an earlier and unusual association with the Air Force:

'I was looking through ACIs (Army Council Instructions) which every army officer was supposed to read, when I saw a request for commissioned artillery officers to volunteer to fly with the RAF as air gunners. I thought it sounded interesting and decided to have a go. The job entailed a course of training in air gunnery, following which I flew on a single Nickel (leaflet) raid over Lille in a Wellington on the night of 5 April 1942. Seated in the front turret, I had a box-like instrument on my knees to watch for variations of the indicator in a dial while over enemy territory. The purpose was to discover if the Germans were using a specific form of radar. I was never quite sure why Ack-Ack (anti-aircraft) officers were chosen for the task. Thereafter I was one of a few army officers sporting an air gunner's wing on my tunic. Some months after returning to my searchlight unit I saw another ACI which announced that army officers could volunteer for pilot service with the RAF in army co-operation squadrons. Evidently at that time they anticipated a pilot shortage. Having enjoyed my brief period as an air gunner I decided to apply. No doubt the previous air experience helped, for I was accepted immediately. They never transferred me to the RAF; I was just seconded, despite receiving an RAF number and taking RAF uniform and rank.'

There were, of course, adventurers, perhaps the most notable being those foreign nationals who clamoured to join; albeit that they felt the cause was just – Nazi Germany was a tyranny that had to be countered. However, the primary motivation for volunteering to fly for the British was the attraction of the 'derring-do' of the fighter pilot, as established by the air aces of the First World War twenty years before. Practically all fancied themselves in the cockpit of a Spitfire. This enthusiasm is well illustrated by the intentions of James Goodson:

'Having survived the torpedoing of the *Athenia* on her fatal western voyage soon after the outbreak of war. I eventually ended up in Glasgow. Not being very pleased with the people who had tried to confine me to the deep, I sought out a recruiting office. The recruiting sergeant was at a loss what to do when confronted by an American who wanted to join the RAF. After a telephone call to a superior he informed me that he thought it would be all right but I would have to swear allegiance to the Crown. I said that wasn't going to be a problem. He then handed me a form and proceeded to outline a few details of what was expected if I were accepted. All seemed simple until he said: "It will be three shillings a day." A quick bit of mental calculation transformed this sum into five US dollars a week. Crestfallen, I stammered, "I don't think I can afford that." He looked at me a little strangely before replying, "Well, that's what the pay will be." Of course, I didn't tell him I thought he was asking me for three shillings a day or my delight at attaining my fondest dream. To think I could join the RAF and fly a fighter plane while actually being paid for doing it! The lovable fools, they could have had my services for nothing!'

Goodson was successful and eventually joined the ranks of one of the three 'Eagle' squadrons, units specially raised to embrace the considerable number of Americans who joined the RAF. Young men from many other neutral countries also joined and flew for Britain, but not in such numbers as those from the USA to warrant special squadrons.

INITIAL TRAINING

Whether you had volunteered or been conscripted, leaving the shelter of the family home to report to an RAF reception centre was, for the majority of young men and women, a step into the unknown, and one faced with concern. The experience of Don Nunn is not untypical:

'Like most 18-year-old recruits I was a bit apprehensive on first reporting to Lord's cricket ground, the London reception centre for aircrew. But it wasn't quite the awesome experience expected. Turning in my civilian belongings I got my first lesson in service dodges. As each ration book was surrendered the reception clerks slyly flipped through and removed any still valid coupons. These were obviously being secreted away for personal use. They may have eaten well but, like the rest of the intake that day, all I got was a plate of soup. Lord's was not quite the harsh regime I'd imagined. In the following days I was even able to sit in the Members' Stand and watch a game. A somewhat incongruous scene as next to we young boys in blue there was a bunch of old gents sipping G & Ts and occasionally applauding; all as if the war had never happened.'

The transition from civil to military life was a rude awakening for many youngsters, particularly girls with a refined background. Maureen Brickett found it an almost traumatic experience:

'The shock horror of my first few days in the WAAF are a lasting memory – having been educated in a Convent where Modesty was the eleventh commandment, I joined RAF Innsworth near Gloucester on November 13th 1941. Our first bitterly cold night in a Nissen hut ended with a "march" to the ablution block a hundred yards or so away in temperatures below zero – standing in the icy concrete shed faced with a long line of wash basins and only cold water and confronted with hardier types stripped naked, I nearly died with embarrassment! I don't think I really washed for a week, just kept sprinkling the talcum powder! When I eventually discovered a bath and hot water, I thought I was in heaven!!!'

Men accepted for aircrew usually spent a few days being processed; which simply meant collecting kit and an introduction to the preliminaries of military drill, while somewhere clerks found an establishment where each newcomer could be sent for initial training. Those destined for non-flying duties generally reported to one of the larger basic training establishments such as Padgate or Cardington where discipline and drill were endured for eight weeks. 'Short back and sides' removed the last vestige of civilian status, as Martin Mason discovered:

'Reporting to the recruit depot at Padgate in July 1940, I spent ten days being fitted out with uniform and having endless inoculations before being posted to a new station, RAF Kirkham, near Preston. Young men took a pride in keeping their hair trim, attending the barber every two or three weeks, but there was no opportunity for me to get a short back and sides at Padgate and Kirkham lacked a barber. The authorities were aware of the problem but had difficulty obtaining the services of a civilian barber. It wasn't until a Sunday morning that one arrived to shear us. A queue of possibly fifty new recruits soon formed. The barber, seeing the daunting task ahead, worked at prodigious speed with his electric shears so that by the time each man was clipped the tail end of the queue was still moving forward to take up the slack resulting from his move into the chair. The effect was that the queue seemed to be constantly moving forward. I, and most of the others, had the quickest haircut of our lives.'

And then there was the uniform. A recruit did not really feel part of the Air Force until he or she had donned the distinctive blue. At the start of the war a male recruit eventually received two No. 1 Dress uniforms, of which one was kept for parades and walking out – 'Best Blues'. Later, one set was replaced with a No. 2 uniform, a blue version of the army 'battledress', and this was used for everyday wear. The initial decking-out would be followed by variations as desired by different branches of the service. Ernest Thorpe had some pertinent observations on dress:

'The war "respectabilized" uniform. Before, if a girl was seen with an airman there was the comment: "Fancy that; well I never." But with dear Uncle George in uniform all this changed. As a member of the RAF Regiment from its inception, I became well aware of the importance of uniform. Uniform dictated who you saluted and who gave the order, "Right dress!"

'With our usual Air Force uniform we were first issued with peaked caps. Our sergeant referred to us as his "bus drivers". We were glad when these were discarded in favour of side caps. Some wore these at an extremely jaunty angle, presenting balancing difficulties. The Air Force pullover, very durable, was often worn in bed for warmth – and I only saw one instance of an airman wearing pyjamas persistently in the worst conditions.

'Our underpants were heavy, knee-length drawers, button-up fronts with brace loops; the male equivalent of the "passion-killers" that WAAFs were reputed to wear. For our shirts, some bought Van Heusen collars as they were smarter, softer and more comfortable; illegal, as was another practice of widening the rather narrow trouser bottoms of the "best blues". This was achieved by putting inverted Vs in the bottom of the seams, giving a slightly flared look. A civilian tailor in Hythe would carry out this work, always sounding us out on the probability of an "invasion", he being a Jew. As the alterations were frowned upon by the "powers that were", we had to take evasive action when sighting RAF Police.

'Providing one was wearing the correct uniform, smartness was encouraged. There was a practice of "stick" man. The smartest man on parade would be excused the guard. A reservist named Parker was always our "stick" man. But he was also a bit of a rebel and they eventually posted him to the Middle East.

'In 1941 I was pleased to make the transition to khaki with more comfortable battledress blouse and the blue boiler suit fatigue dress replaced with khaki denims. Later on, after being on a motor vehicle driver's course, with the usual service cussedness I was given a motor cycle. Breeches and dispatch-rider boots, waterproof jacket and leggings, were topped off by a hated crash-helmet which seemed to be made of papier mâché. How we appreciated civilian clothes when on leave!'

There were few women who were completely happy with all items of the WAAF uniform which, basically functional, gave little acknowledgement to current feminine fashions. At least the issue was plentiful, something which impressed Irene Storer:

'In 1940 there were so many of us that the supply of uniforms ran out and I was issued with two navy overalls, a navy beret and a grey raincoat with an armband. Later on I was issued with proper uniform and received the following: 4 shirts, very roomy in smooth cotton poplin, blue; 8 separate matching collars; 1 black tie; 2 air force blue serge skirts and jackets, both unlined; 2 caps; 1 cap badge; 2 pairs black flat lace-up shoes; 3 wool vests; 2 suspender belts, old-fashioned pink corset fabric about 6 inches deep; 4 bras, same fabric as suspender belts; 4 pairs heavyweight grey lisle stockings; 6 pairs wool winter knickers, black; 6 pairs wool summer knickers, grey, and 1 pair plimsolls. I had never had so many clothes in my life! The greatcoat was double-breasted with a cream woollen lining, but I did not receive one until December 1940.

'The only scope for any measure of individuality was in underwear, and as service underwear was reminiscent of 1914 these were the garments we tried to substitute – with difficulty without clothing coupons. I appreciated the bras and suspender belts, having previously had to wear an uncomfortable corselet; but the knickers were really awful! The only difference between the summer and winter ones was the colour – the winter ones being called "blackouts" after the fabric used to black out windows. A favourite practical joke was to raise a pair of blackouts on a flagpole! I continued to wear my own panties until they needed replacing, when I made some from whatever fabric was available. Petticoats were not issued, and as the serge skirts were rough, many service women made petticoats from cut down nightdresses, old evening dress fabric, or parachute silk – but one could be punished for using the latter. Service women were permitted to wear their own stockings if they were of regulation colour.'

Following reception some recruits found themselves quickly moved on to what, compared with the civilian life they had just left, were primitive conditions. Rumour, that persistent service infection, sometimes voiced a suspicion of exploitation. Albert Benest:

'After reporting to the Air Crew Reception Centre at Lord's cricket ground in London, I was sent to Ludlow in Shropshire. This was really no more than a staging camp until they had sorted out where we were to be sent for basic training. We had to live in bell-tents surrounded by mud, with which we fought a losing battle to keep it from our brand-new uniforms and equipment. It rained most of the time and to keep us occupied we were set to digging trenches which were then piped. The story that went around was that the ground was part of an estate owned by an Air Vice-Marshal who was taking advantage of the available labour to have some free drainage carried out.'

A recruit's early days in the RAF are well summed up in the experiences of James Donson who aspired to fly:

'One's memory of the early days of aircrew training is a hazy recollection of almost continuous movement from place to place – a gathering together process, a few days at one place where we got to know what a sergeant was; some perfunctory drill; inoculations, documentation; then on to somewhere a couple of hundred miles away; more documentation, then after a week or two making sure that we knew our own names and numbers. Sergeants and corporals had only ranks, they never seemed to have names; it gradually dawned on us that the fact was not surprising since, in the view of most erks, NCOs had no fathers. After what seemed an age (some three weeks) we were issued with uniforms. On then to Initial Training Wing (ITW) – yet another journey. When we arrived at our destination we found our HQ was a large comfortable seaside hotel on the Welsh coast equipped with wash-basins, baths, beds and proper loos, none of which any of us had seen since leaving home. We began to feel that at least for a time there would be respite from primitive, makeshift conditions. Life became a routine of early rising, PT, lectures, route marches and meals. Lectures on meteorology, navigation, signals, rules of the air, etc., always took place in rooms about a mile apart and we marched from one to the other in "flights" at the regulation 40 paces a minute. As yet, no one had seen an aeroplane at close quarters but we had a number of lectures on aircraft recognition, no doubt to lessen the shock when we would eventually see one.'

The rapid expansion of the RAF after the outbreak of war and the vast influx of new personnel during the early months, led to Training Command being reorganized as Flying Training and Technical Training. The pre-war facilities were swamped and the situation was met by taking over a wide variety of civilian properties, in particular hotel and holiday camp facilities in the large seaside towns. Although the rigours of 'drill' and 'bull' did not endear these early weeks of service to the participants, there were sometimes compensations. Peter Catchpole:

'One of the good things about the initial training at Blackpool was that at least once a week we were sent to the Derby Baths to swim. This vast place had been one of the pre-war attractions of Blackpool as a seaside holiday centre. About 500 air force fellows would descend on these baths at one time. Only about half had swimming-costumes or trunks, the rest swam nude. It was an eye-opener for an 18-year-old like me, who had led a fairly sheltered life before joining up, that there were so many differences in men; long fellers and short fellers, big fellers and embarrassed fellers. Guards were placed at each entrance to keep the locals out and to watch over our deposited rifles and equipment. However, we heard that the cleaning women who were supposedly kept away from the baths area while we were swimming, had made peepholes through doors and shutters and regularly enjoyed the spectacle.'

One soon learned that there was little regard for individual modesty. No problem if you had been a school boarder, but hard on those from a sheltered background or the self-conscious. There was one particular contact with the Medical Officer that no one liked. Ernest Thorpe:

'In retrospect, "flashing" to order in the "FFI" (Free From Infection) inspection was humorous, but not at the time. "When the MO comes to you, you will drop your pants." Embarrassing, degrading. I sometimes speculated inwardly as to whether the WAAFs were subjected to this ordeal.'

The conditioning programme to which all recruits were subjected had the aim of instilling discipline. Rigorous exercise, menial tasks and constant verbal persecution by the non-commissioned officers (NCOs) in charge was an unpleasant experience. One had to 'take it' for any individual who showed signs of rebelling was branded insubordinate and suffered greater indignities. The general resentment among recruits now and again produced subtle forms of retaliation. Cyril Clifford:

'My original trade was Service Police and in the winter of 1940 I was posted to No. 1 RAF Depot, Uxbridge, the home of "bull", to take a course. The police course was quite interesting and they made us feel the job was very necessary. The camp discipline, however, was very rigid and there seemed to be a senior NCO around every corner waiting to pounce on anyone who stepped off a path or had a button undone. Victims would find themselves in the cookhouse, after the day's lectures, cleaning out baking-tins, etc. Friday night was "bullshit" night when the barrack rooms were scrubbed and polished so vigorously that you could see your reflection in every surface. The Station Warrant Officer would come round inspecting, wipe his finger along the top of a door and, showing us three specks of dust, exclaim: "This place is not fit for pigs to live in!"

'The harsh regime was, understandably, resented although we had to accept it; but for a time we had our little dig at authority. There was a long path from the lecture rooms to the airmen's canteen. If someone saw an officer in the distance he would pass the word along and we would deliberately spread out in a long line so that the officer would have to return hundreds of smart salutes. After a while the authorities began to realize what was going on and we were ordered to form large squads and march between the locations.'

A more daring snub to authority is recalled by Ray Lomas:

'At University Air Squadron we progressed from basic drill to continuity drill. That is, the whole squad went through a drill routine without shouted commands for the series of movements. When the drill corporal shouted "Forward March" we carried on right the way through the routine, having memorized the changes. We reached a pretty good standard. After the UAS we all went to the Air Crew Reception Centre in London and suffered the usual chasing around new recruits had from the NCOs. Getting a bit fed-up with one particular corporal we got together and decided to bring him down a peg. The opportunity arose when we were out on the square in front of some officers. As soon as the corporal gave his first order we went into our continuity routine. It looked perfect to the watching officers but we were ignoring all the corporal's commands and putting on our own display. He was very quiet thereafter.'

An impromptu plot against the PT overseers is recounted by George Irving:

'Squads were marched down to Scarborough sea front where their sergeants could position themselves on the road above to roar out their orders. One morning it was very windy, the tide was in and the sea rough. The squad next to us was composed of "old-timers" who had been in the RAF prior to the war and had remustered for aircrew training. Their sergeant called out "Running time; begin!" so they jogged off along the sea front and appeared to be unable to hear the "About turn" order and just disappeared from sight before their rather red-faced sergeant could get down on the lower road. After calling in at a café for tea and buns, they reformed and jogged back through the town in immaculate formation. Their drill sergeant was very cross.'

Most of the haranguing from NCOs was impersonal but occasionally more direct animosity arose, usually where an individual confronted the authority of an NCO. One trainee who believed he was being singled out devised a novel way of hitting back.

James Donson:

'In order to collect fatigue parties to flatten all the food tins in which most of our rations came, the duty sergeant would find minor defects on daily inspections – like blankets not folded in creases or dust on the waste-pipe under the wash-basin and similar trifles. The occupants of the rooms in which such "unairmanlike slackness" occurred would be issued with 7-pound sledge-hammers for their evening task. One sergeant always seemed to pick on a particular trainee every time. On one occasion the trainee was prepared. When the sergeant stood over him, immaculate in his bearing and appearance, he edged a full tin of corned beef into his pile and brought down the sledge-hammer with full force on it. Smashed corned beef flew in all directions, most of it on the walls but some on the sergeant's immaculate uniform. There was an exchange of words, brief from the trainee, voluble from his tormentor.'

Later many of the sufferers came to realize that the dreaded NCOs of 'square-bashing' days had been encouraged by their superiors to behave in a hectoring fashion. An observation nicely summed-up by William Reid:

'When you were an AC Plonk doing your basic training, you always felt the PT corporals were such hard men. Yet when I met some of them later on they were really such nice fellows. You came to understand that all that shouting and discipline was a necessary part of the conditioning process so that an order was accepted without question.'

A facet of training days which few escaped was guard duty. This usually inflicted discomfort and boredom, although in Eddie Wheeler's first and only commitment to this role tedium was soon dispelled:

'A water-tower which supplied the Yatesbury camp was located on a hill surrounded by trees on the other side of the main road to Calne and was viewed as a potential target for saboteurs. Hence the necessity to mount a guard throughout 24 hours daily. My turn for guard duty on the water-tower arrived and the weather was foul, bucketting with rain, and I was assigned for night duty from 6pm to 6am next morning. The shifts were two hours on and two hours off, the rest period to be spent in a tent adjacent to the water-tower. Our Lee Enfield .303 rifles were issued by the sergeant of the guard and live ammunition seen for the first time. Two guards were to patrol round the tower, meeting each other at about 10-minute intervals. The usual challenge procedures were outlined by the sergeant. On approach to the tower persons were to be challenged: "Who goes there, friend or foe?" If no response, the challenge once again. After the second challenge if no reply, then fire!

'Patrolling at night in pouring rain – surrounded by trees – was the most soul-destroying job one can imagine. My boredom was suddenly broken by a distinct rustling in the trees. Petrified, I am sure my challenge "Who goes there?" was but a whisper. Further noises emanated from the trees – could be two or three assailants – but still no response to my next hysterical challenge. Panic-stricken at the thought of the tower being attacked during my patrol, I released the safety catch on my rifle, aimed at the area from whence the distinct noises came, and fired. There was a thump within the trees and my heart sank – "God, I've killed someone." The sound of the shot brought the other guard and the sergeant running with shouts of "Bloody hell!, what was that?" Shaking like a leaf, I was rooted to the spot while the sergeant investigated. He returned with the news that I had shot a local farmer's cow which had strayed into the trees.'

FLYING TRAINING

After basic training those who would eventually join a ground trade went to one of the technical training establishments – seven out of every ten RAF personnel. Men accepted for aircrew proceeded from an Initial Training Wing to an elementary flying training school. Here would-be pilots came face to face with the realities of taking to the air in a machine which, as in the case of Philip Knowles, temporarily tempered their enthusiasm:

'In August 1942 we arrived at No. 18 Elementary Flying Training School at Fairoaks for our first flying experience, in Tiger Moths, and to be graded for training as either Pilots or Observers. At our first meal a collection was made for a wreath for an unsuccessful student, which was very cheering. Later that evening we were paraded at the edge of the airfield for guard duties when a Tiger Moth started a take-off run downwind, careering all over the place. What fun we thought, an Instructor giving us a demonstration of crazy flying. However, the Tiger turned and started climbing at an angle which even we knew was impossible. It then stalled straight into the ground, with fatal results. The pilot was a ground-crew member who had apparently been rejected from Fleet Air Arm training and wanted to give a demonstration of his flying capabilities. Our first task was then to guard the wreck, with particular regard to the pitot head protective cover, which was still in place, thus preventing any air speed indication. For several days our landing approach was close to the wreckage – a chastening symbol.'

However keen and competent to fly, there was one problem that did not manifest itself until actually taking to the air for the first time – airsickness. An unco-operative digestive constitution put paid to several flying careers. It was a question of degree and could be conquered. Hugh Fisher had no intention of quitting:

'When I began my flight training as a Wop/AG I quickly discovered that I suffered from airsickness. My instructor sent me to the Medical Officer, who asked a few questions and told me to eat barley sugars and the problem would go away. So I did as I'd been told but on my next flight I was sick again. The Instructor wasn't very pleased and said: "Didn't I tell you to go to the MO?" When I told him I had, he said, "Well go again." So off I went. The MO said: 'Didn't you come and see me yesterday?" I told him I had and what happened. I was again told to go away and eat barley sugars but it made no difference and my instructors continued to complain. A corporal said dry bread was a cure; I never tried it. However, later on I discovered that eating dry fluffy biscuits before a flight seemed to help. It took about six weeks before my stomach finally settled down. Even then I was never really comfortable when flying, particularly if there were a lot of turbulence. Now and again I would be airsick, but I managed some 1,600 hours flying.'

There was nothing quite as exhilarating as one's first solo flight, although that did not mean acceptance as a pilot. An average one out of three failed to make the grade in the initial flying course and these men usually went on to navigation training. Not everyone had the necessary aptitude for flying an aircraft although acceptance depended very much on the instructor's judgement. Even past the first stage one could be 'washed out' at a later date as happened to Cyril Clifford:

'To avoid wastage of places on flying courses, those hoping to be pilots had to do a grading course of 12 hours' flying on Tiger Moths. I'd flown about ten-and-a-half hours' dual and was sitting in the crew room on my own when an officer instructor came in. He asked me if I had flown that day and when told I had not, he took me up. After an hour or so's instruction, including landings and take-offs, we came down for the last time and taxied to the petrol pumps. I thought we had finished for the day and awaited a verdict on my capabilities as a pilot. When the fuel tank was full the instructor got the pump attendant to swing the propeller. When the engine was running he shouted down the speaking tube: "Do one more circuit and bring it back to dispersal."

'Determined to do my best, I taxied carefully to the take-off point, did the cockpit check, looked around to see if anyone was about to land, and then turned into wind. Full power and up to 1,950 revs. Line up on something on the horizon and keep pedalling the rudder bar to keep straight. Stick forward to raise the tail then centralize. "Unstick" trim for climb and watch the airspeed. At 500 feet throttle back to 1,850 revs. At 1,100 feet level off, re-trim and throttle back to cruising revs, 1,750rpm. It was only then, on relaxing my concentration, that I realized there was no helmeted head above the front cockpit: I was on my first solo.

'I completed the circuit and made a reasonable landing with only the slightest of bumps. Having satisfied my instructors I was sent to Elementary Flying Training School in Canada, but my instrument flying was not considered good enough to allow me to continue to the next stage. However, I had the satisfaction of knowing that I had soloed in quicker time than did a number of distinguished RAF pilots.'

Instructor pilots were often older men or those 'rested' from operations. It was a demanding task, particularly at EFTS, with perhaps a score of take-offs and landings a day. And one had to be ever wary for unexpected action by students. Ian Glover of No. 14 EFTS:

'One had some strange explanations from student pilots for their actions. The most memorable occurred one beautiful, warm, sunny day when landing at Hockley Heath. This satellite to our main station at Elmdon was really nothing more than a large meadow. As we came down I asked the pupil in the rear cockpit of the Tiger Moth how he knew when to level off. "When I can smell the clover, "Sir!" came the cheeky reply.

The usual 10-week course at EFTS was followed by an advised 16- (later 20-) week advanced flying course at an SFTS (Service Flying Training School) where the aircraft types were predominantly Miles Masters or North American Harvards for single-engine training, and Airspeed Oxfords for twin tuition. Training proceeded apace, often at far from ideal locations and in poor weather, which increased the number of accidents involving neophytes. 'Near thing' incidents were experienced by the majority. The pitfalls of the trainee pilot were many. George Irving:

'My initial cross-country exercise involved laying out a course to steer from base to the Brecon Beacons and back, noting special "pin points" on the track and time over same, everything having to be logged. We had to take off at three minute intervals so I thought it would be a good idea to arrange with the pilot of the Oxford following mine to fly in loose formation to prevent us getting lost, as two heads are better than one. I arranged to take off and clear the aerodrome, then hang back a bit until he took off and caught me up, before proceeding on the allotted course together. After taking off, I cleared the 'drome and did a slow 360 degree orbit, but the other Oxford never appeared. Finally, I turned back on to the course to steer and completed the exercise on my own.

'On returning to base I reported in to my instructor for the log to be checked. About five minutes later my friend arrived and also checked in. I was just admonishing him about not joining me on the trip when the phone rang in the instructor's office. It was an enquiry from Balloon Barrage Control at Portsmouth about Oxford T1336, which had strayed into their area while the balloons were flying. My friend had taken off after me, but had set his compass on the reciprocal course and had flown into the Portsmouth area instead of to the Brecon Beacons.'

On completion of the advanced course the qualified pilot went on to an Operational Training Unit (OTU) where he flew the type, or similar type, of aircraft that he would use in an operational squadron. OTUs were linked to the respective Bomber, Fighter or Coastal Commands. After completing this final stage of training a pilot would join a squadron in the appropriate Command. Among RAF aircrew OTUs were characterized as run-down organizations, a belief nurtured through experiences while undergoing this part of their training. George Irving again:

'After ten days' leave I was posted to No. 51 OTU at Cranfield. We had both long- and short-nosed versions of the Blenheim; most of them had been seconded to Cranfield from operational squadrons. All looked very tired and jaded. The instructors were on rest from ops and, like the planes, tired and jaded. After three short trips F/O McLure, my instructor, said: "Take it up on your own and for Christ's sake don't bend it when you decide to come down, we're getting a bit short of planes." It was at this stage of my training that I realized that it was not only the Germans we would have to contend with in the war; the other, and possibly the more dangerous, would be the aircraft, their serviceability and the weather conditions. Flying was only called off when the base had to close down through fog or low cloud. It was raining heavily when I took off one night, the cloud base being at 1,000 feet and solid up to 5,000 feet. After clearing this I completed my exercise and was very relieved to get back to base as the aircraft engines felt a bit rough and the weather was deteriorating. I made my report relating to the exercise and notified the ground crew as to the state of the aircraft and the suspected "mag drop" on the engines. Returning to the crew room I met Sgt Martin Johns who was leaving to take off on a similar mission. I informed him about the weather conditions, also that if he was assigned to use the same Blenheim to give it a thorough check before taking off as it had been running rough. Half an hour after taking off he crashed and both he and his navigator were killed.'

The aircraft at OTUs may have been wanting, but so too were some of the fledgling aircrews. Exceptionally so in the incidents witnessed by Don Nunn:

'The day our crew arrived at No. 29 OTU, Bruntingthorpe, we witnessed a Wellington over-shoot and crash off the end of the runway. We learned it was the second time that week the crew had crashed while trying to land – no one was hurt. Group obviously had misgivings about these fellows and sent down a screening officer to fly with them. Off they went, only to crash again while trying to land.'

Too often OTU accidents brought tragedy, such as that witnessed by Eddie Wheeler while instructing at No. 18 OTU, Finningley:

'Standing outside the flight offices one evening, we watched as a Wellington was taking off with a pupil crew going solo for the first time. As the plane lifted off at the end of the runway, the port engine cut out and the aircraft struggled to gain height. One of the pilot instructors near me said, "For God's sake, don't turn into the dead engine!" At about 1,000 feet that is exactly what the pupil did and one officer exclaimed, "He's had it!" As the Wimpy turned, probably in the hope that he could get on to the end of the runway and land, the plane flipped on its back and dropped like a stone. There was a thud followed by an explosion and a huge pall of black smoke. Six young men with high hopes would never see their first operation. During four years of war I had witnessed so many similar instances, but one was still shaken each time it happened.'

In Bomber Command there were Heavy Conversion Units (HCUs) to ease the path to large four-engined aircraft. These also had foreboding reputations and not without cause as Gerry Hatt discovered:

'In my case I was far more apprehensive at the Con' Unit than on operations. My Halifax Heavy Conversion Unit posting was Wombleton. Having found the billet I'd been allocated, I walked in, chucked my kit bag on the bed and then noticed a bloke sitting on the next one looking miserable. In an effort to be sociable I joked: "What's the matter mate? It can't be that bad." "You're new here aren't you?" he said. "Yeah," I replied. He said: "I've done three bloody cross-country's and come back by train each time. On three consecutive trips I've baled out, ditched and crash-landed." The bloke was right. It was positively hairy there. The first time my crew went out solo we had to come back on three engines. On another occasion we all had to bale out. The chop rate was pretty high. There were probably other reasons for the high casualty rate, but the state of the aircraft was the main one in my opinion. The Halifaxes were usually old and well worn, having done a great many flying hours. Also, they were the early production models with the unstable tail unit.'

On finally reaching a squadron, training was by no means a thing of the past. To be sent on a course was almost SOP (Standard Operational Procedure) as new techniques and equipment were introduced. In the early days the training courses were often instituted to improve basic trades where weaknesses were identified, notably air-to-air gunnery. The benefit of sending a power turret gunner to practise flexible gunnery, as in Alan Drake's case, is questionable, even if no Blenheims were available – but it provided a bit of excitement:

'In October 1939 we W/Op Air Gunners were packed off from our squadron to No. 2 Armament School, Manby, to receive three weeks' air gunnery training.

The School used Fairey Battle monoplanes and Hawker Hind biplanes. The Hind had open cockpits with little protection from the icy blast of slipstream. Communication between the gunner and the pilot in front of him was usually by hand in view of the engine and air noise. The gunner's cockpit was surmounted by a Scarff ring to which was fixed the Lewis gun used for air-to-air firing at drogues. Normal procedure was for the gunner to tap the pilot on the shoulder at the commencement and cessation of firing so that the pilot knew when to hold the aircraft straight and level or when to dive or climb away. On one occasion, after I had ceased firing, I turned to tap the pilot's shoulder with the flat of my hand but somehow managed instead to give him a hefty box on the ear. He gave me one hell of a look and promptly turned the Hind over on its back. The result was sheer panic on my part trying to make sure I had secured the Dead Man's Hook to the bottom of my 'chute harness and to prevent anything loose from falling out. Not content with scaring the life out of me, I also received a rollicking from the pilot on landing before he departed, nursing his sore ear.'

The estimated aircrew demand was such that arrangements were made for training to be carried out overseas in Commonwealth countries, most notably Canada and eastern and southern Africa. This not only eased the strain on UK establishments, but offered a better environment for elementary and advanced flying training. Those who had this experience were almost universal in praise of their hosts. Tom Minta:

'The generosity and hospitality of the South Africans was something I am unlikely to forget. From our ship we were put on a train in Cape Town and sent north to Bulawayo in Rhodesia. When the train stopped at Mafeking to refuel, we found the station platform lined with trestle tables filled with cakes, fruit, lemonade and so on. The people were wonderful, they really spoiled us, took us round the town in their cars and returned us to the train when it rang its bell. This kind of hospitality was to be repeated on many occasions at the various stations in Rhodesia.'

The largest number of training establishments for RAF aircrew outside the UK were in Canada where, as in Africa, the experience was akin to an adventure holiday after the blackout and rationing of the UK. Many trainees 'never had it so good' and took advantage of the situation when about to return to the Old Country. Len Barcham:

'I did a fair amount of my training in Canada and, when qualified and commissioned, I returned to England with a certain quantity of goodies; things unobtainable in this country at that time; silk stockings, nylons, dress lengths, perfume, etc. A good proportion went to my current girl-friend who, in typical feminine fashion, became suspicious: "Have you been faithful to me?" she asked. I gave her the perfect answer – "Frequently." '

In general, the Canadians treated the British trainees royally and endured with understanding the occasional incident that put them and their property at risk. D. A. Reid was privy to one mishap that could have had nasty consequences:

'In 1944 I was sent to Canada for training, taking a course as a Bomb Aimer at No. 5 Bombing and Gunnery School, Dafoe, Saskatchewan. The usual bombing exercise had pilot plus two U/T (under training) bomb-aimers with a load of 12 practice bombs in an Anson. The bombs had a small charge, sufficient to make a bang, flash and smoke that would mark the point of impact for the aimer some 10,000 feet above. Each trainee dropped six bombs singly, taking turns.

'One night, as the Anson banked over Dafoe town to head for the target, I looked down in the nose and saw my mate, Ginger, drop the release "tit" on the floor. The bomb-release light went out as a practice bomb descended on to Dafoe town. We abandoned the exercises and returned to base; Ginger was a very worried man.

'Next morning a townsman arrived at the main gate and was taken to the CO. Presently Ginger was called to report to the Office. We all expected the worst. A little later Ginger came back grinning. The bomb had detonated just outside the bedroom window of the Dafoe man's wife. She had been in labour at the time with a doctor present. The doctor said it was the quickest delivery he'd known!'

The Canadians' most common complaint was about low flying. Unauthorized low flying was a punishable offence but the temptation was too great for many trainees; Peter Culley being one of those apprehended:

'The exhilaration of low flying was my downfall. The first reprimand came through scaring the daylights out of a repairman who was up a telegraph pole stringing wires. He, or someone, reported the number of the Fairchild Cornell I was flying from Alberta Elementary Flying Training School. My next piece of devilment was taking too close a look at an Indian reservation, for which I was also reported. My final undoing, however, was while on a three-leg solo navigational flight from my Service Flying Training School at Estevan, Saskatchewan. I had met an interesting girl who came from a small town and decided to pay her a visit. After finding the place, I thought it would be fun to take the Anson down the wide main street. I did this three times – level with the rooftops. Unfortunately, the performance was viewed by one of our instructors who happened to be on leave visiting this particular town. A couple of days after the incident I was notified by the instructor, on his return to the unit armed with aircraft number and time of the "attack" that this serious misdemeanour was a Court Martial offence. However, this officer was a great fellow and, after playing down the incident, I was allowed to re-muster to Trainee Airgunner. Following a short period of training, my career as an airgunner proved to be no problem for the next three years – as I could only fly as low as the "Skipper" decreed!'

There was an even more favoured location: the United States. Britain was offered by the US Government arrangements for pilot training, initially at civilian establishments and, after America became involved in hositilities, at a number of US military bases. William Reid was one of the early trainees:

'My flight training was done at Lancaster in the Mojave Desert. We arrived before America entered the war. Then the Japs hit Pearl Harbor and you'd have thought California was about to be invaded and the place laid waste by air raids. In those first few weeks the Californians got into a bit of a panic as if their shores were about to be invaded, yet once they decided to do things then no one could touch them. People's attitude to the military changed rapidly. At one time it wasn't everyone who would pick up an Army hitchhiker, but after Pearl Harbor the civilian population couldn't do enough for them. Then suddenly servicemen were the most important fellows around. We couldn't have had better treatment and were always being asked about the war back in Britain. When Bomber

Command flew the first thousand bomber raid you would have thought we had actually taken part in it ourselves, the way they fussed over us. When we went into town we wore our best RAF "blues" and many local people thought the albatross insignia on our shoulders were wings and that we were already pilots. Of course, we didn't disillusion them. There were always invitations. And when they said come to supper they really meant it. It wasn't said in the non-commital way we do over here. There was no lack of genuine hospitality.'

Evidently the mode of instruction varied and some pupils found certain aspects wanting. William Drinkell:

'After elementary instruction I went to the United States under the Tower's Scheme whereby RAF pilots earmarked for Coastal Command were trained by the US Navy and brought to a standard where they gained their wings. After some basic flying on Naval Aircraft Factory N3N biplanes, we went to Pensacola for an advanced course, finishing on Catalinas. The US Navy instructors never taught me to handle an aeroplane as if it were an extension of myself. Everything was by numbers, a sequence of detailed exercises. For example, you were instructed how to do a loop at such and such a speed and with precise directions. No one told you you could carry out the same manoeuvres at different speeds and using different techniques. They took me through to my wings in an efficient manner, but never taught me the love of flying. Years later, when I became an instructor, I always wanted my students to love flying first. If they did then the rest would follow easily.'

The wide open spaces and clear skies of the United States certainly provided safer flying training than in Britain but, inevitably, the pupil pilots gave their instructors some anxious moments. Stanley Ward:

'The experience of being sent across the Atlantic to undertake pilot training in Oklahoma is something I am unlikely to forget. Nor do I think one of my American instructors will forget me. We did our advanced training on Harvards – AT-6 Texans the Yanks called them. Nice aircraft; a joy to fly. Well, on this particular occasion we were taking off dual, me in the front and the instructor in the back. As we lifted off the ground I selected Gear Up but it didn't come up. Now our training was that before you select Gear Down you always closed the throttle momentarily so as to activate the warning horn. You then opened the throttle up, selected Gear Down, closed the throttle again momentarily and if there was no warning horn you knew the gear was down and locked. Anyway, we are just off the ground and I had selected Gear Up with no apparent response. So I said to the instructor: "Gear still down, Sir." He replies, "Okay, select down," meaning for me to go through the sequence again to see if the wheels would come up next time. So what do I do through force of habit? Close the throttle. No problem when you're letting down to land, but we were just off the ground and climbing towards the hangars at the end of the field. In the brief moment it took for me to realize my folly I saw the hangars suddenly loom large and several guys on the apron running for their lives. With the throttle full open again we did miss the top of the hangar but not by much. It would not be kind to repeat the instructor's comments from the back seat.'

And, of course, there were always the adventurous who broke flight regulations, as Philip Knowles recalls when at No. 1 British Flying Training School:

'On 22nd June 1943 I was flying an AT-6A (Harvard) on a night cross-country from our base at Terrell, Texas, to Shreveport, Louisiana, and back with another cadet, Alan Lamberton, in the back seat navigating. It was a lovely clear starry night and as we approached Shreveport the city lights were spread out in front of us. Everything was under such good control that I asked Alan about trying a slow roll. He agreed, so I had a go. Half-way round there was a great commotion from the rear cockpit and a terrible smell. I thought we were on fire and was relieved to get back straight and level without seeing any flames. The aircraft was behaving normally, but there were fearful curses coming over the intercom. It turned out that the rear relief tube was blocked and had been used – some time ago! When we inverted it emptied itself over Alan and his navigation board. The smell was unbelievable, even with both hoods open, and we had an hour's flight back to Terrell. That was bad enough, but what could we say to the next pair who came out to take the aircraft on a similar trip? We could not admit to night aerobatics!'

However, it was not always the pupils who were in error as John Peak found out at No. 13 SFTS:

'There was a Standard Beam Approach flight on the airfield with Harvards specially fitted with the necessary radio equipment for beam flying, and the perspex of the rear cockpit, under which the pilot having instruction on instrument flying flew, was green. The pupil wore red goggles enabling him to see the instruments – albeit with a red tinge – but looking out through the green perspex was just a black void.

'A relief airfield at Brada, 10 miles south-west of our base at North Battleford, was fitted with the beam equipment. Pupil and instructor would take off from base and fly towards Brada where the instructor handed over to the pupil who would then have to intercept the beam and turn on to the correct course to carry out an instrument approach to the airfield. While training we would not waste time by landing but would climb away for another approach. These training sessions would last for about 1½ hours and were quite mentally exhausting. On the other hand, the instructors, who each had four pupils allocated to them, used to find it rather boring. One particular instructor, whom we liked a lot, was on a rest between operational tours on Spitfires over Europe. To relieve the monotony he would start the session by taking off from base and when clear of the airfield would drop right down to zero feet and fly for several miles over the prairies before climbing up to 3,000 feet and handing over to the pupil to fly the beam. When the session was over he would again take over, return to base and do a wheel landing – as soon as the main wheels touched he would open the throttle and hurtle down the runway racing car fashion, closing the throttle just in time to turn off at the end of the runway and taxi in.

'On one occasion when we were night flying SBA, I was No. 3 to fly and while No. 2 was flying No. 1 came back to our living-quarters and warned me that the instructor had a bottle of whisky with him and had got through most of it. When I reported to the crew room, everyone was having a coffee break except our instructor who was asleep in a corner. Most instructors were briefing the next pupils to fly, but when my instructor came to he just said, "Okay, let's go."

'He had the engine running and was taxi-ing almost before I had strapped in, did a fast turn on to the runway and we were airborne! As soon as we had cleared the airfield he switched on the aircraft's landing lights, dropped right down on the "deck" and repeated his daylight performance with corn stubble flashing by inches below in the glare of the landing lights. After a while he climbed up to 3,000 feet and said, "Okay you have control, carry on doing back beam approaches." We had to get experience at back beam approaches which meant approaching the airfield from the opposite direction, where you then did not have the benefit of the outer and inner markers. This was fairly straightforward, provided other aircraft were also doing it to avoid approaching in opposite directions.

'After I had done two of these approaches, there had been no sound or comment from the front cockpit and I concluded that my instructor must be asleep and not keeping a lookout for other aircraft. The thought then struck me as to whether the others flying were also doing back beam approaches. I therefore decided to raise my red goggles so as to see outside; I had just done so when there was a loud roar and I saw the exhaust flames of what must have been another Harvard going in the opposite direction. I waggled the stick violently and a sleepy sounding voice said, "I have control." He flew back to base and did one of his racing car landings, but misjudged his braking and ran off the end of the runway amongst the scrub before returning to the perimeter track and taxi-ing in.

'The next morning all four who had flown with him were called into the flight commander's office and told that when the ground crew put the plane away in the hangar they found that a picketing hook situated beneath the wing had been torn off, together with the panel to which it was attached. He asked if we had noticed anything about our instructor's flying that night. We all replied, "No Sir." I believe he was grounded pending an inquiry, but we graduated shortly after and were soon on our way home to the UK, so I never knew the outcome.'

The Drill

CREATURE COMFORTS

Some two million men and women served with the Royal Air Force at some time during the 1939–1945 War, a large proportion of whom, at the time, considered boredom the main feature of their war. This view was not confined to the non-flying section. A reappraisal, half a century on, finds the majority declaring it to have been an experience that they would not have missed. Patriotism and duty aside, the fact remains that the result of tedium was that the individual's main occupation became personal welfare. Paramount in this situation was sustenance, for the pleasure of eating and drinking was often marred by scarcity, monotony and poor cuisine; sometimes to a point where it became almost obsessional for the deprived. For every station with a good mess, it seemed three could be found where the reverse was the case. Perhaps it was a matter of opinion or palate, but there were messes where the meals left a lasting impression. Roy Browne:

'The food at Skellingthorpe was absolutely appalling. Dreadful stuff; all slop. I think it was the cooks, not the ingredients. Some brave corporal did get up one day and voice his disgust to the Orderly Officer but things never improved. It must have ranked the worst food in the RAF.'

For Maureen Brickett it was the method of serving rather than the food that made meals so awful:

'My first breakfast in the WAAF: the enormous dining hut . . . orderlies shouting '"ats orf" . . . picking up a plate at the end of a long queue and receiving a slice of liver, a ladle of gravy, two slices of bread, a pat of butter and a spoonful of jam all piled on top of each other. Having found a place to sit and fetched my tin mug of tea from an urn marked "sweetened tea", I returned to my place to find everything a soggy mess in a sea of gravy, half cold and fast congealing, but nevertheless eating what I could because I was so cold and hungry!'

Sentiments echoed by Ernie Edwards:

'It wasn't so much the food as the way it was prepared and served that was the problem. You queued up at the counter and the mess staff came along slapping it on your plate; a bit of lukewarm mutton with lukewarm gravy and synthetic mashed spuds, all flopped together in an unappetizing mess. We got this day after day. To be fair, there must have been 500 senior NCOs in our mess. How the devil the kitchen staff coped with it all I don't know. I think the reason the meals were so poor was that the kitchen staff were overloaded with work.'

Small units, where the cooks did not have the pressure of numbers, offered better fare. The problem of poor food or poorly prepared food appears to have been more acute on large stations. This was particularly so in Bomber Command where two or three thousand personnel had to be catered for on a single station. The monotony of the meals was a common grouse – although this cannot have been John Everett's initial reaction:

'After completing training as an engine fitter I was posted to No. 102 Squadron at Topcliffe. My first meal in the Airmen's Mess was quite an experience. I sat down with a plate of sausage, cabbage and potato. Cutting into the cabbage I hit something hard and retrieved a three-inch rusting nail. Other diners were amused at my comments about cabbages having a high iron content. I wasn't, but didn't like to complain, this being my first time in the mess.'

In fairness, the problem of running kitchens and a mess on the scale demanded at most large stations was fraught with difficulties. In order to improve matters many mess administrators attempted to impose timed servings to take the load off kitchen staff and thus improve the cooking of meals. At some stations this was stringently applied as Albert Herbert relates:

'Seems that on No. 115 Squadron too many aircrews were coming into the Sergeants' Mess for meals after the appointed time period. Late meals were anathema to the Mess Sergeant, so all late meals had to be asked for by presenting a chit from the squadron adjutant. Well, the crew of a particular friend of mine came in late and behold – no meal chits. So the Mess Sergeant told them there would definitely be no meals served to them in the sergeants' mess that night. This did not please the crew who had returned from an operation and suffered debriefing, particularly my friend Val, who thundered at the Mess Sergeant: "Who the hell are you? You must have been the cook at the Last Supper!" Quick as a flash the MS replied: "Yes, I was, and Judas Iscariot had no meal chit – and he got no dinner either!"

One of the incongruous things about service life was that one might move from a station where meals were limited and lifeless to one of plenty, where cooking was excellent. At one location the 'grub' was so good it even had a soporific effect. Dennis Baxter:

'The food at No. 17 ITW Scarborough was good. Plenty of plum duff and the like and the problem arose of keeping awake at the lectures after lunch. We were given navigation lessons from a pleasant ex-schoolmaster named F/Lt Stirling. Half the class would usually nod off, but he didn't seem to worry unduly about the snoozing. Sometimes he'd drop a ruler on the floor or rap on a table to try and wake people up. He could have made it very difficult for the offenders, but as far as I am aware he never reported anyone for being asleep. His attitude was: if you want to learn you can, the choice is yours.'

At those stations where meals left much to be desired, personnel endeavoured to supplement RAF fare with refreshments from civilian sources. Thus many sought out the local cafés and restaurants in off-duty hours. In the early months of hostilities expense was the only problem, but as rationing became more severe civilian eating-places had little to offer – apart from what was 'under the counter'. Jim Double:

'In 1943 I was a member of staff at No. 10 Radio School, Carew Cheriton, South Wales. Across the road from the main gate there was a wooden building known as "Smokey Joe's", a café run by a very jovial cockney. Cooked food – bacon, eggs, sausage, etc., could always be obtained although officially rationed. However, it was not unknown when part way through a meal for the plate to be whisked away from under you, to be replaced once it was decided that a food inspector was not on the scene.

'When the liberty trucks returned from Tenby at night the café would be inundated with airmen and WAAFs getting tea, coffee or a sandwich. Cheese sandwiches were 7 pence each, rather expensive, but as Smokey pointed out, he had to have sufficient funds for any eventuality.

'One Monday morning, when off duty, I dropped in for a coffee and was asked by Smokey to help count out 100 £1 notes. He had got to attend the Magistrates' Court at Pembroke Dock, having received summonses for no less than 28 food offences! He estimated £100 should cover it. Later in the day I met him again, wearing a beaming smile, to be told: "Tell everyone to be in the Plough tonight; I will pay." '

Even the normally figure-conscious WAAFs sought to supplement their diet in civilian establishments. Maureen Brickett:

'I was stationed at RAF Turnhouse near Edinburgh, but as a Clerk Special Duties working in the Operations Room, I never actually lived on the station. We were always "people apart" and were billeted in big and usually very elegant houses which had been "taken over". Edinburgh was a land "flowing with milk and honey" compared with London. There were two restaurants in Princes Street, Mackies and MacVities, where you could eat to your heart's content at any time of the day, the most tempting and delicious savouries or pastries! I was 8 stone and 3 pounds when I joined and three months later I had put on three-and-a-half stone! One day one of the RAF flight sergeants was showing a group of "resting" pilots around Ops and laughingly pointing at me said, "There's the best TWO girls in Ops," and the nickname stuck!'

At various locations a shortage of accommodation necessitated RAF personnel being billeted with civilians. In such circumstances those involved usually dined royally, mothered by the lady of the house who was glad of the extra rations provided. Unfortunately, this was not always the case as Peter Catchpole relates:

'With the large intake of RAF trainees at Blackpool, many of us were found billets in the area. With three other fellows I was sent to a guest-house whose owner was paid by the RAF to sleep and feed us. They obviously didn't want to take servicemen and we were given a tiny little room with three bunk beds and fed on the minimum that these people could get away with. Every Saturday for dinner, without fail, we each had a small meat-pie sitting on a plate of gravy – no vegetables or anything else. The place was taking in Lancashire holidaymakers for a week's stay and while we were faced with the meat pie these civilians would sit down to a good Saturday dinner. It got so that some would take pity on us as their week wore on, and slip us food. Anyway, I think the rations allowed by the RAF were probably being used for the civilian guests. I've never wanted to eat a meat-pie since.'

On airfield sites out in the countryside, the proximity of farm and garden produce found many a Nissen hut with a cooking stove and makeshift larder for off-duty additional meals. Eggs, rabbits, game and vegetables were bought, scrounged or pinched in the nearby villages. There was always an airman from a country background who would be willing to draw a pheasant or gut a rabbit ready for the pot. Little was sacred to those feeling a bit 'peckish'. Frank Clarke:

'I was stationed at Wellesbourne Mountford, Warwickshire, on 'C' Flight Wellington IIIs at No. 22 OTU. Close to our dispersal point was an old Nissen hut used as a repair shop and for sheltering from the rain. Somehow we acquired a pet goose who became very tame and friendly with the regular members of our Flight. However, if a stranger came along the goose would go for him and chase him away. It could be quite vicious. When NAAFI time came and we were working, the goose always gave a warning call to tell us the van had arrived. It was then first in the queue to obtain a bun or some tit-bit from one of the NAAFI girls. The bird used to follow us around, coming over to the aircraft dispersal area and sitting near us while we worked. Woe betide any stranger who arrived; a guard dog could not have done a better job. We had him for about 18 months until one Christmas when, sadly, he disappeared. No doubt he ended up on someone's dinner table.'

The sources of some fare were surprising. On 2 September 1943 two Hurricane squadrons attacked with rockets the Zuid Beveland lock gates in the Dutch islands. Meeting fierce opposition, four aircraft were lost and several others damaged. One of the latter was the Hurricane of No. 137 Squadron's CO, John Wray:

'Once I thought I was out of range of fighters I settled down on course and took stock of my damage. My aircraft had been hit in a number of places; at the time I did not realize how badly. Also, I had a wound in my right arm, although I didn't find this out until after I had landed. My eye was travelling around the aircraft looking for damage when suddenly it lighted on a duck hanging by its neck close to the wing tip on the leading edge. During the operation and escape I had obviously picked it up. After landing back at base my ground crew took possession and had it that night for supper!'

When it could be passed off as a communication or training flight, aircraft were often used in the cause of enhancing a mess larder. A ploy used by Tom Minta when at Headquarters, 19 Group, Coastal Command:

'The mess made one old penny on each drink and as we were not too keen for this money to go to central messing, every now and then we had to have a party. I thought it would be nice to have some lobsters so I took a Proctor and flew down to Portreath where I knew I could buy some from local fishermen. The lobsters were put in a basket in the back of the Proctor and off I went back to Roborough. After I'd been airborne for about 15 minutes I suddenly noticed control movements unconnected with my own movements of the stick. It was the damned lobsters which had somehow escaped and were all over the floor and pulling on the wires with their claws. I flew the rest of the way just hoping one didn't get jammed in the controls.'

After food, a pint and a fag were often the means of making service life more tolerable. A limited supply of beers were available on most stations through the good offices of the NAAFI, but airmen generally preferred to get off station to the pubs for the local ale. In England most public houses were tied to a local brewery and only stocked its brews. Hence the attraction of a particular hostelry was often a case of how the beers suited the palate. True, Guinness, Bass and other special bottled beers were also available in most pubs, but the airman's pay kept him to draught 'mild', 'bitter' and the like. Beer was another commodity in short supply and publicans tended to evoke their own brand of rationing with 'under the counter' supplies for favoured customers. Thus you had your regular pub knowing continued loyalty would ensure access to the liquid reserves.

Beer was also the favoured drink with officers, a 'noggin or two' with pals in the mess was a way to spend an evening. Spirits were in even more limited supply and a luxury even on an officer's pay. Scotch became a totally 'under the counter' commodity. There were other sources if you chanced to be stationed in the right area, as Ken Campbell discovered:

'While attached to No. 489 (RNZAF) Squadron, Royal New Zealand Air Force, equipped with Hampden torpedo-bombers, I was stationed at Wick, Caithness, up in the north of Scotland. At that time Caithness was a dry county, pub-wise that is; weather-wise it was something else! Wet, wet, and wet most of the time, with lots of Scotch mist and low cloud. There was no local place – apart from the mess – for off-duty airmen to chew the fat and put the world to rights over a pint of ale. So by far the greater part of our crew's leisure time was spent tramping across the surrounding moors and heather – weather permitting. An extremely pleasant pastime too, seldom encountering another living soul, apart from the sheep who were docile enough; the epitome of quiet perfect peace.

'Out walking one rare fine day and feeling "peckish" after covering several miles, we chanced upon one of the well-scattered crofts. Hoping we would come across the occupier and be able to buy a snack of some sort, I gave a gentle knock on the door and awaited some kind being to answer my call. The portal was duly opened and a grizzly-looking old crofter appeared. "Good morning Sir," says I, "Would it be at all possible for me and my pals to buy a snack and a drink please?"

"You'll get nothing here bar a drop o' goat's milk. I've haaerd aboot ye canny Customs and Excise frae yon Edinburgh," said the sage, casting a beady eye over our uniforms.

"A glass of milk and a sandwich will do fine, thanks; but, Sir, just to put your mind at rest, we're not Excise men from Edinburgh. We are airmen from Wick RAF station taking a stroll on the moors:"

"Airmen frae Wick eh? Ye've nay been sent to spy on an old honest crofter then?"

"No, we are truly from Wick airbase."

'After much thought and careful soul-searching the old boy reached a conclusion: "Och, well noo laddies, come away in and sample a wee dram o' Hamish's special brew."

'Inside his croft, Hamish reached behind a sack of spuds and produced a bottle of his "special brew" and forthwith proceeded to pour out four very liberal tots. Raising his glass aloft Hamish, with a broad grin on his craggy face, chirped: "Lang may ye lum reek the noo airmen frae Wick." "Lang may ye lum reek, Hamish," heartily chanted three weary but contented airmen frae Wick. Lang may ye lum reek – long may your chimney smoke. What a wonderful salutation; far better than our half-hearted English "Cheers".'

While not every airman drank, there were few who did not smoke. The cigarette habit was unquestioned; smoking was the adult thing to do. A packet of Weights or Woodbines in the erk's top pocket, Players or Gold Flake were a step up the social ladder, and if you aspired to be thought a cut above the rest then it was Craven A or du Maurier. While it might be claimed to be a matter of taste, the brand price had more bearing on choice – an officer concerned with his image would never dream of smoking Weights or Woodbines. They said a cigarette put one at ease, relaxed you; few recognized the need as an addiction to nicotine. Smoking was, of course, officially never allowed on duty and this put strain on the would-be chain-smokers. Jim Swale of No. 295 Squadron recalls one desperate individual:

'Special ops meant that we had little sleep for two nights and a day, and Taffy was very young and very, very tired. After our egg (for night work), bacon and beans we felt satisfied; but not so Taffy. Taffy could not exist long without fags and there was not a single fag to be scrounged from anyone in our section at Rivenhall. Most of us preferred pipes in which we smoked Balkan Sobranie – three bob an ounce at the NAAFI. Taffy said, "I'll nip down to Kelvedon, I think I know where I can get some fags." He departed on his bike; we went to bed. Some considerable time later he had not returned. Anxiously, we went looking for him. We found him still seated on his bike and propped up against a thicket in a low ditch on the way back from Kelvedon. He was fast asleep in the hot sunshine! We also saw that there was a rectangular shape in his left-hand tunic pocket.'

Smoking around aircraft was strictly taboo, a court-martial offence. Fuel fumes pervaded most aircraft and so the fire hazard was very real. Even so, there were individuals who took the risk as they just could not do without a fag. John Everett:

'I was working on a Halifax in one of the Topcliffe hangars late one evening. Beside the aircraft I was fixing there was another Halifax and a Stirling in the hangar. The only other person around was an engineer from Handley Page who was in the other Halifax disconnecting fuel pipes. Suddenly I heard a shout and a lot of commotion and saw this chap fall out of the fuselage door with his clothes alight. I jumped down and looked for something to smother the flames. "Don't worry about me," he said, "I'll put myself out. The plane is on fire; try and put that out." I ran for the extinguisher up near the hangar doors. The thought of what would happen to three heavy bombers and the hangar made me run as fast as I could. Climbing in through the fuselage door of the Halifax I found the inside well alight. Luckily I was in time as the flames had not really taken hold of anything inflammable and I was able to use the extinguisher to put them out. I then remembered the burning man but found he had been able to smother the flames and he didn't seem harmed. He was more concerned about there being any other witnesses to this incident and was relieved when told we were the only two people in the hangar. I had no wish to get him into trouble but somehow I had to account for the fire extinguisher being emptied. For my trouble he gave me 5 shillings – a lot of money in those days – which I used to start a Post Office Savings Account for my small daughter. No wonder the engineer was anxious to keep the incident quiet; I discovered that although working with petrol and having it all over his clothes and splashed around the fuselage of the Halifax, he had actually struck a match to light up a cigarette!'

How the pleasures of alcohol and nicotine rated against the pursuit of the opposite sex was very much an individual case. RAF aircrews certainly had a reputation of being Casanovas among British services, even if there is little evidence to prove them more romantically adventurous than the army or navy men. Perhaps this reputation owes something to advertisements depicting a spruce airman, by a well-known hair-dressing, leading to the other services' quip of 'Brylcreem Boys' for the RAF. That aircrew were thought by some to be womanizers is illustrated by George Irving's encounter with a doctor:

'I was sent to the RAF hospital at Halton, near Aylesbury for tests as my eyes were rather inflamed and did not improve with the normal treatment by the MO. At Halton I was given a very thorough eye test and blood samples were taken. In fact, I told them if they took any more I would demand a blood transfusion. On the third day the ward doctor came on his rounds and said: "We haven't found your trouble yet but you're clear of VD." I told him that I wasn't in the least surprised as I didn't sleep around or go out with naughty girls. He replied: "We always test you flying types just in case."'

Perhaps the MO's attitude had been influenced by seeing something akin to the information Eddie Wheeler found displayed at Newton:

'Walking into the crew room one morning, I spotted the serviceability board bore the names of girls in Nottingham, many of them familiar to us, with details of their sex prowess, dates when they should be overlooked, whether they were married or not, and whether overnight accommodation was available. This information was updated almost on a daily basis and it needed to be consulted before embarking on any blind dates.'

On the other hand, romance most certainly flourished for many young men met their future wives while serving. A good proportion of WAAFs married airmen they knew in the Service and with whom they worked. This was to be expected. There were some unusual introductions to girls, however, like that Tony Murkowski had:

'At Andrews Field we had to do readiness duty to scramble if a flying bomb was reported. Jerry was launching them from aircraft at this time, the winter of 1944. One morning I had been stuck in the cockpit of my Mustang near the end of the runway for nearly an hour and was getting very thirsty. Then, when a "Sally Ann" van arrived at a nearby dispersal, I could see the airmen collecting big cakes and getting mugs of tea. This made me feel even more thirsty. So I called out to the ground staff mechanic who was sitting on my wing, "Go and ask that girl how about a cup of tea for the pilot." So he went across and presently this good-looking girl comes with tea in an old mug. I wanted to pay her – it was a penny a mug – but because I'm strapped in I couldn't get a hand in my pocket to get a penny. So she says, "That's all right." I say, "Okay, thanks. Let me take you out one evening to repay you." So we fix a date to meet in the town. Well, it is dark in the winter evenings, no lights because of the blackout, but I'm there and I wait and she doesn't turn up. Okay, too bad. Then I see her on the airfield a week later and ask her why she don't turn up. She says, "You never turned up!" We find that I had

misunderstood her directions. We must have been waiting on opposite sides of
the street and did not see each other in the dark. It ends well; we got married.'

PAY, LEAVE AND PROMOTION

Next to appetite and creature comforts, pay and leave frequently occupied the
mind of the airmen. A humble aircraftman (AC 2) received two shillings a day as a
new recruit. His 'keep' was, of course, found by the Air Force and the pay
amounted to little more than pocket-money. It allowed the purchase of a packet of
cigarettes, a round of sandwiches and two pints of beer. Different grades and
promotion brought better pay and there were rises as the war progressed. Aircrew
received a higher rate; even so it provided less remuneration for NCOs than many
war-work civilian labourers were getting. John Studd was surprised to hear a
justification for this:

'I was drinking in the pub one evening when I was asked by a gentleman with
an Irish accent, who said that he worked on the airfield, how much I was paid as a
sergeant bomb-aimer. When I told him 15 shillings a day he said: "I get more than
that – but of course it does include danger money for working on the runways."'

Pay was always meagre – roughly a third of what US servicemen of
equivalent rank received when they arrived in Europe – but Albert Herbert
recalls an additional source of income:

'Operational aircrew in Bomber Command could qualify for a five shillings a
day leave grant from the Nuffield Fund, which could be anything from one in
four to one week in eight, depending on the attrition in their squadrons.
Personnel receiving awards such as the DSO, DFC and DFM, got £10 for each
"gong" and another for each bar to that medal. The NCOs would keep their
money, but the officers were expected to give theirs to a Benevolent Fund.'

Officers were not alone in being expected to contribute to some deserving
cause. Despite their low pay, other ranks were often solicited for hand-outs,
notably for some station fund, occasionally in a manner that appeared obligatory.
One such instance was strongly resented by George Watts:

'As we filed out of the Watton hangar after pay parade, an officer and an
NCO would be sitting at a table collecting sixpences for the sports fund. As we
"erks" were working seven days a week, sports were not for us. Only officers and
WAAFs had the time to use the tennis-courts and other facilities. Deciding this
was not fair, on the next occasion I refused to pay. The officer immediately
reprimanded me, but when I asked if that meant the levy was compulsory he
declined to answer and simply took my name and number, implying that I would
later be called to account for my action. Nothing more was heard of the matter
and when the next pay parade came round their takings were down considerably.
I had spread the word.'

More than one comparative newcomer to the Service encountered a situation
where there was a suspicion of being the victim of a racket. Ray Howlett:

'Reporting to Uxbridge for posting after initial training, we were mystified
when at our first payment we were charged for "barrack-room damages". None of
us saw any damage or any reason for the two shillings deducted and felt like

breaking a couple of chairs to get our money's worth. I wondered at the time if it was a fiddle to boost the NCO's pay!'

There were no hard and fast rules on leave for ordinary airmen. It was normal to receive a week's embarkation leave before being sent abroad to the Middle or Far East but some ground men in the UK, stationed far from their homes, were never afforded an opportunity to see their families throughout their wartime service. The majority were able to take advantage of a '48' (48-hour leave) allowed and administered by the station at which they served. There were no travel allowances for these and one had to get home and back as best one could. John Everett:

'Weekend passes and hitch-hiking have a place in wartime memories. Of the varied lifts, mine included an ambulance, a hearse and the back of an empty brick lorry which left me half choked with red brick dust at the end of the journey. We had a "Geordie" airman on the base who walked along the railway line at Thirsk and thumbed a lift by goods train to Newcastle.'

The return to camp following leave could be a fraught business if delay threatened to make one late. Ken Brotherhood was one of many who had this experience:

'Given a weekend pass, I decided to visit my girlfriend in Manchester. Leaving RAF Lindholme I travelled to Doncaster and then on to Manchester with a mate. Although we had arranged to meet at the station on Sunday and return together, my mate was nowhere to be found so I set off back alone. It was necessary to change at Wakefield and after alighting I asked a porter where to catch the train to Doncaster. Small and stocky, silver watch-chain complete with medallion spread across the front of his waistcoat, he stroked his moustache, pushed his cap to the back of his head and said, "Eh lad, tha'll have to go over t'other side." A guard was poised with green flag and whistle beside the train standing at the opposite platform, so realizing it was about to depart I dashed over the footbridge and just got aboard in time. We chugged along, stopping at various stations, but when we reached Barnsley I realized I was the only person left in the carriage. Feeling a bit concerned I called out to a female porter on the platform, "What time do we get to Doncaster?" "You won't get to Doncaster on this train," she replied. "it's going into the sidings now until morning." I think she saw my look of despair and took pity on me because after a few more questions she said: "The engine is going back to Wakefield. I'll ask the driver to give you a lift." He agreed and off I went, riding on the footplate, where I enjoyed a mug of tea and a bacon sandwich. It was also explained that when the Wakefield porter had said "the other side", he meant another station on the other side of town. Hitch-hiking on a locomotive was a novel experience and saved me from a late return to camp and the trouble that would have brought.'

Vic Holloway while stationed at Montrose was one of the less fortunate where taking leaves was concerned:

'For the four years that I was stationed in Scotland my home was in Hampshire, too far away for a 48-hour pass. We did find means of getting a longer leave though. Because of the difficulties in travelling, any man who lived in the Western Isles was allowed to count his 48-hour pass from the time he arrived at Mallaig or the Kyle of Lochalsh to board a boat, through to the time when he arrived back in those ports to go back to his station. The drill was to leave camp and go to Perth and spend a night there. Next day to catch the train to Inverness and spend a night there, then on to the Kyle in the morning. When you arrived at the ferry you had your leave chit date-stamped. Forty-eight hours were spent on Skye and you arrived back at the Kyle to have your pass stamped again to be within the allotted time. Another couple of days were taken to go via Inverness and Perth back to Montrose so that leave had been extended from 48 hours to six days. I did this with a friend on several occasions and others were pulling the same trick. Somehow the authorities never got wise as to what was going on.'

Aircrew received more generous leave, generally between postings, with at least a week after completing an operational tour. The length of leave depended very much upon the availability of personnel in a particular command to which assigned, the more so in the final 18 months of the war. In some circumstances the Air Ministry were particularly generous. Rex Croger:

'After I got my wings in Canada I returned to the UK early in 1944 and was sent on a month's leave. Just before it was up I received a letter telling me I had another month. Eventually I had four months' leave before finally being posted to an OTU. At that time there were obviously more pilots than needed.'

Another beneficiary of an extended leave was Tony Spooner, who eventually ascertained the reason why:

'Being on the staff of Admiral Pridham-Whipple, Vice-Admiral, Dover, for D-Day operations was an interesting experience, but once the Channel was secured and the "fake" invasion across the famous Straits of Dover a thing of the past, there wasn't any need for the liaison appointment. When I mentioned this to the Admiral, he promptly told me to go away on "indefinite leave".

'The possessor of a conscience has disadvantages. After several weeks of blissful leave I began to worry. "Could an Admiral send a S/Ldr on indefinite leave? Would Coastal Command be looking for me?" I duly reported back to HQCC. "Oh dear. Not another of you. I suppose you also want to get back to a squadron. You see, the trouble is that not enough of you S/Ldrs got yourselves killed during the immediate D-Day period. We reckoned on quite large numbers. How about going to Transport Command? They are looking for Air Traffic Controllers. It could get you another stripe soon." In the end, I was posted to assist a Wing Commander in HQCC and he didn't know how to occupy his hours. Apparently not enough Wing Commanders had been killed either. It was a tough war for the planners.'

The benefits of rank were obvious and there can have been few AC2s who did not aspire to eventual elevation to AC1, however lacking in ambition. Promotion not only meant better pay and privileges, but was an acknowledgement of one's standing, something to be proud of. For ground men and women attaining promotion could be a very lengthy business, whereas for aircrew it could sometimes be meteoric, the result of heavy attrition. Bill Japp:

'When four captains of No. 14 Squadron were killed in a night-flying accident in 1943, Ron Gellatly literally found himself promoted from Flying Officer to Squadron Leader overnight!'

Although a wanting necessity in many battle depleted squadrons, the elevation of an experienced NCO to commissioned officer status was not so easily achieved. Roy Wilkinson, then a Hurricane pilot of No. 3 Squadron, was one such case:

'On 15 May 1940 we were doing some low strafing (which we should not have been) when the CO was hit by an Me 110 and shot down. I managed to shoot down the 110 and by chance to blow up an ammo' lorry at the same time. By the time I got back to our base at Merville, Officer Commanding 'A' Flight, Flt Lt Walter Churchill, had received confirmation from the front line that the CO had been shot down and that I had got the Me 110 and the ammo' lorry. "So," he continued, "as the senior flight commander, I am now the CO; and you Wilky, are now 'A' Flight Commander." "I can't do that you know, Sir; I'm only a Sergeant and you've got a couple of Flight Lieutenants there." "There's a war on now," he explained, "King's Regulations are thrown out the window! I'm the boss now so do as I say. You're our top scorer by far; you are now the flight commander. I've seen Bunny Stone and the other officers and they are quite happy to fly behind you. In fact, I shall probably fly behind you too, for you to lead the squadron."

'When we were evacuated back to the UK the Air Ministry told the Boss that he could not list a sergeant as OC 'A' Flight. He replied, "I can. I've done it. I told you to make him a flight lieutenant a fortnight ago and you didn't, so he stays there." Air Ministry tried to compromise by saying, "Let him do it, but don't put him at the top of the list on squadron Daily Returns." But the CO stuck to his guns and for a couple of weeks I continued to command 'A' Flight as a sergeant pilot. Then a signal arrived and I was commissioned as a flight lieutenant back-dated to when I had taken over in France.'

Promotion enabled the bright and successful to elevate themselves to ranks above their former superiors, a situation that the latter naturally did not relish. Thus due promotion was not always quickly forthcoming if those handling 'the papers' felt their position threatened. An instance of this was encountered by Steve Challen:

'In July 1940 I was sent to No. 1 OTU at Silloth near Carlisle, along with several other recently qualified AC2 air gunners. Our course instructor was a Sergeant Air Gunner, Busby by name, who we thought had the rank because of his duty. He told us about the Air Ministry Order which was promulgated December 1939 making all qualified aircrew no lesser rank than Sergeant. This particular AMO was not to be seen on any notice-board where such things were usually posted. Was someone sitting on it? Inquiries at the Orderly Room drew a blank. Inquiries to the Station Warrant Officer produced an abrupt dismissal. A deputation from we "plonks" finally gained an audience with the adjutant who was a little "put out" but said he would look into the inquiry. The AMO was posted some days later, causing a rush to the stores to draw enough tape to provide chevrons for both sleeves. The "permanent" NCO staff in the Sergeants' Mess didn't take kindly to the invasion of these "jumped-up" volunteer aircrew. Everything had obviously been arranged for we were allocated tables apart and a "second sitting" in the dining-hall. A division was also evident in the lounge area of this wooden building. "Okay, just passing through. Life on the squadron will be better," we consoled ourselves.'

The granting of commissions, particularly after training, was a contentious subject among aircrew, with many men believing that the decision was made on your background and not solely your ability. Certainly there were instances of this as noted by George Irving:

'Prior to completing the course at Cranfield we had to attend an interview for officer selection. We had been told at the commencement of our training that the granting of commissions depended entirely on our individual efficiency during training. Of the 43 pilots who finally completed their training, only eleven were granted commissions as Pilot Officers. It was noted that all of these had been educated at public schools. We others were given the rank of Flight Sergeant.'

Experienced civilian fliers, exalted scientists, notable business executives and the like who joined the RAF were often bestowed with a rank and task which the authorities thought fitting to their status. There was a suspicion of the 'old pal's network' in some of this; the managing director of a food manufacturing concern, who had never moved out of central London, given a squadron leader's uniform was one example. Such bestowals of rank were resented by those RAF regulars and VRs who had come up the hard way – and suffered by very senior officers who experienced the lack of military formality often exhibited. Tony Spooner:

'At the outbreak of war, the large Brooklands School of Flying civil flying organization concentrated its considerable staff of flying instructors at the RAF aerodrome at Sywell, Northamptonshire. By pulling in instructors from Brooklands, Sywell, Dunsfold, etc., it had about 50 civilian instructors. On 1 September 1939 we were all put into uniform according to which RAF Reserve we served. Some curious rankings resulted with the Deputy Chief Instructor becoming Flight-Sergeant Goldsmith with dozens of RAF officers under him. We had just the one bar. This became our joint mess with officers and sergeants mixing freely; as we had done the day before.

'Duncan Davis, who part-owned the Brooklands organization, appeared as a F/Lt while his local manager appeared as Wing Commander Mackenzie. Soon we were visited by a very senior officer, Air Chief Marshal Sir John Steel. Duncan and Mac were doing their best to explain to their distinguished visitor that we were really all civilian pilots "dressed up for war". It wasn't going down too well, especially as Sir John was critical of the usual "lunch-time snort" which we were having between the morning and afternoon sessions of battling with our pupils. To appease the visitor, Duncan decided to introduce him to a well-known peace-time pilot, Ken Waller, who had figured prominently in the famous race to Australia in 1934 in the original DH Comet. Now Ken was one of those who was wearing his brand-new Sgt-pilot's uniform. He was also a languid, affable chap who called nearly everyone "Old Boy". He was glad to be introduced. He rose gracefully from his chair. "Glad to meet you, Old Boy. Now it's my turn for a round. What will it be, Old Boy?" Somehow Air Chief Marshal Sir John Steel was not impressed by his brief meeting with the renowned flying instructor.'

The disciplines imposed by rank were an accepted part of the service. In combat units the division between officers and other ranks was not so rigidly imposed, particularly in crews with a mixed complement of officers and NCOs.

Basic training establishments tended to have the most authoritarian regimes for reasons already outlined. Interestingly, the most common prejudice against officers among other ranks is that reflected by George Watts:

'As to officers, I found the fliers and regulars much easier to deal with. War service ground officers were usually pompous and arrogant being ex-solicitors, council clerks and the like. We called them Penguins (no wings and flat feet). But this also applied to several NCOs in the same mould.'

The RAF, like the other services, had its share of those bestowed with temporary commissions who used their rank belligerently and to enhance their own standing. Those officers more involved in leadership than administration were generally of a more understanding nature, but the popularity of any commanding officer really hinged on the character of the individual. A good CO could be firm yet be seen still to be a good sort, a reputation which, once established, became known throughout his command even by those who had no direct contact with him. Vic Holloway:

'The CO at Montrose was one of the Coleman family, the mustard people. A great man and popular with all of us. The winter of 1940–41 was hard with lots of snow. He had all 1,200 men on the station out on the runway marching up and down in lines until we had trampled the snow down hard so flying could be resumed. And the CO was there, tramping up and down with us until the job was done. He liked his bit of fun too. At an officers' party I once saw him stand on his head and then drink a glass of whisky while supporting himself with the other hand. Of course, as an other rank I wasn't supposed to have been around to see this.'

Station Commanders also had sufficient rank to be able often to effect retention of personnel who enhanced their domain. Mick Osborne:

'The Station Commander at Martlesham was very keen on football and when he learned I had been a keen amateur player before joining up he soon had me in the Station team. Called The Robins, we were one of the best in the district and had a lot of success against other RAF and local teams. I went to Martlesham in 1941 as a rigger on the Air Sea Rescue Flight and stayed there for over three years. I'm sure this was because the Station Commander made sure I didn't get any postings as he wanted to preserve his football team.'

The workload of commanding officers in operational units was considerable, involving them in both administration and combat leadership. Even so, many impressed their men with the attention paid to an individual's welfare. James Donson, a pilot in No. 500 Squadron, gives an example of this:

'At the beginning of April 1942 we started operations in earnest under a new CO, W/Cdr D. F. Spotswood. Under his guidance the squadron was transformed and a vast amount of work was done with a corresponding boost to morale. In the first ten days of April my crew and I flew five anti-submarine patrols each lasting some 5½ – 6 hours. On the last one I had experienced one or two sharp spasms of stomach pain, but when we reached the limit of our patrol and turned for home the pains became more frequent and intense. We sent a message by W/T and some 2½ hours later we landed, closely followed down the runway by an ambulance. The squadron MO came on board and I was taken to the local hospital and had my appendix removed the same day.

'After about a fortnight I returned to the squadron. When the station MO saw me he glanced at me from his chair and, without a word, filled in a small piece of paper and handed it to me, made a dismissive gesture with his hand and I left. After a moment or two I read the chit, which simply said, "Fit to return to duty. Height limitation 4,000 feet."

'I made my way over to the squadron offices and went into the crew room where I was cheerfully greeted by the few aircrew who were in there awaiting the time of their next take-off. After a brief rest I went in to the office of my Flight Commander and told him I was fit to fly again. "So is my dead grandmother," he replied and disappeared at once. He reappeared almost at once and said, "The CO will see you now." As I entered the CO's office he was looking at the MO's chit which I had handed to the Flight Commander. His frown became more menacing. He had bushy black eyebrows, black hair and a formidable black moustache, all of which could make him look like an approaching thunderstorm. "This piece of bumf says you are fit to fly." He then looked me up and down. "It so happens that I am about to take off for a short air test to keep my hand in, you can come with me." As he was getting up from his chair he said, "My parachute is over there," indicating a corner of the room, "Pick it up for me, I'll just get my helmet from the locker." I walked over to the other side of the room and tried to pick up the 'chute. Try as I would I could not raise it beyond knee level. "Leave it, come and sit down." He opened the door and said quietly to someone in the orderly room, "Bring two cups of tea."

'He then went on to talk to me, questioning me closely about exactly what the MO had said to me, what examination and tests he had carried out on me, etc. I told him exactly what happened. During this time the tea came in and he talked of many things and asked me a host of questions, mostly concerned with service life, including, surprisingly, how did I feel about being under the command of someone younger than myself. That few minutes told me more about him than I realized at the time – that he wanted from everyone the best that they could give and that he was determined that they should be, as far as possible, happy and comfortable in the service to give it. He ended the interview with. "By the way, I am sending you on 14 days' leave. Flight Sergeant Frewen is flying to Liverpool tomorrow with his crew to be interrogated by the Navy into a possible sub' kill. Go with him, it will cut down your journey a good deal. Call at the orderly room in the morning for your travel warrants. Doc Gordon will be back from leave when you return and we'll see how you are then." Years later, I was not surprised to learn that a new Marshal of the Royal Air Force was Sir Denis Spotswood.'

COs were also faced with restraining the exuberance of junior officers, many of whom took a delight in trying to outwit authority or engage in pranks that officially would be classed as unbecoming. Few would deliberately confront their CO in this way, but it could happen by accident. Tony Spooner:

'Few pilots could have had a more varied and interesting war than I. Yet it was due to knocking over my Commanding Officer. It was my misfortune, as I then saw it, that I happened to be a pilot/navigation instructor at the outbreak of war. Being young and foolish, I wanted a more active piloting role. However, the great need was to create pilots and navigators quickly and in large numbers. So there I was. Moreover I seemed destined to spend the entire war instructing as the school which I served (No. 2 School of General Reconnaissance) was moving to Canada. I had my sailing date. Our training airfield, Squires Gate, Blackpool, a pre-war racecourse, was narrow. It was raining "cats and dogs". My Anson had no screen wipers. As I came in to land at the end of another detail, I espied a figure walking across the airfield. To teach the miscreant a lesson, I side-slipped the Anson straight at him, only kicking on opposite rudder at the last moment. It worked a treat. The man, in an officer's raincoat, broke into a trot and slipped in the mud. The last I saw of him, he was floundering like an abandoned turtle.

'"The CO wants to see you," I was informed upon arrival. "And me him, I want to report some silly clot. . . ." The CO was about the only Wing Commander in the RAF with the ribbon of the army's Military Medal upon his tunic. During the First World War he had been, so I was told, a Regimental Sergeant-Major before transferring to the RAF or RFC. Certainly he retained an appropriate stentorian voice. So fierce was this "bark" that he had been nicknamed "Woof-Woof".

'"Come in," he roared, in response to my knock. There he stood, covered in mud. He was a Wingco, I was a freshly commissioned P/O on probation. I tried in vain to point out that it was all his own fault; how dangerous it was to walk across the landing area in pouring rain. I was off the boat immediately. I never got to Canada. Nevertheless I had a fascinating war, flying everything from Tiger Moths and Spitfires to Liberators and Dakotas; survived three tours of ops and became a liaison officer with the Navy; all due to knocking over my Commanding Officer.'

Sometimes even squadron COs were not above being intimidated by those of very high rank and position as the following anecdote from John Wray shows:

'He was an Air Chief Marshal, the Inspector General. When he visited units he always picked on one particular subject upon which he briefed himself extensively, there would be no chance that you would know more about it than he did. If you tried to pull the wool over his eyes you'd had it. He always mentioned other things first, in passing, then suddenly the question. All the time he was catching imaginary flies as he spoke; clapping his hands together here and there. Most disconcerting for those being interrogated, already sitting on the edge of their chairs.

'He arrived at my Wing and I'd got the word through underground sources that the question was to be cleanliness of aircraft. I passed this on to my anxious squadron commanders. He always flew himself, accompanied by his white-faced PA. I met them and we proceeded to the first squadron. We sat down with the squadron commander and the action started. Details of operations were sought, did they like the aeroplane, etc.? The squadron commander's voice was now high-pitched as he eagerly tried to provide what he thought was the right answer. Suddenly, "What about cleanliness of your aircraft. How do you clean them?" "With petrol, Sir." "And do you find that satisfactory?" "Oh yes Sir, its gets them very clean." "Have you ever used Gunk?" "Oh yes Sir." "And how do you find that; does it clean the aircraft better?" "Oh yes Sir, it's very good, much better than petrol." The Air Chief Marshal was now catching flies: "That's interesting," he said, "It's not yet been issued to the Service."'

If an opportunity to take advantage of authority presented itself there were always those quick to act. Any innocent new to a unit or station was fair game as Tom Minta discovered:

'After arriving at St. Eval, a brand-new Pilot Officer on my first squadron, one of the early duties assigned to me was as officer in charge of church parade. Some 150 men were mustered, and off we went behind a band to the church which was close to the perimeter track. At the church, like the good bright boy I was, I stood in front of the parade and called out: "Fall out the Roman Catholics and Jews." I walked into church with about five blokes!'

RED TAPE AND INITIATIVE

Bureaucracy is despised, chiefly because of its impersonality. The mechanics of administration engender bureaucracy and, applied to a service through which two million men and women passed in six years of war, often became impersonal and sometimes a dispenser of the irrational. It seemed that there had to be a form and a number for everything. But errors were inevitable and once entered into the system were difficult to erase. The service number bestowed on each man or woman was a typical example of this, following a clerk's slip of the pen or finger on the typewriter. Tony Spooner:

'It all started when my newly wed wife said: "Isn't your number 740827?" When I nodded she went on: "Why then do they pay me my little wifely allowance under a different number, 740824?" I examined her Allowance Book. It was all too true. There she was married to Spooner A. Sgt-pilot 740824. I was new to the Air Force but not so new as to imagine that it didn't really matter. "Suppose," I thought, "that Spooner A. Sgt-pilot 740827 went missing, would the kindly RAF then pay a pension to the wife of Spooner A. Sgt-pilot 740824?" Something told me that they wouldn't. It would be bad enough to get the chop but doubly so if my "nearest and dearest" couldn't later collect.

'Thus began a fruitless correspondence. The more letters I wrote, the worse the situation became. On one occasion, thinking that perhaps a little humour might work where logic had failed so miserably, I signed one of my letters:

Spooner A. Sgt-pilot 740824
Spooner A. Sgt-pilot 740827
Spooner A. ACII

'At an earlier stage of my life I had been an insurance wallah and had passed the exams of the Associate of the Chartered Insurance Institute. At that time being an ACII was regarded as a "good thing". Back came a letter addressed to Air Commodore Spooner A.

'Relief seemed in sight when one day my CO informed me: "Spooner, you are up for a commission tomorrow. See that you clean your buttons properly for once and report to the Board at ten hundred hours." I soon became Spooner A. Acting Pilot Officer on probation, with a number of 82848. In this exalted rank, I was even allowed to pay my own wife an allowance. My troubles were over.

'But were they? Within weeks I began again to be haunted by my *alter ego*. A "Spooner A. Acting Pilot-Officer on probation, number 82948" began to appear. Until war's end I never knew which I was. Nor do I know which one of us was demobbed after it was all over. For all I know, the other must by now be the oldest PO in the RAF; perhaps with a whacking big pension, too.'

Many are the horror stories of clerical errors and the tribulations that followed. There was another common occurrence – to judge by the number of examples encountered. A recruit would be instructed in one trade, only to be posted to take up an entirely different trade. Likewise aircrew would end up in assignments for which they had not been trained. These changes were often deliberate and of necessity as there were no personnel available at the time to fill a particular demand. There were, however, to be irritating orders which could only be the result of blind administration. Vic Holloway:

'I joined the RAF Auxiliaries in 1938 as a driver and regularly drove RAF transports before being called up about three weeks before war was declared. Then three months were spent at Locking in Somerset driving just about every type of vehicle on the station. The next thing was an order to report to Blackpool for instruction in driving motor transport!'

It frequently appeared that postings were based on the whim of some clerk rather than meeting an actual requirement. 'You felt like pawns in some giant game being played out on a map of Britain – whom shall we send where next?' was the disillusioned comment of an airman who maintains he was shifted six times in six weeks. Tony Spooner also had an experience akin to this:

'Half-a-dozen of us were posted from Squires Gate to an airfield miles from anywhere deep in the heart of East Anglia. We were to report "at once". It was November 1940 and the London *Blitz* was at its worst. This had disrupted the British rail system. Our train came to a halt at a station near Leamington. "No trains to anywhere tonight" greeted us. More for a joke than anything else we inquired where "that little train was going". It consisted of a couple of ancient carriages pulled by a small tank engine. It had steam up. "Oh him; nowhere special. Have a word with the driver. See if he can help you." The driver was helpful. He could not possibly get us to East Anglia or to London but he would agree to take us to Northampton where we all had friends, but only if we paid him a night's lodging there. It was swiftly arranged. However, just as we were marvelling at the *ad hoc* manner in which the rail system was operating, we found ourselves defeated. A larger group had outbid us and had persuaded the driver to take them to Leicester!

'How the rail system managed to operate in this way I never discovered. Nor did we discover why we had to report to Bassingbourn "at once". When we eventually did get there, about two days late, they had never heard of us. Two of us were promptly posted to Lossiemouth instead. That train journey was also quite an event. At one time about 20 of us were "seated" on the floor of the luggage van of a panting train in the highlands with one dear old soul complaining that she had a first-class ticket. At Lossie? You guessed it. They, too, had never heard of us. Also, they only trained whole crews. However, after some delay they did teach us to fly Wellingtons. Whereupon we were posted to PRU at Benson to fly Spitfires!'

There were forms for everything and even forms to acquire forms. 'Too much bumf' was an oft-aired complaint at all levels. Records were necessary but some people's requirements for paperwork could be very frustrating. Alfred Pyner was one who suffered in this way:

Above: His Majesty King George VI in the uniform of Marshal of the Royal Air Force. (Official.)

Right: Billet fire escape enjoyed by Rex Croger (front) and friends while training in Canada. Note Air Gunner's brevet on Army uniform.

AIR MINISTRY,

WHITEHALL, S.W.I.

21st July 1943

MESSAGE FROM

THE SECRETARY OF STATE FOR AIR.

You are now an airman and I am glad to welcome you into the Royal Air Force.

To have been selected for air crew training is a great distinction. The Royal Air Force demands a high standard of physical fitness and alertness from its flying crews. Relatively few attain that standard and I congratulate you on passing the stringent tests.

You are, of course, impatient to begin and you naturally ask, "When do I start?" Your order on the waiting list is determined by your age, date of attestation, and so on; and you may be sure that you will not be overlooked when your turn comes.

While waiting, go on with your present job, or if you are not in employment, get a job - if possible one which helps on the war effort.

You will want to know why you, who are so eager, should have to wait at all. I will tell you.

The Royal Air Force is a highly organised Service. In the first line are trained and experienced crews whose stirring deeds and dauntless courage daily arouse the admiration of the world. Behind these men and ready to give them immediate support are the newly-trained crews fresh from the schools. In your turn, you and other accepted candidates stand ready to fill the schools. Unless we had a good reserve of young men, like you, on which to draw, time might be lost at a critical moment and the vital flow of reinforcements would be broken.

I hope this explanation will help you to understand. The waiting period should not be a waste of time. There is much that you can do. You are very fit now or you would not have been chosen. See that you keep fit. Work hard and live temperately. Learn all you can in your spare time about the things you must know if you are to be efficient later on in the air. The more knowledge you gain now the easier it will be when you come to do your training.

In wishing you success in the Service of your choice, I would add this. The honour of the Royal Air Force is in your hands. Our country's safety and the final overthrow of the powers of evil depend upon you and your comrades. You will be given the best aircraft and armament that the factories of Britain and America can produce. Learn to use them well.

Good luck to you!

Archibald Sinclair

SECRETARY OF STATE FOR AIR.

Left: Patronizing and unctuous letter sent to those accepted for aircrew to caution against possible delay in call-up.

Right: Most WAAFs considered the cap the best piece of their uniform. The smile is Maureen Brickett's.

Right: Ernest Thorpe in dispatch rider's gear astride an Ariel motor cycle. The beret was both practical and comfortable and dispatch riders were the first RAF personnel to be issued with this headwear which, eventually, superseded the forage cap.

Left: *Right dress! Even the girls did not escape drill. (Official)*

Right: *Ivan Mulley while at AVRC. The white cap flash was the distinctive mark of those accepted for aircrew training. Once having passed through ACRC and ITW to pilot or specialized training phase, the flash was tucked down inside the forage cap fold as an indication that one was no longer a complete sprog.*

Below: *Black on orange striped Fairey Battles used by the bombing and navigation school at Moffat, Rhodesia, 1943. (J. Heap)*

Above: *The popular Harvard (AT-6 in US terminology) advanced trainer over the Canadian wheatlands. (R. Croger)*

Left: *Pilot Officer George Irving, 29 August 1941.*

Right: Sergeant Ken Campbell, 1942.

Below: The visit of King George VI to Malta in 1943 included this drive up Kingsway toward Porta accompanied by Lord Gort, VC, the island's Governor. A souvenir snap from Graham Smith's album.

Left: Warrant Officer John Strain. (K. Campbell)

Right: Corporal Irene Storer.

Below: Dame Laura Knight's painting of a WAAF balloon site at Coventry features Corporal Irene Storer's Flight at work securing their charge. Corporal Storer is on the right. The bed, complete with concrete blocks, is shown behind the girls. This painting hangs in the Imperial War Museum, London.

Left: Pilot Officer Peter Thomas, first Nigerian pilot commissioned in the RAF.

Top right: The Sergeants' Mess at Marham airfields Norfolk, 1940. Fortunate were personnel posted to inter-war built stations such as this where barracks and messes were substantial and heated. (H. Kidney)

Right: Jim Donson and members of his Hudson crew outside one of Stornoway's cold Nissen huts.

Left: Sergeant Leonard A. Johnson. After his tour in Bomber Command he returned to the United States and was commissioned in the US Navy. He lost his life while in the comparatively safe job of operating flying-

Above: The wreck of Fortress WP: 0 at Kinloss. There were at least twenty hits from cannon-shells and bullets on this aircraft.

Top right: Sergeant Mick Wood (left) and Harry Sutton (right), a picture taken at Kinloss after the crash-landing.

Right: Wellingtons, the workhorses of Bomber Command during the early years. These are aircraft of No. 214 Squadron at Stradishall.

Left: Stanley Tomlinson, in centre of door nearest camera, and men of 149 Squadron pose beside Stirling OJ:K at Lakenheath. Patch forward of tail fin is the repair of battle damage sustained on 5 November 1943.

Bottom left: Nose decor of 'Friday The 13th', veteran No. 158 Squadron Halifax, when this aircraft was on display to the public at a site just off London's Oxford Street, summer 1945.

Below: Sergeant Steve Challen, Canadian volunteer, in 'flying togs' early 1941.

Above: Morgan Hewinson with other members of the crew.

Left: Flight Lieutenant William Reid, VC.

'Early in 1941 I was posted to Finningley, Yorkshire. As was always the case in the Air Force, if you were a latecomer you were an outsider; those already there were entrenched in comfortable places. So I found myself an LAC in charge of the flying wing stores for a new OTU being formed to handle the Avro Manchester. We had just one example for familiarization purposes. As it always seemed to have one engine removed it never flew. This and an assortment of other types and equipment was inherited from No. 106 Squadron which provided the basis of the new unit. At Finningley the main stores was still on a peacetime footing; the war hadn't disturbed the service's love of paperwork. I was confronted with a huge pack of volumes known as the RAF Vocabulary – spare parts books for everything under the sun. There was an even bigger pile of documents which were amendments to the first heap. Vouchers had to be filled out in triplicate and unless the paperwork was correct there was an inquest on every request or movement.

'One day I had to dispatch a rogue aircraft engine to the main stores. My training was that all plug holes had to be sealed to keep muck from getting into the cylinders while in transit. As I had none of the proper bungs I screwed in some sparking plugs I found, before the engine was hoisted on to a small lorry and sent off. The main stores would not accept it as there was no voucher for the sparking plugs!

'I was angry at this bit of red tape and not very happy when someone rang up to say he had put in an order for a table for his office two or three days ago and where was it? This only added to my irritation that someone should be fussing about a table when I was up to my neck in dud engines. I turned to my helper and asked him to look up the application adding: "There's some bloody bloke here who doesn't know there's a war on!" The following morning an arm with a lot of rings on it appeared round the door and a voice said: "I do know there's a war on." It was the Wing Commander Flying. He had evidently overheard my aside. But he took it as a joke; in fact he put me up for promotion to corporal. Only they now had to supply someone for an overseas posting and, of course, last in was first out. I went to South Africa.'

There were important records, such as those covering airworthiness. Trouble could rightly result from any breaches in this respect; aircrew safety could depend upon listing the correct information. James Kernahan had good reason to remember Form 700:

'In 1941 I was a flight mechanic, airframe, at Wigtown in Scotland, a training airfield. Taking charge of an Anson one evening, I gaily signed the Form 700 (which gave the serviceability status of the aircraft) on the word of the mechanic I was relieving, that he had performed the necessary inspection. The Anson was scheduled for a cross-country to Blackpool and back that night and when the crew arrived one of them moaned that he didn't want to go as he was missing a date. I consoled him with: "That's all right, you'll be back soon, the undercarriage doesn't work." So away they went. About a quarter of an hour later the Anson appeared in the circuit, came in to land and the undercarriage collapsed!

'Having finished my six-hour shift, I was awakened in my Nissen hut by an SP and taken to the station flight office to face a number of officers. By then I had a good idea what this was all about. One of the officers asked me to repeat exactly what I had said to the aircrew member of the Anson and why. I explained that it was just a joke and that we had been told always to put on a cheerful face for aircrew for it was not desirable for any man to fly if unhappy or stressed. They accepted my explanation and there were no questions on my signing the Form 700. That was the last I heard of the incident. But it was a lesson to me on how careless words could bring trouble.'

Much of the paperwork had to do with regulations, the need to establish and maintain order. But regulations were a handy excuse for many people to take no action, a bastion against initiative. Far too often when a change was patently desirable nothing was done. Albert Heald became involved in such a situation:

'The transport at Ridgewell before the first squadron moved in was limited to a crash tender, an ambulance and a few light vehicles. We found the crash tender was fitted with a speed governor on the carburettor as an economy device, restricting the speed of the vehicle. In December 1942 No. 90 Squadron arrived, but the first Stirling to land ended up with a collapsed undercarriage on the runway. The crash tender driver set off immediately as I and others clambered aboard. We started yelling "put your foot down" although we knew the thing would only do about 30mph flat out and due to lack of acceleration it took a considerable time to reach that speed. Additionally, we had to drive halfway round the perimeter track and then down the main runway to reach the crashed aircraft. Fortunately it had not caught fire, but received a spraying of foam just in case. Ironically the position where the Stirling came to rest was almost opposite the tender's parking place, but muddy conditions prevented a short cut across the grass. It was plain that if the aircraft had burst into flames it could well have been burned out by the time it was reached. The situation was brought to the notice of our administrators, but no action was taken.

'By coincidence a similar accident occurred sometime later while I was on duty with the crash tender. As the ground was frozen rock hard we took a short cut to reach the disabled Stirling – which again did not catch fire. As the action was against regulations there was an investigation as to why we had driven over the grass as opposed to the authorized procedure of going round the perimeter track. The result was removal of the carburettor governor and the construction of a hard road to the runway to enable the tender to take the shortest route. It took someone breaking regulations to get the administrative bureaucracy to act.'

Despite a system which often mitigated against individual enterprise, the inventive and the opportunists were in evidence and their actions were at times acknowledged by their superiors. An unusual example of initiative is recalled by Philip Knowles:

'In the spring of 1944, No. 650 Squadron, based at Cark-in-Cartmel, was involved in target towing for the Army, who were firing mainly with Bofors AA guns. Our Martinets were fitted with a winch mounted with its axis horizontally across the front of the rear cockpit. The towed-target operator (TTO) used this winch to let out the flag target on a steel cable, controlling it with a brake. The cable was wound in again by a small windmill (outside the port fuselage), which could be rotated so as to face the slipstream and power the winch.

'One army unit was particularly accurate and shot away four targets in quick succession, each time requiring the cable to be wound in and let out again with the new target. In this process the winch brake overheated and caught fire. With no fire extinguisher, Corporal Hall, the TTO operator, had to make use of the nearest equivalent with which nature had endowed him. This was successful, the Martinet got back safely and Cpl. Hall was commended by Group.'

A less fortunate incident was of Ken Campbell's making:

'The hydraulics of the Blenheim Mk IV were somewhat unique. The central system allowed two separate functions to be activated; one, power to operate the undercarriage and flaps (air brakes); the second supplied power to the gunner's turret. Unfortunately, however, not all at the same time. The drill was for the skipper to select wheels and flaps for take-off. On becoming airborne and well clear of the ground, the hydraulic power was transferred to the turret and the guns were brought on stream. Back in the circuit preparatory to landing, the switch was turned to make the undercarriage and flaps live again.

'On the morning of 13 January 1941 the squadron was assigned to a daylight escort job for a bunch of Coastal Command strike aircraft heading out over the North Sea to the enemy coast. During pre-flight briefing the Wing Commander reminded crews of the opposition's latest ploy, a hazard experienced by crews reaching home base on completion of recent sorties – as if we needed reminding! – Old Adolph's fighter boys had come up with the most delightful little party piece. As our Blenheims neared base and manoeuvred into position to make the final approach prior to landing, wheels down, a brace of bloody Junkers 88s swept in from nowhere and shot the hell out of us. Couldn't do a darned thing about it – no operating turret d'ya see?

'As was the usual routine after the main briefing, a question and suggestion session followed the essential operational flying tactics and planning. At this stage I feel it is time to mention that a tiny minority of the navigator and pilot fraternity looked upon air gunners as a pretty thick mob. Most notably such views were held by the odd callow youths with oodles of egg-head qualifications and fresh out of school or college. Gunners thick? – no way!

'Back to the briefing room where the Wingco had just finished talking. I stood up, touched my forelock and half stammered: "Sir, after the skipper has committed himself to landing with wheels down and part flap would he re-select the turret and we rear-gunners could very soon put a stop to Jerry's little skylark." I swear I saw the Boss grin happily and murmur: "By God, he's got it. The sergeant at the back there has solved the whole ruddy problem." Like I say, air gunners just ain't so stupid after all.

'I was rewarded for my brilliance by being made lead gunner in a vee formation of three for the escort. The operation was highly successful and all aircraft returned to base. Undercarriages were lowered and locked, turrets re-selected. It was great, all we rear-gunners were having a ball, firing the guns like they were going out of style. The Ju 88s buggered off right sharpish. I felt mighty pleased and smug with my day's work.

'We landed. The pilots couldn't extend full flap as the system was still tied in to the turrets. All three Blenheims ploughed through the hedge at the far end of

Bircham Newton. I dodged the de-briefing. I thought the air might be pretty solid around the Operations Room area. Maybe the sergeant at the briefing room was after all inclined to be on the thick side. Even so, I don't reckon the Wingco and the rest of the boffins were over brilliant for going along with such a bloody silly wheeze in the first place.'

There were also ideas that were too daring. Or, in the case offered by John Wray, decidedly suicidal:

'My squadron commander was a man of original thought. One night we were in the crewroom listening to Lord Haw Haw when the lights went out and a series of loud bangs told us we were under attack. The hangar caught fire so we picked ourselves up and rushed in to try and rescue our rather heavy aircraft by pushing them out on to the airfield. In the morning we came down to survey the scene and were surprised to see that one of the aircraft had six feet missing from one of its wings. No one recalled us hitting the doors in our hurry to get them out of the hangar and so we went inside to see if we could find the piece of wing. We did not have to search very far for there was a big hole in the hangar floor, and when we approached it and looked down we saw an unexploded bomb lying at the bottom weighing about 500lb. We all made off at high speed with one exception, our Squadron Commander. He had suddenly been struck with an idea that, in those circumstances, would have never occurred to any other rational human being.

'He called to his retreating adjutant, a meek and mild man of a shy and retiring disposition. "Come here," he said. "Go and get some rope and some airmen; we will get this out, have it emptied, paint it red, cut a slot in it and use it as our squadron post box." The adjutant remonstrated as best he could with an individual who was used to getting his own way, but to no avail. He had just returned with a length of rope and some very reluctant airmen when, fortunately, the Bomb Disposal Squad turned up. They were absolutely livid when they saw what was about to happen and sent everybody packing.

'Our station commander was a man of few words, but each word had a telling effect. He read the Riot Act to my squadron commander, who had heard it so often before that he knew it by heart. For our squadron adjutant he reserved the unfairest of jibes: "If you want to mess about with unexploded bombs, I'll get you posted to a Bomb Disposal Unit." Needless to say, within the week we had a splendid new squadron post box – a 500lb bomb, painted red with a slot cut in it through which one posted one's letters.'

BASES AND BILLETS

Peacetime Royal Air Force establishments provided reasonably comfortable accommodation for both officers and men. Many had centrally heated quarters, spacious messes and good recreational facilities. But a goodly proportion of the RAF's 'wartime warriors' were never fortunate enough to be posted to one of these stations, and, if serving in the UK, most likely only woke to view a Nissen hut ceiling's curved corrugations. The rapid expansion programme following the outbreak of war necessitated requisitioning large country houses, seaside hotels, furniture warehouses and redundant shops for use as barracks and to provide training and operational facilities. More than 2,000 establishments ranging from small listening-posts to vast storage and maintenance depots were used by the RAF in the UK from 1939 to 1945. Of the total, well over 500 were airfields or airstrips, less than 100 of which dated from pre-war. Therefore the most likely airfield billet would be one of the prefabricated huts, perhaps wood and felt or asbestos panelled if you were lucky, but more probably a Nissen hut with damp concrete floor. The old hands, like Morgan Hewinson, knew that one had to look after oneself, addressing the situation with the following unofficial dictum:

'Basic rules for aircrew on being posted to a new station:
1. Find comfortable accommodation.
2. Find the cycle store.
3. Find the Mess.
4. Report in. In that order.'

For comparative newcomers there was often little opportunity for choice; you went where you were told. Archie Elks:

'After we had done our signals and gunnery training we were posted as Sgt WOP/AGs up to Llandwrog, North Wales. When we arrived an NCO took us across to some Nissen huts which looked absolutely awful – dripping wet with water on the floors. He said, "That's where you'll be living. These are unfit for human habitation." Always being quick to meet sarcasm with sarcasm I quipped. "All right for aircrew then." "You're dead right!" he snapped back, and stormed off.'

From 1941 most new airfields in the UK were built to handle multi-engined aircraft to a Class A standard with paved runways and roads and accommodation for 2,000 souls. Each had facilities to make it self-contained, with electric power, water and sewerage if local services failed. Each Class A airfield cost about £1 million, a prodigious sum at the time, when labourers earned 30 shillings a week and a new bungalow might be raised for £500. The airfield building programme was, at the time, the biggest civil engineering feat ever undertaken in the UK; but due primarily to haste, the quality and nature of construction left much to be desired. Material shortages found many structures still incomplete when airfields had to be occupied. Obtaining further action to get matters put right was a frequent frustration. The solution devised by one enterprising officer faced with a problem was noted by Tom Imrie:

'I think RAF Polebrook must have been put together fairly quickly as during the summer of 1941, when there were frequent thunderstorms, the camp roads – particularly in the area of Squadron Headquarters – became flooded. The station commander, Group Captain Evans-Evans was obviously getting little help from "Works and Bricks" so, ingeniously, he retrieved a rescue dinghy from one of the Forts, put in three WAAFs and floated the lot on one of the ponds which had a road below. The photographs he sent to the Air Ministry did, I believe, bring immediate results.'

Airfields were constructed the length and breadth of the land, wherever the topography was satisfactory and, in the more rugged areas, where it was not. The locations of several airfields, particularly those for Coastal Command, were very much 'last resort' where a base was needed to better the range of aircraft that would operate from it. One such was Stornoway, which left a lasting impression on Jim Donson:

'At Kyle of Lochalsh we embarked on one of MacBrayne's ferries, which still serve the islands, and arrived at Stornoway at around 1am. A lorry drive and we were at the airfield in the early hours. After a makeshift meal we were shown to our quarters. Nissen huts surrounded largely by peat bog. Unfortunately no beds or lockers had yet arrived so we were obliged to make up our bedding on the floor. Travel-weary after the tedious two-day journey from Norfolk, we fell asleep at once, to be awakened a couple of hours later by a great clamour on the iron roof of our hut. This was to be our alarm-call every morning – sea birds in great numbers trying to alight on the slippery rounded roof in a high wind. After another hour or two of fitful dozing, a knock on the door was followed by the entry of the duty sergeant announcing that he would return in half an hour to escort us to the mess for breakfast. This we thought strange. We soon learned when we joined some half-dozen other new arrivals the reason for what at first appeared to be "Nanny" treatment. All the huts were linked by narrow paths which had been built by putting tons of hardcore into the peat and it was essential to keep to the paths. This applied all over the station, roads, runways, dispersals and so on. I found often that landing on either runway was rather like landing on a jelly. Proof of this was to be seen later when the pilot of a Liberator (the only one I ever saw land there) in turning at the end of the runway to taxi back, found that one leg of the main undercarriage sank slowly through the surface causing the Liberator to come to rest on one wing. There it had to stay until the runway had been sufficiently reinforced to enable the use of jacks and cranes to liberate the Liberator!

'The weather at Stornoway was another matter. I once had the job of flying with a new pilot, both to check him out and to familiarize him with the airfield and its surroundings. His only comment after landing was, "This is supposed to be July, does it piss down like this all the time?" I assured him there was a break, lasting maybe an hour, at some time during each week.'

One advantage of the large number of airfields dotted around the UK was the presence of a ready haven should the weather turn bad. In rugged country, thick cloud often hid hills and the prudent pilot did not penetrate the murk over high ground if he could avoid it. But dropping in to land unannounced at strange places could bring hazards, as Philip Knowles discovered one stormy summer's day:

'In July 1944 ground crew members of No. 650 Squadron, target-towing at Cark-in-Cartmel, attended a course to improve aircraft servicing efficiency. Since this was measured by the number of flying hours achieved per month, the pilots were encouraged to make flights whenever possible for whatever reason. As one result of this policy I was ferrying a squadron member to Glasgow to go on leave.

'On the far side of the Solway Firth the solid cloud base came down to the sea and it was obvious that we could not get to Abbotsinch. I decided to divert to Carlisle, where my passenger could get a train. This was a grass naval airfield with Sommerfield tracking providing a form of runway. I was surprised to see large white crosses near each end of the runway, but assumed that they represented aircraft carrier limits for Fleet Air Arm training. I received no signal from the ACP hut at the downwind end of the runway, but came in anyway. Just as I touched down I saw (a) a number of men leaping up from the runway; (b) the ACP hut was a builder's hut, and (c) there were large spikes sticking up from the tracking all around us.

'Fortunately we hit neither men nor spikes, but I got a terrible dressing-down from the naval Station Commander ("Didn't you see the white crosses?"). I got another rocket on returning to Cark, as my diversion had gone unreported and my failure to arrive at Abbotsinch had set off a search operation. Not a good day.'

The proliferation of airfields also produced the trap of which Horace Nears quotes an example:

'One night a guy came back from ops and there was a little bit of cloud sitting on top of Lasham so Flying Control told him to divert to Odiham. The pilot replied that there was no need to divert him as he could see the Lasham runway clearly. Flying Control agreed to let him land and switched on the floods. They waited and waited and finally became concerned when no Mosquito arrived. Not half as concerned as the pilot of the Mosquito when he found he had landed at nearby Odiham!'

Many of the pre-war airfields were situated in areas where they could not be extended or developed to meet the requirements of operating larger and heavier aircraft. Some prestigeous aerodromes were quite primitive by later standards. Tony Spooner:

'The American had crossed the Atlantic for the first time. Pan Am had flown him to the Shannon. Here he was taken to the land airport to board a Dakota for London. After an uneventful flight, the young RAF pilot of this aircraft, having safely landed at Croydon, recently restored to its original role of "London's Airport", was about to taxi in when the American burst into the cockpit. "Well done skipper. You made it OK but what happened. . . .?" The pilot looked puzzled. "Nothing happened. We've arrived. This is London Airport. . . ." "Oh gee, my mistake. I thought that we had come down in a field!" And so, of course, they had. Croydon was nothing more than a rather bumpy grass field; devoid of any runway and with a huge hollow at one end in which a Dakota could completely disappear from view from the Tower.'

Among the pre-war airfields was one originally formed from low-lying meadows that had a peculiar distinction which Morgan Hewinson exploited:

'The airfield at the School of Air Support at Old Sarum was a very special field. It had a watch tower to one side and a "land where you please" policy. What was unusual about it was the enormous crop of mushrooms it produced. Aircraft landed only infrequently, so with a promise from the watch tower controller to warn of approaching aircraft, one would go out on to the field in the evening armed with a large bag or container to collect the next morning's breakfast. Of course, the inevitable happened. No warning from the tower. It must have made a very funny spectacle; one small dark figure in the middle of the field not knowing which way to run as the light aircraft sped towards me. I felt as a snail must when being chased by a goose.'

Oppos

CELEBRITIES AND CHARACTERS

If one performed fairly mundane duties, day in and day out, for five or six years, the highlight of service could be coming face-to-face with one of the great names in history – an occasion remembered and recounted with pride. This was the case for Desmond Jenkins:

'Being a cook was a fairly uneventful job; most of my time with the RAF was spent in kitchens. The most memorable day of my whole service was Christmas Day 1944. I had been badly burned in a kitchen accident and was rushed to the burns unit of a large hospital just outside Brussels. That morning, while sitting in a bath of saline water having my chest and arm burns treated by a medical orderly, we were informed that Field Marshal Montgomery was going to pay a visit to the hospital and I had been one of those selected to meet him. This was a great thrill for a humble LAC and I was happy to sit in my bath of warm water, particularly as there was snow outside and the day was very cold. The press men were present and while waiting for the Field Marshal one of them took my photograph. It was a couple of hours before the great man arrived but it was worth the wait and a memorable experience. With the excellent Christmas dinner that followed, washed down with a few bottles of beer, it was an enjoyable occasion, despite my burns. A few days later an aunt, who was a nurse in a military hospital outside Cardiff, happened to be looking through a copy of *The Nursing Mirror* and to her amazement saw the picture of me in the saline bath. This was the first my family learned of my accident because I had been unable to use my hands and write home.'

An audience with the great could come about by chance circumstances; such as befell Graham Smith while walking to Valletta on a bright day in early 1943:

'The hot dusty road to Malta's capital seemed its usual long hike. The prayer was always a lorry of some sort, anything on four wheels would do. Lo and behold the answer to the prayer, a gleaming car with a pennant flying on the bonnet; chauffeur-driven. Field Marshal Lord Gort, VC, Governor of the Island deigning to stop and offer a lift to a mere LAC! "Hop in my man," came the gentle-toned command. I was put at ease immediately by his general manner as he enquired how long I had been on the island and asked for my overall comments connected with my stay, which covered the dark days right through to the rapidly improving state we had reached at this juncture of the conflict. The journey into Valletta seemed but brief as the Field Marshal chatted animatedly, especially when I mentioned that my father had served under him on the Western Front during 1914–18. He almost sounded as though I could have been referring to a fellow officer – not just Corporal Smith, one of the many thousands of men under his overall command.'

Even if you were not fortunate enough to encounter the truly famous, a crossing of paths could still be a memorable experience. Len Barcham:

'While on courier work I was stranded in France on Christmas Eve 1944 when our aircraft sustained damage taxi-ing over rough ground. After a Christmas of onion sandwiches I finally scrounged a lift back to England on the 29th in an American Dakota piloted by a Lt Geiger. Our destination was Bovingdon where Geiger put up a real black. On his approach he was given many red Very lights from the runway control van which he apparently chose to ignore, having failed to notice a Liberator behind him doing its usual long low approach. The Liberator eventually had to "go around" again. When we got into flying control the reception was not friendly and I was jolly pleased I hadn't been piloting. The Liberator was Churchill's and he was in it, just returning from the Yalta Conference!'

A souvenir linked with the famous is treasured by Hugh Berry:

'When volunteers were required for cinema projectionists I was accepted as this had been my civilian occupation. Eventually I was teamed up to operate Mobile Cinema No. 12, an Austin 3-ton lorry equipped with 35mm projectors, screen, petrol generator and all equipment to make it self-contained. Our job was to visit RAF establishments behind the North African battle lines and give the boys a film show. On one occasion we were playing to wounded in a Benghazi hospital and learned that in the audience was Lady Rosalinde Tedder, wife of the Air Commander-in-Chief who later became Marshal of the RAF Lord Tedder. Afterwards she kindly signed our Completion Certificate, a form required by the authorities in Cairo to prove we had actually given a performance. Lady Tedder didn't have her glasses and inadvertently signed on the line marked Comments but added "A very good show – liked by all." The next day she flew back to Cairo, the plane crash-landed, and she was killed. I still have the carbon copy of what was probably her last signature.'

Then there were those who actually knew the famous. Sid Cottee:

'While instructing glider pilots at Weston-on-the-Green I shared a hut with a tall, well-spoken chap with black wavy hair, named Desmond Leslie. I didn't know a lot about him but he took himself off to London a lot and had a good line in civilian clothes. One morning he didn't turn up for duty until around 10 a.m. The Flight CO, Flt/Lt Ridout, a ruddy-faced, bald-headed, experienced pilot who had once flown biplanes on the Northwest Frontier, properly let Leslie have it, demanding to know why he was so late. "Matter of fact," Leslie explained in his deep, cultured voice, "I was dining with the PM at Chequers last night and when I came to leave the guards wouldn't let me out." Ridout obviously didn't take kindly to having the mickey taken out of him by one of his tug pilots. "Why the ****** ****** didn't you go back and wake Winston up and ask him what the ****** password was?" he exploded. I didn't know it at the time, but Desmond Leslie was telling the truth; he was Winston Churchill's nephew.'

During the course of hostilities many famous people who had distinguished themselves in civilian life joined the RAF. The most popular were those who had made a career in entertainment or sport, becoming well known to the public through exposure at the cinema, on the radio or in newspapers and magazines. Thus it became a point of interest to relate that you served under Richard Murdoch or that Dan Maskall was your PT instructor, although such names would probably only mean something to your contemporaries. For others there was, and remains, a certain pride in having been in close proximity to one of the RAF's own famed; men such as Guy Gibson, Douglas Bader, Leonard Cheshire, Johnny Johnson and so on. There were also those in RAF service who had distinguished themselves in the First World War or in other spheres of aviation. A few were not only renowned for their deeds, but for their eccentricities. A famous individual encountered by Tom Minta was most certainly in the latter category:

'I was posted to the Central Flying School at Upavon. Not to learn to fly but as a mechanic to look after the many different types of aircraft they had there, ranging from current service types like Spitfires and Wellingtons to the new Stirlings and Manchesters. George Stainforth, Schneider Trophy winner and world air speed record holder, was the CO of the flight responsible for writing the Handling Notes for all new aircraft. George was quite a character. He would arrive at the hangar in the morning with a Sealyham and a pet fox both on leads. There were a couple of stakes in the grass with rings to which he tethered the fox while he was on duty. George would occasionally go home in the station "Spit", taking the Sealyham with him. His arrival back on Monday morning often featured a series of low passes, upward rolls and inverted flying as he beat up the place to make sure we were fully awake. Then he would land, taxi over, get out, lift up the flap just aft of the pilot's seat – which normally held the radio – and extract a basket in which was the Sealyham. The dog was retained by four pieces of elastic from its collar to each corner of the basket. It didn't appear to suffer unduly from the aerobatics but he did tend to walk sideways for a bit when he was put on the ground.'

Tom Minta was later – while serving with No. 58 Squadron – to encounter another extraordinary character who became something of a legend:

'One morning I was in Operations waiting to be briefed, when the CO said, "Oh, Mint, I want you to take a passenger with you tonight. Wing Commander Cohen. He's from Command and wants some first hand experience." Cohen turned out to be 68 years old and a distinguished First World War airman with a DSO and MC among his medal ribbons. This was the time when the U-boats had started coming out in packs. Because of the risk of cross-fire if we happened to come on a pack we tried to arrange that there were other aircraft in the vicinity that could be directed to make an attack. On this occasion we were called in by someone else but he had been shot down by the time we got there. Cohen was on the front gun so at least we felt he had seen a bit of action. We got back to Holmsley near midnight after about an 11-hour haul, debriefed and had sandwiches in the mess. Cohen said he'd like to see me in the Ops Room at 9 next morning. After a short, sharp sleep I made for the Ops Room, still somewhat tired. Reporting that I'd been asked to be there by Wing Commander Cohen, I was told: "Oh yes, he's left a message. He's awfully sorry but he decided he'd go out with the Beaufighter boys early this morning." I was more than a little taken aback and remember thinking that I hoped I'd be as spry if I made 68.'

Lionel Cohen's intrepidity and energy were remarkable for a man of his age. Recognition of this was his DFC in 1944. At 70 he was the oldest man to receive this award. Every command had its celebrities and, it seems, there were few units without a colourful character or two. This was particularly so on operations where stress and relief continually fluctuated and the latter was expressed in unrestrained conduct. Often a man whose air discipline was exemplary would be the life and soul of the mess on the ground. Such individuals are remembered with a mixture of affection and admiration by more sober comrades who never tire of recalling connected exploits. Typical is Ken Campbell's anecdote of a squadron star:

'Warrant Officer John Strain, a No. 489 (RNZAF) Squadron pilot at Wick in 1943, seldom made an error as a skipper when airborne in his Hampden, especially during an operational flight. However, it must be said, away from the flying scene the happy-go-lucky Johnny was guilty of dropping the occasional clanger.

'Among his many activities, "J.C." (as he was widely known) took a very keen interest in, and had a good working knowledge of, all his aircraft's equipment; not merely in the cockpit but bombsights, guns, navigator's paraphernalia, radios, etc. In line with this knowledge, Johnny liked always to see his aeroplane neat and tidy, he hated clutter which could impede quick access and exit should any emergency occur. He took a look around the inside of his aircraft two or three times a week to make sure all was up to scratch. It was during one of these informal "look arounds" that Johnny was in the vicinity of the rear turret, checking that there were no gash ammunition cases lying around, when he saw he was not alone. Beyond the rear gunner's position the fuselage of the Hampden narrowed so that it was an all fours job to progress further up towards the tail. Johnny could see the rear end of a prone instrument man who was in the process of servicing the master compass, which was situated just about as far back towards the tail as one could go. The repairer was intent on the delicate job and did not appear to be aware of Johnny's presence. Never one to miss an opportunity for a laugh, Johnny quietly stretched up the fuselage and prodded the instrument bloke sharply and firmly between the buttocks. "How's that for dead centre, chum?" quipped the practical joker, as the startled technician did an abrupt about. It was Johnny's turn to be startled; the betrousered WAAF instrument specialist was not at all amused!'

COMMONWEALTH AND ALLIED MEN

The Royal Air Force became a veritable mix of nationalities as the war progressed. In addition to British stock, there were a large number of volunteers from the Empire and Commonwealth, whose countries eventually supplied the complements for whole squadrons. Airmen who escaped the occupation of their European homelands were numerous enough to be formed into units with special national associations. There were also several hundred United States citizens who volunteered for aircrew, some of whom preferred to remain in the 'Raf' after America became involved in hostilities. Finally, there were the odd volunteers from other neutral countries, mostly attracted by the adventure of combat flying.

The first Commonwealth squadron in the RAF was No. 75 which, in April 1940, was designated as a New Zealand unit to be manned mainly by aircrew of the Royal New Zealand Air Force. Other Commonwealth designated squadrons followed; predominantly Australian and Canadian, and although personnel were part of their country's own air forces, they functioned under RAF command in the UK. As there were shortages of Commonwealth personnel trained in specialist trades or aircrew duties, these squadrons always had a varying number of British nationals on strength. Conversely, men from the Commonwealth and Empire were frequently to be found in RAF units.

During the early days a 'We of the Mother country know best' attitude prevailed in many quarters within the RAF which was, understandably, irritating to those from overseas. Mick Wood was involved in one incident that smacked of this bias:

'On the cold and foggy Boxing Day morning of 1940, a bus arrived at Uxbridge with the first batch of pilots from Australia. From the headquarters building came a Wing Commander demanding to know who we were and whence we had come. Someone explained that we were 32 pilots arrived for OTU training, having reached Scotland from Canada on the previous day. "And what is that uniform you are wearing?" "The Royal Australian Air Force uniform," we replied. "Well, you can't wear that here," he snapped. With that the entire 32 of us re-boarded the bus with a scarlet-faced Wing Commander feeling much put down by this batch of insolent colonials. Presently the matter was put right. The Station Commander appeared, welcomed us all and we were taken to the mess for lunch. With hindsight the mistake was probably reasonable. At that time the RAAF issue greatcoat had been cut for use by the post-First World War airmen who occasionally went about their duties on horseback; besides which the colour of the cloth was much darker than that worn by the RAF.'

A more blatant touch of prejudice was encountered by Vincent Elmer in a reprimand he received:

'The second morning after our contingent of ground crew men arrived at Middleton St. George we were allowed to go down to the hangars to see what Wellingtons and Halifaxes were like. Our training in Canada was only on basic trades and we had never been anywhere near any operational aircraft. We were going to have to learn our job from the RAF lads as we went along. There was a No. 420 Squadron Wellington loaded with incendiaries and HE bombs parked in front of a hangar. After looking it all over with great interest from outside, I decided to explore the interior and climbed up the ladder under the nose. Fascinated by the equipment, I moved along to the bomb-bay. Here I was too inquisitive and somehow managed to set off the flotation bags which were for use in a ditching. With the hiss of air going into the bags I made a hasty retreat back to the nose. There I was confronted by an RAF Flight Sergeant who had heard the hissing and was not at all pleased. He made his contempt for Commonwealth help very plain: "God blimey. You ruddy colonials! We should send you all over to

Hitler and the Luftwaffe. You'd soon mess things up and this war would be over in a hurry." '

Such an outburst was simply the normal habit of finding a convenient reason to distance oneself from the offender. Relationships between Commonwealth airmen and their British counterparts were generally excellent – many RAF men preferred to serve with Australian or Canadian squadrons. For young men making their first overseas journey, wartime Britain and its customs took a little getting used to. Vincent Elmer again:

'British plumbing was a joke to most Americans and Canadians, but my introduction wasn't at all funny. Soon after arrival in England I took the opportunity to visit a pub. Whether it was an effect of the beer consumed I do not know, but I had an urgent need to visit the toilet. The flush system was like nothing I'd seen back home and I couldn't find a handle. Finally I figured that the chain, attached to what looked like a cistern high up the wall above the toilet, must be the flush control so I gave it a pull. Nothing happened, but as there was a bit of resistance I gave it a real hard tug. A little too hard for the chain and just about everything attached to the other end came straight out over the top of the cistern and a cascade of water with it. The landlord didn't have a very high opinion of Canadians as he strove to check the flood.'

Apart from Canadians, Australians, New Zealanders and South Africans, there were representatives from just about every country in the Empire. A darker face among air crew was not that rare. One individual endeared himself to Jim Double:

'On 1 October 1941 I was posted to No. 3 EFTS at RAF Watchfield, near Swindon, Wiltshire, and on arrival was allocated the top bed of a double bunk. It was late in the evening and I found the bottom bed was occupied by a Nigerian who was fast asleep. He proved to be a distinctive character!

'He was Peter Thomas, son of a Nigerian chief who had, I learned from Peter, sponsored several Spitfires. Peter had been passed down from many previous courses to join the new intake! It was quite normal for him to get lost regularly while solo. Strangely, he would choose to land on the only ploughed field around and across the furrows to end up on his nose! He would come trudging into the billet late at night having been fetched home yet again! When we suggested he would get washed-out, his reply was always – "My father will buy some more."

'Halfway through the course it was wound up and we were transferred to the Arnold Scheme in the USA, but Peter remained at Watchfield. This lad had trained at an English university, but still insisted, should he get into combat, the enemy would not kill him as he would turn into a wild boar! After I returned from the USA I saw a photo of Peter Thomas of Lagos, the first Nigerian to be commissioned in the RAFVR; he had got his wings. Sadly, I later learned that he had been killed in a flying accident with a Spitfire. I still keep his photo.'

Then there were the men from the occupied countries of Europe: Poles, Czechs, French, Dutch, Norwegians, Belgians, Yugoslavs and Greeks, all of whom had specially formed squadrons linked to national identity; the most numerous being the Poles with fourteen squadrons and the French close behind with twelve. Here too there was a proportion of British personnel to fill trade vacancies or to ensure the necessary liaison. Polish pilots, particularly those in fighters, had a reputation for being a wild bunch but tenacious combatants; records show they achieved considerable success. As in the case of Commonwealth personnel, several men from the occupied countries served in RAF squadrons because there was no requirement in one linked to their country; but also sometimes through choice. These individuals often endeared themselves to the British airmen. John Wray recalls a man who won his admiration;

'This was a Free French Air Force Lieutenant in one of the squadrons in my Tempest Wing. He was small in stature, unprepossessing and wore rimless spectacles. Although he spoke good English, he was of a quiet and retiring nature. None of this was surprising because he had been a master in a school in a small village in France. The outbreak of war and the subsequent battles across France, resulting in the capitulation of that country scarcely touched him. He continued to teach, considering this was his job. However, when the Germans came to his village he became so incensed by their behaviour that he escaped to England and joined de Gaulle. So, to look at he didn't really measure up to what most people considered a pilot should look like. In fact, he wasn't a particularly good fighter pilot and those who had him flying as their No. 2 had an uncomfortable feeling in the seat of their trousers!

'Now the Tempest was a great fighter aeroplane, but she did have some annoying little habits. Like most women she did not like being kept waiting. If, for example, one had to wait to take off for any length of time because other squadrons were landing or taking off then, if you were not careful when opening the throttle for take off, at best you received a shower of oil over your windscreen and at worst the engine would stop. One day our Frenchman, taking part in an operation with his squadron, had to wait for take-off while a Spitfire Wing landed. When the Tempests eventually took off, our Frenchman's engine stopped halfway down the runway. He stood on his brakes but went off the end of the runway and turned over. I rushed out with the fire tender and ambulance, though fortunately the aircraft did not go on fire. However, unlike an upturned Spitfire where a few lusty airmen under the tail could lift it up to allow the pilot to be released, the Tempest was much heavier and so we had to get a crane, all of which took time.

'When eventually we lifted the tail the Frenchman dropped out, his right hand completely severed. This had come about when, realizing he was going to turn over, he instinctively put up his right hand to protect his face. The glass screen on his gunsight cut off his hand. Without a word, he jumped to his feet and started to walk towards the ambulance. Suddenly he turned round and walked back to the aircraft, he got down on his knees and reaching inside pulled out his parachute. He stood up, threw his parachute over his shoulder and walked to the ambulance. I saw him six months later in the bar of the Park Lane Hotel, fitted with an artificial hand. It is to my eternal shame that I have forgotten the name of this little French schoolteacher with the heart of a lion.'

And then came the Yanks. Many young Americans had joined the RAF before their country found itself at war with Germany, mostly by volunteering for the RCAF. Americans turned up in every RAF command and quickly earned the respect of those with whom they flew. There was a certain amount of glamour attached to the image of Americans, as most British ideas were derived from the cinema where Hollywood dominated. A friendly, outgoing nature was the general impression left through initial contact, but the ladies sometimes had their expectations of glamour squashed. Alan Haworth:

'My skipper, Johnny Johnson, was a Texan farmer who went up to Canada early in 1941 and joined the RAF. He was a burly, good-natured guy who, being a Sergeant, was issued with boots whereas I, a Pilot Officer, had shoes. On Saturday nights when we were not flying, together we went to dances held in the upper hall of Haverhill town hall. The floor of the hall must have seen a lot of use because it was worn quite smooth, but had hard knots in the wood which protruded as bumps. During the course of those dance evenings in the summer of 1942 Johnny's feet got rather hot so he would take off his boots and dance in stocking feet. But as he was afraid his boots might be pinched if he left them in the cloakroom, he insisted on tying the laces together and wearing them round his neck while he danced. I cannot remember him making many conquests among the Haverhill belles!'

The cockpit of a fighter was the main attraction and not at a loss to recognize the political and propaganda value of letting United States' nationals fight the Luftwaffe, the Air Ministry formed three special American fighter units identified as Eagle Squadrons. These were ultimately transferred to the United States Army Air Force (USAAF) when this organization commenced operations from the UK in the summer of 1942. By this time the RAF was battlewise and prepared to act as mentor to their American cousins. The general expectancy among RAF personnel was that US airmen would be much like themselves apart from different accents. The reaction on finding that Americans had different attitudes and outlooks on many aspects of both the military and social scene brought – behind their backs – mild disdain, ridicule and even a little resentment. The new allies were welcomed, but many RAF officers reserved an opinion. The stories were many. James Donson:

'In July 1942 I was involved in flights from Stornoway to set up a navigational beam for an operation known as "Mother Hen". The purpose was revealed when one day a B-17 Fortress appeared with a dozen P-38 Lightnings in formation, soon followed by similar air reinforcements from America via Greenland and Iceland. There seemed to be little room on the airfield while the P-38s were being serviced and refuelled. It was our first meeting with any Americans and we immediately discovered that their attitude was more informal than ours in the officers' mess. One entered in full flying kit, including calf-length, red leather, high-heeled boots with spurs. He removed the bulb from a light socket, plugged in an electric razor and proceeded to shave. Those RAF officers present did their best to look unconcerned and refrained from comment in the best interests of this welcome new alliance.'

There is no doubt that Americans had their preconceived ideas about the British and were somewhat surprised by many aspects of wartime Britain. If we found their military conduct casual they were undoubtedly amazed by the antics that transformed many an RAF officers' mess as Tony Spooner observed:

'One evening in the summer of 1943 a B-17 unexpectedly dropped in at
Turnberry after a flight from the USA via Greenland and Iceland. The crew were
invited to stay the night. Later that evening we decided to introduce the pilot,
who hadn't been in the UK before, to our particular mess game of stripping down
to underpants and carrying out a circuit of the room via the chairs, tables, rafter
beams, etcetera without touching the floor; made more difficult by carrying a
lighted newspaper. He entered into the spirit of the game but was obviously
astounded by our antics. It transpired that before leaving the States he had been
briefed not to expect too much overt friendliness because of our natural reserve.
Hence his repeated muttering as he went round the course of, "Heck, where's all
this British reserve." '

Nevertheless, what were seen as the idiosyncracies of their new allies became
the subject of many a mess anecdote in RAF establishments, often embellished to
add the correct trans-Atlantic flavour. An accomplished raconteur like Hamish
Mahaddie could make delightful play with an occasion he recalled:

'I was supposed to be fielding for a scratch baseball team and was put out as
far away as possible so as not to interfere with the play . . . when a Fort landed at
Oakington. A funny little gentleman with a baseball cap, smoking the last of a
cigar, got out and approached me, stopping a few yards away. He put his hand in
his battledress jacket and pulled out a very large John Wayne-type hand-held
cannon, pointed it straight at me and asked: "Say Bud, do you speak English?" I
replied that being a Scot there was some doubt about that. He then asked what the
name of the town behind me was and I said it was Cambridge. He said: "Is that
the same as Yale and Harvard?" and I said, "Good gracious, no, there is a lot of
doubt about that." He then asked in which direction was Alconbury and, having
got a taste for the jargon, I said: "Just go down this trail a piece for ten, maybe
fifteen miles, and there you will find Alconbury." He then put away the hand-held
cannon, got back in the aircraft and took off. We heard later, however, that he
was very lucky because many aircraft of that squadron landed in France where
they didn't speak English! But very rough old Germanic Saxon. . . .'

The American fliers were integrated into the British system of flying control
and also adopted many other RAF procedures. RAF personnel acted as
instructors until such time as the Americans could provide their own. Although
much was new and strange, the Americans learned quickly. Inevitably, there
were some individuals who were not easily led from more casual ways as Bill Japp
discovered:

'When a new US B-26 Marauder Group arrived from America in 1943 the
crews had to be instructed in the Flying Control and R/T procedures used in
North Africa. A number of RAF Marauder pilots were assigned to fly in the right-
hand seat to check out the American captains on these procedures on completion
of their course. This revealed that at least one of the Americans wasn't convinced
of the necessity of correct radio procedures. I was flying with a pilot who went
through all the formalities for take-off correctly and was cleared to proceed in his
aircraft "D-Dog". As we were going down the runway, from the B-26 behind us
came the laconic inquiry to the tower control: "Say, can I follow that rollin' dawg
now?" '

For some RAF stalwarts the assessed shortcomings of US airmen remained a convenient moan, just as there were those US personnel who preferred to see only the worst side of the British, but eventually there were few RAF men who did not come to acknowledge that their USAAF counterparts were making a major contribution to victory. Perhaps the relatively higher pay and the attraction British women had for Americans invoked a little jealousy, but practically every RAF man who had first-hand experience of US servicemen found them likeable. American benevolence was famous too, as Harold Southgate experienced:

'When stationed at Defford, with the Telecommunications Flying Unit (TFU) in the later stages of the war, it proved quite difficult and time-consuming to use public transport for returning to Colchester on leave. Knowing there was a USAAF base at Boxted just outside the town, I had the idea of trying to arrange for someone to fly me to Boxted in order to get home quickly. This was surprisingly easy to arrange as an experimental flight with a Lancaster. It took 45 minutes to fly to Boxted where we received immediate permission to land. My aircraft took off back to Defford while I reported to the Control Tower to be greeted warmly and asked where I was heading. Told that I was going home to Mile End, about three miles from the airfield, the Duty Officer immediately rang for transport and within minutes a jeep arrived and conveyed me to my front door. Total time less than one hour compared with the seven to nine hours if I had come by train. Never had a bad word to say against the Yanks after that!'

ATTITUDE TO SENIOR SERVICES

The air of vanity which pervaded RAF personnel, in spite of belonging to the Junior Service, was also reflected in inter-service rivalry. Predominantly good-natured, one never missed an opportunity that arose to score points off the Army or Royal Navy. Tony Spooner gives an instance:

'As was the custom, when a group of RAF officers became accustomed to a station they adopted a certain bar. It became their off-duty "drinking hole". So it was at Blackpool. The staff of the School of General Reconnaissance there adopted the Casino Bar. To our horror, we were "invaded" one night by a group of very "la-de-dah" army officers in full regimental dress. They must have been Hussars or some such judging by their colourful uniforms with much chain-mail around their young shoulders. It was too much to bear. One of our lot sidled over with a sweet, innocent expression and inquired: "Would you young gents mind settling a bet for us simple RAF folks. Which of the colliery bands do you all play for?" '

Naturally the japes were not all one way. Tony Spooner again:

'Thanks to really foul weather there was no air activity by either side over Malta on Christmas Eve 1941. The beer flowed. I had been working in close co-operation with the Fleet Air Arm squadrons at Hal Far, only a few miles from my own base at Luqa, and it was natural, when the booze was running out at Luqa, to pay them a visit to see how their booze supply was coping. Their supply seemed unending, their hospitality was generous and I was soon incapable of driving myself back to Luqa. "Not to worry, old chap. We'll put you up. . . ." The accommodation was by far the most palatial I experienced in Malta. Sheets (long forgotten around Luqa), a huge dry room, a real bed and they even supplied me with red silk pyjamas. Soon I was dead to the world and it would have taken a bulldozer to have awoken me. It was only next morning, when a startled orderly roused me to advise me that the officers were about to serve the men with their Christmas dinner, that I learned that I had spent the night in the bed, and in the pyjamas, of the Station Commander – a naval Captain. I didn't visit Hal Far again.'

The frequent use of 'pongo', 'squaddie', 'fish-head' and other such terms for soldiers and sailors underlined the slightly contemptuous view RAF 'bods' had of the sister services. On the serious side there was considerable co-operation in many spheres – the Army Co-operation and Airborne Forces squadrons which involved mixed Army/Air Force teams. Likewise Coastal Command liaised with naval establishments. There was also an interchange of personnel to fill specific needs if one service had a surfeit and another a dearth. Fleet Air Arm mechanics were used to service Stirlings in airborne squadrons. These were remembered with affection by Jim Swale of No 295 Squadron:

'A number of Fleet Air Arm lads joined our airborne operations squadrons at Harwell just before D-Day and stayed with us when we moved. Few had ever been to sea anyway. We, however, were literally "at sea" for some time, as their nautical terms kept us in a state of high amusement. The plum being, "Are you going ashore tonight?", which meant a visit to the towns and villages around Rivenhall. We called them matelots, a mixture of sarcasm and endearment I suspect. It did not really matter, for they were good lads. Two who had been warned not to ride their bikes behind Stirlings waiting for take-off clearance at the end of the runway, just ignored the warning. As they pedalled behind one of these aircraft the pilot put on full boost. The result, two matelots and two bikes blown across the airfield like paper bags, causing damage, a broken arm and multiple bruises.'

Whether Army, Navy or Air Force, there was an unspoken bond between all servicemen, past and present, as Albert Herbert discovered:

'With my "half wing" and stripes up, I passed out of Madley, No. 4 Radio School with a posting to London. I popped into the tea bar at Liverpool Street Station for a cuppa and a sandwich. When I went to pay my bill and gave the old lady behind the counter my half-crown, she said that I must be proud to be a pilot and that she hoped I'd shoot down one of those Germans for her. I didn't want to disappoint her by telling her that I was a wireless operator not a pilot, so as I picked up my change I said "I'll try" and left to catch a bus. When the conductor came round I discovered the old lady had short-changed me and I only had half the fare. Embarrassed, I explained to the conductor that I was on my way to my next posting and had nothing more in my pocket. He took what I had and gave me a wink. When I got off the bus I noticed he had a DSM and '14-18 ribbons on the breast of his jacket. Then I understood why he let me ride the whole way to my destination. "Thanks mate," I said.'

WOMEN'S AUXILIARY AIR FORCE

The Women's Auxiliary Air Force came into being as an adjunct of the Royal Air Force two months before the outbreak of war. Broadly, its purpose was to use women in a supportive role, in suitable duties where they would release men for other work. Initially these duties were few and chiefly of a domestic and clerical nature, reflecting the general male view of a woman's place in society. The supposed frailty and subordinate role of WAAFs was reflected in the Air Ministry's view that they should be paid a third less than most equivalent male ranks and receive a smaller food ration. In reality, like their male counterparts in air force blue, WAAFs came in all sorts and sizes, many with healthy appetites and not lacking in physique or physical ability. By all accounts a few were more worthy of belligerent duties than many males who had to shoulder rifles. Irene Storer encountered one such individual while training:

'In our entry was a girl of voluminous proportions and with thick, wiry vermilion hair. She turned all conversation into an argument during which she soon ran out of words and let fly with her fists which had some weight behind them! We all kept our distance if we could. From somewhere she had received a black eye over which she wore a black patch. We were all marching along past a brick wall with a line of airmen sitting on it when one of them called "Hello Nelson". She hesitated then stopped and we all thought she was going to pull the man off the wall. She changed her mind, however, and carried on marching. I suppose she reasoned that it was not worth a charge just as we were about to be posted to our sites.'

There were, apparently, misgivings among some senior RAF officers about having women in the service at all. The chief concern being that feminine charms would distract men from their duties. Certainly romances occurred but RAF personnel who served alongside WAAFs quickly came to appreciate their contribution to the war effort and thought of them first as workmates. Indeed, the general dedication and efficiency of these girls earned them considerable respect among both airmen and officers. Rex Croger's assessment of those encountered in No. 26 Squadron is not untypical:

'Most of the squadron transport was handled by three WAAF drivers; they took us to our aircraft and collected us on return. They were fine, good-looking girls. We went swimming with them in the Solent now and again. They didn't bother about costumes! But it was all decent fun; the relationship was platonic. We were all good mates.'

The pre-war morality, where the majority of British women preserved their virginity until marriage, was challenged by wartime pressures. For servicemen the knowledge that there might not be a tomorrow undermined sexual restraint. Being removed from parental influence and on stations where men predominated, some girls did engage in unguarded amorous affairs. Elsie Lewis was a WAAF Nursing Orderly who saw the result of such liaisons:

'There were a few young girls who got into trouble. Usually the new recruits who had been at boarding-school or strictly brought up. To them life in the WAAF was comparative freedom but they didn't know how to cope with it. One girl started to develop a tummy but said it was due to a gnat bite when the MO made another suggestion. When she said she hadn't been with anybody and insisted it was a gnat bite he commented to me: "All right, we'll have to wait won't we Lewis. Nine months should see who is right." An NCO was heard to murmur. "It must have been a bloody big gnat." '

Such happenings involved only a small minority; for the most part chastity prevailed. Many girls volunteering for the WAAF were young and of comparatively sheltered upbringing; even a little naïve when it came to the crude world of servicemen. While men would modify their language and conform to accepted behaviour in the presence of WAAFs, there was many a kindly joke at the girls' expense behind their backs. This example from John Wray:

'My station Equipment Officer was a well-known businessman who would shortly be returning to civil life. I was on one of my tours of the station and dropped in on him to have a chat and a cup of tea. While we were talking a knock came on his door. "Come in," he said. The door opened and in walked a young WAAF. "Please Sir, where can I get felt?" The Equipment Officer and I dared not look at one another. "Go down the passage", he said, "and speak to the Sergeant, he will help you." Once the door closed we both exploded!'

It would also be wrong to imply that the WAAF was characterized by the young and innocent. The average age was 23 years and a goodly proportion, if conscientious in their duties, were high-spirited enough to flout regulations if they thought they could get away with it. Fraternization between officers and other ranks was not encouraged and there was a certain amount of risk involved in pursuing such harmless associations as Eva Sizzey discovered:

'I was friendly with a WAAF officer and at her invitation went out for a trip to St. Ives when we had some time off. On return, a boyfriend of hers gave us a lift in an Air Force vehicle. My cycle was put on top of the roof. When we got back to Oakington and into the WAAF site, as he drove round a corner my cycle fell off right in front of our Orderly Officer's van and she ran over it. My officer friend made out the cycle was hers, while I hid down behind the back seat of the vehicle we were in. If I had been found out it would have been "jankers".'

Punishment of WAAFs was a peculiar business. Legally a girl had the right to refuse to accept punishment and could discharge herself from the service. A situation that understandably was not given prominence and was unknown to many girls. WAAFs subject to disciplinary charges usually appeared before their RAF Station Commander or his deputy. John Wray relates a skilful piece of manoeuvring when erring with a penalty:

'Mine was the only squadron on the station and so when the Station Commander was on leave I had to act as such as well. I carried out these duties, mainly, by calling in at SHQ each day to deal with any business that the adjutant had for me. One morning he said, "We have a WAAF on a charge of losing a Service bicycle." These bicycles, issued to those whose duties required them, were not supposed to be used for private purposes. Needless to say, they were. This WAAF had taken hers down to the local pub and somebody had pinched it. I sat in my office looking very formal and the young WAAF was marched in by the WAAF Flight Sergeant, accompanied by the WAAF Officer. The usual procedure of identification of the accused was followed and the charge read out. She had absolutely no defence. She had done it and the bike was lost. I gave her a reproving lecture on responsibility for public property, delivered with great pomposity. I went on to say, "This is a very serious offence and so I am going to make you pay for the cost of replacing this bicycle." This was about £4.

'She, being on about four shillings a day, burst into tears and was led sobbing from my austere presence by the Flight Sergeant and supported by the WAAF Officer. When the door closed the adjutant said, "You can't do that. You have exceeded your powers. You can only dock her a maximum of a day's pay." "Oh dear!" I said, "We had better have her back." A red-eyed WAAF was then marched back and I said to her, "I have reconsidered my decision and have decided to be lenient with you, you will pay four shillings instead of four pounds." '

The WAAF constituted more than 15 per cent of the overall personnel strength of the RAF. At peak strength in mid-1943 they numbered 181,835 of whom one in 26 was an officer. While largely a volunteer force and drawing girls from all walks of life, commissioned WAAFs tended to be middle or upper class, several with academic qualifications and, like the other women's services, among the officers one could encounter the daughters of important people. George Irving:

'I made an awful "black" one evening at Bradwell Bay. We had retired to the lounge for coffee and dinner and joined a group "chatting up" some WAAF officers, one of whom offered me a cigarette. Just as I was about to take one I noticed it was a Craven A, a type I disliked to smoke. So I apologized in what I thought was a humorous way by saying, "Thank you very much indeed but I never smoke Craven As. I think they are awful." She looked at me in rather an odd way and carried on her conversation with the others. Later, when it was time to leave to go on patrol, one of our chaps came to me and said: "You rotten bastard, just as I was doing a nice line chatting up that lovely brunette you go and offend her." Nonplussed, I asked how. She had only offered me a cigarette which I declined because it was a Craven A. Jock then told me the lady in question was Miss Carreras, whose father owned the tobacco firm producing Craven A. Next evening I was able to apologize to her for my lack of tact in refusing a cigarette. I must have been forgiven because she presented me with a full 20 packet of Craven A, saying, "It's time you stopped smoking that other rubbish; try these again."'

Whatever the background of a WAAF officer, an RAF other rank did not have to salute her unless he chose to, another reflection of prejudice in a male-orientated service. What would become identified as feminism was never really evident in the wartime WAAF, but many girls found intelligent comradeships among their WAAF associates. Irene Storer:

'One evening I went into a hut and found the girls listening to "The Brains Trust" on the wireless. I was surprised. "Come on Corporal," said one girl, "It's "The Brains Trust tonight." I sat and listened and found that they turned the programme into a discussion group cum questionnaire among themselves, with much laughter. It was amazing. A thought struck me that we could organize our own "Brains Trust", which we did, with me thinking up the material for it. It was great fun and what a lot I learned about those girls in that pleasant way. One could put up with such hard work and deprivation in living conditions when you shared it with people as sensible as those.'

As the months passed so the duties and trades in which the WAAFs predominated multiplied. By VE-Day WAAFs served in some 85 defined categories ranging through clerical, store-keeping, vehicle driving, engineering and barrage balloon handling. A vital task in which they excelled was air traffic and operational control. WAAF were to be found in most control rooms on combat, Sector and Group stations. In these duties many became very familiar with squadron loss and achievement. Another aspect of this is recalled by Maureen Brickett:

'Working in Ops was a fascinating experience – we were almost always busy and the work was varied and interesting, but of course there was a sad side to it – often groups of young and glamorous pilots would come to see "the other side of the job" during their "resting periods"; sadly on their return to flying duties many of them were shot down – what a dreadful waste it all was.'

The most physically exacting trade in which WAAFs figured was that of Balloon Operator. Not only did work on barrage balloon sites demand physical strength, it frequently meant exposure to the worst excesses of UK weather. Louise Howell:

'Being in Balloon Command was a hard but rewarding job in every way. We were a small band of twelve to each balloon, always sited on the outskirts of a town, usually in a park. We did everything ourselves, even making up the guy ropes and splicing steel cables. The times I dreaded most were periods of bad weather and high winds. On these occasions we were out most of the night, turning the nose of the balloon into wind whenever it varied. One wild night I got caught up in the tail rope and suddenly sailed ten feet into the air; not a very pleasant experience.'

During 1942 the WAAF became the major source of personnel in Balloon Command, serving in more than 40 operational squadrons at strategically important locations throughout the UK. Each balloon site was normally in the charge of a WAAF Corporal, an exacting command for what could be a dangerous job – steel cables downed many balloon operators as well as enemy aircraft. The following is Irene Storer's account of a hazardous event:

'Then came the day when, at about 12.15 I left the office to go and see how the lunch was faring. The phone rang and the LACW dashed into the kitchen calling. "Storm-bed Corporal!" "What?" said I. It was a lovely day. I told the duty cook to keep the dinner warm and ran outside. The sky was clear except for a few clouds away in the distance which were rolling together like a speeded-up film and heading for us. I called to everybody "Storm-bed!" They all dashed to their positions and we had that balloon down in double quick time, which was none too soon. I stood as near as I could to the winch driver saying, "Slow down, now speed up again," and so on. We all had our eyes glued to the balloon. Suddenly a civilian woman ran screaming on to the site and made straight for me. I couldn't have anything to do with her at all, the situation was dangerous enough as it was and anything could happen if I were distracted. The duty cook heard her and ran up and grabbed her away from me. She kept shouting "Come and shift this balloon." She was taken to the kitchen where she explained that a balloon had caught fast on her chimney pot and her house was full of smoke. The cook asked her if it was ripped, because if not then it was full of gas which could set fire if she did not go home and put her fire out. She could see it was obviously not our balloon. She went home after the cook had promised to inform HQ of her address.

'We had just finished bedding when a freak wind hit us. I made everybody sit on chairs round the balloon, each of us watching a section of it. Every time anyone saw something slip or come unhooked she dashed up and re-fixed it. The concrete blocks banged up and down on the bed making an awful din. It was over an hour before we were able to leave it in the hands of the guards and go in to partake of a belated dinner – during which we watched balloons sailing away in the air, some with sandbags hanging on them and we all thought it looked very funny. Those balloons could have come from anywhere and must have broken away before the rip-line was tied to the bed. Later we learned that ours and the one at Arboretum Park were the only ones saved in Derby. I think it was Coventry that lost every one. I was glad HQ had given us the order in good time.'

Two members of the site team had to stand guard over the balloon night and day, come fair or foul; usually the latter in the British climate. This could be a miserable task, particularly as protective clothing appeared to be available only in large sizes. Louise Howell:

'If there were small sizes for the WAAF I never saw them. Every Monday morning a lorry delivered clean overalls. When the pile was thrown out there was a scramble to find a pair to fit. Needless to say, being only 5ft 2in I always ended up with one a foot too long in the legs. As for being dressed for night guard duty, which each of us had to do, two hours on, four hours off, any German who invaded our site would have died laughing at the vision he encountered. I had to stand all the time because I couldn't sit down in all the gear I was wearing. This consisted of a pair of slacks over my pyjamas, a sweater, seamen's thick socks, that came nearly to my thighs, Wellington boots, an oilskin coat that hung down to my feet and with the sleeves turned back to my elbows, and all topped with a sou'wester hat that was so big it fell over my eyes whenever I moved. Last but not least a truncheon to take on intruders and a whistle to call for help!'

While WAAFs proved their worth in many and varied duties, they were not permitted to fly aircraft. Knowledge of this led to many aircrew being surprised in a similar way to the incident described by Frank Cheesman:

'One fine morning in mid-1942 the inmates of No. 11 (P) AFU, Condover, were agog with anticipation by the rumoured visitation of a Mosquito aircraft that very day. At this time the Mossie was largely an unknown quantity, so to speak, to the general public and even in the RAF by no means commonplace, so its appearance at this training unit was looked forward to with no little interest. Although all had heard of its achievements and capabilities, few had been fortunate enough to see one at close quarters. Now was their opportunity. Mixed with a natural curiosity about the aircraft itself was an understandable interest to see just what type of superior being the RAF considered suitable to fly this fabled aircraft. The general opinion was that only pilots of above average ability and great operational experience would qualify. With these thoughts in mind groups of airmen and WAAFs, all of whom had contrived some reason for their presence on the airfield, gathered near the expected parking spot as the Mossie seemingly hurtled round the circuit with the pilot inspecting the airfield and awaiting a "green" from the Control Tower. The critical audience noted with approval the smooth final approach and touch-down as, despite the high speed, the main wheels merged with the runway in a noiseless and smokeless union. An absolute "greaser" of a landing which seemed to bear out their view that only the best pilots were to be entrusted with such a "hot ship".

'The Mossie turned off, made for the marshaller and switched off. After a while and with the ladder in place the pilot made his exit. There first appeared a pair of bootees into which were tucked dark blue trousers. "Hell," said someone, "the Fleet Air Arm." The next forecast was, "A bloody Aussie." Both were wrong as further steps revealed a strikingly good-looking and rather shapely young lady of the ATA. Shock and confusion reigned for a few moments at this turn of events, the major sufferers being the more male chauvinists present. Among the rest discussions of a comparative nature broke out vis-a-vis the attractive lines of the Mossie and those of its driver. The latter was a comfortable winner. There ensued some chat with the pilot until some self-appointed Galahad, looking at his watch, said, "It's nearly lunchtime so we'd better check you into the Tower and then go to the Mess for a drink and meal. Sorry there's no transport but, not to worry, I'll borrow a cycle for you." "Oh no," was the dismayed reply, "that's no good. I NEVER LEARNED TO RIDE A BIKE." I think she finally made it on someone's handlebars, backstep or crossbar!'

Many excellent women pilots flew with the Air Transport Auxiliary ferrying aircraft, but the ATA was not part of the RAF. Indeed the expertise and experience of these ladies – who regularly handled a score of different types – was far in advance of the average RAF pilot. While WAAF were not permitted to fly aircraft, the need arose for flight trained nurses to accompany patients on air ambulance flights. These volunteers became the only WAAF recognized as aircrew – even if not officially classified as such. There was one crucial hurdle to acceptance, flight compatability. Muriel Anderson:

'Having volunteered to be an operating theatre assistant in the WAAF, while waiting for a posting I was sent to work as a nursing orderly at Winthorpe near Newark. As nothing more was heard, it was suggested by an MO that I might like to volunteer for air ambulance work, for which recruits were then being sought. This sounded interesting so I applied and after a week or so received orders to report for an air test. Obviously they first had to find out if I was going to be airsick.

'The appointment was on a Monday and the preceding weekend I had been out cycling in shorts and been badly bitten by mosquitoes. Allergic to the bites, my legs became so swollen I had to have injections and bandages. I was not very comfortable when arriving for my first flight and even less so when I was taken out to a Lancaster bomber and instructed to climb over and sit on the main spar. The pilot was Squadron Leader "Mickey" Martin who, although I didn't know it at the time, was one of the surviving Dam Buster pilots. We took off and headed out over the Wash. Although I felt fine, if a little nervous, the crew must have found it unusual to have a girl on board and were intent on getting a laugh out of the occasion. The undercarriage was lowered and I was told that we were about to land on a cloud. Mickey Martin's next joke was to mention that one engine on the starboard side had stopped. I looked out and saw the propeller blades were stationary, which didn't give me any concern, but the next thing I knew the other propeller on that side had been feathered. I daren't look out at the port wing. Anyway, this gave the crew a good laugh and we returned to earth safely with no signs of airsickness on my part.'

The air ambulance WAAFs were a select few who did sterling work on the continuous shuttles ferrying wounded from continental airfields back to England during the final nine months of hostilities in Europe. Muriel Anderson again:

'As a WAAF air ambulance orderly I flew regularly with crews on Nos. 512 and 575 Squadron Dakotas bringing back stretcher cases and walking wounded from the Continent. As the only members of the WAAF on regular flight duties we were, I suppose, something of a novelty but we were well accepted, if subject to a bit of leg-pulling now and again. Jimmy Edwards, the comedian, was one of the pilots I flew with and Al Bollington, the famous London organist, was another. On flights when we had no wounded aboard I used to think Bollington flew with his feet on the rudder pedals as if he were still playing an organ, the way we zig-zagged about sometimes. His favourite prank was to ask me to go back to the galley in the rear of the aircraft and get him some coffee. As soon as I got back there the Dakota would bob up and down and the coffee went all over the place. When I returned without the coffee and he complained, I politely told him where it was if he still wanted it!'

The Line

WAR AND ETHOS

When, on 3 September 1939, war was declared on Germany by Britain and France, the rank and file of the Royal Air Force were fairly confident that they could give a good account of themselves, a view generally shared by the British public. High Command, with the benefit of Intelligence reports, was not complacent, but did not fully appreciate the weaknesses of the RAF in certain areas. In fact its opponent, the Luftwaffe, not only possessed a greater number of modern aircraft, in most respects technically more advanced than the RAF's best, but had developed better operational tactics. Regular RAF airmen while dedicated, proficient and confident, were to a large degree unaware of what was stacked against them. As John Wray points out, the majority faced the unknown:

'In 1939 only those few who had been in the First World War knew what war entailed. Some, of course, had chased tribesmen in the Middle East and India, but in the main none of us had the remotest idea what it was going to be like when the shooting started. We had read books and we had seen *Wings*, *Dawn Patrol* and other films that gave one some idea but, as one was to learn later, the real thing is very different. So, when we went to France in September 1939 and were told that we were to carry out reconnaissance over Germany, it was realized that we might be about to find out. We were to go at night, an interesting thought because I had more night flying experience on the Blenheim than anybody else in the squadron, and I had ten hours. My flight commander had clocked up four hours. Added to this was the fact that our navigators had more or less been recruited off the street and sent on a short course where all their navigation was DR over the sea. Our gunners were good wireless operators, though inexperienced in the art of shooting at other aircraft. Because we couldn't operate out of our small grass airfield at night we had to go forward to Metz and take off from there. We would fly to Metz, three aircraft for each night sortie. Once there we would be briefed, and then hang around for the rest of the afternoon until it was dark. On one occasion it was a lovely sunny day and quite warm. The three crews had been briefed about a trip to Hanover, and we were all lying on the grass in the sun, our Blenheims lined neatly wingtip to wingtip *à la* peacetime. After all, this was 1939 and the war was not a month old.

'Six French Curtiss Hawks taxied out and took off in formation and climbed to about 3,000 feet. They then flew backwards and forwards across the airfield in various "pansy" formations. Although the front line was not all that far away, it could just as well have been peacetime. Their flying added a delightful buzz to the lovely summer day and helped us to relax and dream of cricket on the green and lovely popsies. The scene was enhanced when an aged Dewoitine biplane taxied out with two people in it to carry out a series of circuits and landings. What a lovely scene.

'Suddenly there was a great whoosh as if the Demon King had arrived. He had, in the form of a Me 109 going like the clappers at nought feet. Of course, none of us had seen a German aircraft before and we were frozen where we lay. We watched in fascination then with realization as the 109 started to chase the unfortunate Dewoitine around the circuit. Needless to say, the Curtiss Hawks, completely unaware of the drama that was unfolding below them, continued to fly backwards and forwards across the airfield, changing formation. After the first burst of fire the pilot of the Dewoitine realized something was amiss and he endeavoured to take avoiding action. Suddenly, he blew up in a ball of flame and crashed into the middle of the airfield. The 109 was gone. One would like to say that this all took about ten minutes, but in reality it was more like three. However, the effect on all of us was dramatic and lasting. We had seen what war was really like.'

During the early years of hostilities RAF men were frequently at a disadvantage in pursuing operations and it is much to their credit that in the circumstances they acquitted themselves so well. Although the junior service, the RAF status was elevated by the direction the conflict took. If the Royal Air Force had no meaningful public identity before 1939 it most certainly had six years later. In part this was the result of patriotic propaganda which had presented the fighter pilot as the saviour of the nation in the Battle of Britain, and the bomber crew as the resolute avengers of the *Blitz*. But there also existed an image of a gallant airman with a squashed cap at jaunty angle, handlebar moustache and silk scarf, uttering nonsenses like 'Wizard prang' and 'Piece of cake'. This caricature arose from customs and jargon created during those savage years, but it became the most distinctive of all British service types.

Although the RAF was the world's first autonomous air force, by 1939 it had few practices derived from its own traditions. Mess rituals, yes, and some indigenous slang. Mostly conduct was modelled on Army and Navy ways. After the declaration of war, customs, attitudes and language quickly developed that gave the RAF the foundations of its own folklore. The extent and colourfulness of RAF slang made it famous. While a little was inherited from other services, much was self-originated, although the sources of particular sayings are obscure. Air-to-air and air-to-ground radio communication necessitated code-words for simplification and confidentiality. Some of these terms were adopted as slang. A cautionary service publication called *Tee Em* (using the phonetic form for TM standing for Training Manual) made use of this jargon to sweeten its lesson and played a large part in its dissemination. Observers of the scene suggest that slang was heard much more extensively in fighter messes than in those of other commands.

The supposed British predeliction for understatement was to be found in its most exaggerated form in the RAF. 'Dicey dos' – dangerous situations – were commonplace in both flying and combat, and anyone who started to relate his adventures with too much enthusiasm would be told to stop 'shooting a line'. Such was the stigma of being classed a line-shooter that it became an accepted part of air force life to play down any personal experience. Presumably this attitude produced the art of pronounced understatement practised by many RAF air crew. Similarly, 'stiff upper lip', the overly calm and collected attitude portrayed by the British serviceman faced with danger, appears to have been accentuated in the RAF. Instead of getting in a 'flap' when a serious situation arose, one endeavoured to make a dismissive or humorous comment. An example of this is given by Horace Nears of No. 613 Squadron:

'The Squadron was on a stand down and a grand station piss-up had been organized in the airmen's mess. Most of us were not feeling our best when, about noon next day the Tannoy blasted forth requiring Black Section to report to the crew room immediately. That included me and, with a few of my oppos also suffering hangovers, I staggered along to the crew room where the first person we met was the Doc. He had a great box of barley sugars and said: "Here, take a handful of these, they are guaranteed to cure anything." My regular pilot didn't turn up and I was sent on the trip with a spare Squadron Leader we called The Count. Apparently it was an urgent request to clobber some SS troops down near Limoges, quite a long ride, and we had to have under-wing tanks on the Mossies. Switching fuel in tanks in flight was quite a procedure. You took off on the internal outers, emptied these and then changed to the internal inners. When these were getting low the juice was pumped out of the under-wing tanks into the internal tanks, switching back to the outers and finishing up on the inners. All went well until I was doing the last change. Twisting the cocks I felt something go loose and come away in my hand. Out came a long rod with a collar and a bit of pipe on the end. So I nudged The Count and held the thing up. "What the hell is that?" he asked. "It's one of the petrol switches," I replied. He then wanted to know what tanks we were running on. I said I didn't know because I was in the process of changing from the near empty outers to the inners, our last full tanks. So he just grins and says, "Oh well, pass me a couple of barley sugars and we'll hope it does the trick." '

If a humorous quip was the way to weather anxiety, it was also used to meet adversity and horror. The remark overheard by John Everett of No. 102 Squadron would have been considered outrageous had it not been uttered by a flier regularly exposed to the same risk of death as his subject:

'There were several crashes around the airfield and if you were one of the first on the scene the sights were grizzly. A Halifax hit a house while coming in to land, burned and exploded. On top of the rubble lay a giant's skeleton. I assume that heat had caused it to stretch. Someone said this was the pilot. A friend of his who was present at this grim scene remarked: "Well, I won't be playing cricket with him this evening." I suppose you had to adopt that sort of attitude to be able to cope with such dreadful sights.'

Minimizing one's own contribution or performance while praising a fellow comrade was a feature of British reserve in all armed forces. Because of the interdependence of aircraft crew members this attitude was particularly prevalent in the RAF. The following accounts solicited from the pilot and the navigator of a No. 90 Squadron Fortress, long after the event described and without either man knowing the other had been approached, illustrates this facet. First the pilot, Mick Woods:

'Four Fortress Is and crews from 90 Squadron went on detachment to Kinloss on 5 September 1941. The aim was to attack and destroy a German battleship then berthed in Oslo. An attempt was made on the 6th, but at that time Oslo was under ten-tenths cloud. Four aircraft set out on the 8th in a loose formation. Three of these aircraft were intercepted by Me 109s over the south-west coast and two were shot down, one crashing in Bygland and the other into the sea. The third Fortress climbed swiftly and the bombs were jettisoned. This aircraft was attacked soon after at a height of some 30,000 feet. Two engines were disabled, one of which caught fire but this went out. The aileron control was destroyed which made a turn difficult. The floor in the navigator's compartment was holed and his maps and instruments were sucked out. The fighter broke off his attack – it was suspected that his ammunition was exhausted – and came alongside before returning to his base. Previously enemy fighters had difficulty in reaching and staying at the high altitudes at which the Fortresses flew. But, fortuitously for the Luftwaffe, its only operational units with the Me 109T model, having longer wings and better altitude stability, were based in Norway.

'The navigator had memorized two radio beacon call signs on the Scottish coast and with these and the radio compass, guided the aircraft to a landfall by which time the height had dropped to 1,500 feet. The pilot then ordered the navigator and wireless operator to leave by parachute, but this was ignored with the remark, "We would rather stay with you." With one gunner dead and another severely wounded, it was decided to attempt a downwind wheels-up landing at Kinloss. The tyres were punctured and the flaps were not expected to be fully operable. At that time Kinloss was grass and the risk of fire was less there than on the sealed strip at Lossiemouth. With much firing of red Very cartridges the aircraft made a downwind approach over the bomb dump to be confronted with an OTU Whitley taking off in the opposite direction. Without flaps the aircraft floated longer than usual before settling down in a cloud of dust. The CO_2 bottles had been fired in the engine nacelles and there was no petrol fire on impact. An American Master Sergeant remarked that two hundred thousand dollars had been spread across the grass. It was thought that it was the first ever wheels-up crash landing of a Flying Fortress. The pilot recommended the navigator for a DFM for his efforts when all seemed lost. This was refused as there was not an officer witness on board at the time.'

Harry Sutton, the navigator involved:

'Mick Wood was magnificent in his handling of our shot-up Fortress, bringing it back and making a superb crash landing. No one had any idea what would happen when we hit the deck; when it was of paramount importance to get the wounded out as quickly as possible in case the whole thing went up in flames. Thus I removed a hatch aft of the cockpit and braced myself ready for the crash. The moment we "grated" down the runway, I shot out of the hatch and round to the rear of the aircraft. However, the ambulance boys, who had been following us, beat me to it. When Mick emerged and joined me his first remark was: "You had me worried for a moment, Harry. You got out so quickly I damn near ran over you!" '

In truth the individual sublimated his feelings and expressions because of an ingrained sense of duty. One was there to serve King and Country and willing to give one's life for the nation and the cause of democracy. Fellow aviators were in the same situation, faced with the same stark reality. So why make a fuss? Act matter-of-fact. One might be frightened but duty was something not to be shirked. A certain amount of pride was involved in duty too. For aircrew duty was paramount; others depended upon you whom you could not let down. An illustration of the value of this conscientiousness is given by John Wray:

'I was in a Blenheim IV squadron which hadn't had the aircraft very long. Other squadrons more experienced on the type had some nasty accidents due to one of the engines failing on take-off. At Wyton five aircrew had been killed in one day. We had already lost one pilot attempting a single-engine landing and we had had one or two instances of engines stopping in the air, although pilots had managed to start them again. I was carrying out a photographic survey of London flying at 15,000 feet. My gunner from my open cockpit days was with me in the front of the Blenheim and was bringing me up on my start points and levelling the camera, etc. He was an AC1 Fitter by trade, aged about twenty and married. I was also just past my twentieth birthday but unmarried. We were just coming to the end of one of our runs and were over Colchester when the starboard engine failed, and there was no way I could get it started again. Not trusting my port engine I decided to make an emergency landing at Eastchurch, a grass airfield.

'Landing successfully, I drew a lot of interest from the Eastchurch personnel because the Blenheim IV was still quite new. I asked the CTO if he could have my engine attended to. For an hour the engine was checked and eventually run up. Ignition switches were checked and as all seemed well I decided to carry out an air test. There then followed the dramatic scene of the 20-year-old officer saying to the 20-year-old aircraftman, "Now, I am going to carry out an air test and as anything might happen I am going alone; you are a married man and so I want you to stay on the ground." To which he replied, "Sir, it is my duty to come with you, whatever the risk." As we climbed into the cockpit I said to him, "Directly we are off the ground you pull up the undercarriage, then I can keep one hand on the control column and one on the throttles." We taxied out, opened up to full power and bounded across the grass. After the aircraft rose and the wheels came up, there was a cough and a bang as the starboard engine stopped. Had my gunner not been there to retract the undercarriage we would not have been one of the few to survive an engine failure on take-off in a Blenheim.'

Seeing others display courage and fortitude was an important factor in lifting one's own morale, particularly in an operational situation. Combat units with high morale invariably had one or two intrepid and resolute individuals who inspired the other personnel in the face of adversity. The small and intimate nature of the squadron – the RAF's basic unit – helped build that necessary spirit of determination and confidence. Even when suffering severe attrition the *esprit de corps* of many squadrons was remarkable. There were, of course, demoralized units, but in many cases the causes were other than combat misfortune. Tedium often played a major part, where personnel felt their duties made no worthwhile contribution to the war effort. This was particularly so during the early years of the conflict. John Sharman, in charge of an RAF Regiment detachment, reflects this viewpoint and identifies a personal change of attitude:

'Manston was often the first touchdown for damaged aircraft returning from ops. In consequence it had what must have been the largest aircraft cemetery in the country. Witnessing so many crashes and with nothing but setbacks and bad news from the war fronts, our gun team felt very low. Early one morning in 1942 I was awakened by a tremendous roar – the ground literally shaking. I dashed up the mound upon which my Bofors were sited and there, across the airfield outside headquarters, were about 60 Spits warming up, ready for take-off. This scene was an eye-opener and did wonders for morale. I turned to my corporal and said: "Do you know Corp, we're going to win this bloody war!" For me it was the turning-point.'

The prospect of being killed was very real. Combat losses were given in the Press and on radio. Within the service, briefings and periodic reviews would reveal the number of sorties so that an idea of the rate of attrition could be assessed. But such matters were rarely mentioned unless in light vein. However apprehensive one might be, there was an underlying belief that one would survive, it would always be the other fellow who would get 'the chop'. As a natural counter to the prospect of the dangerous trade followed, crews away from operations attempted to make life one long party; their hallmark was exuberance. Many drank liberally and engaged in wild pranks. Authority recognized this as a psychological safety-valve and was tolerant. Religion was the succour for some, although generally of a private nature. Individual demonstrations of religious faith were rarely made in public. There seemed to be an unspoken acknowledgement that one would cause embarrassment by calling on the Almighty's help before your fellows. However, those who showed deep conviction were respected, as Cyril Clifford observed:

'On a navigator's course at Portage la Prairie, Manitoba, Canada, I shared a large hut with many other students, mostly like myself, re-mustering. The first night we were preparing for bed and indulging in the usual noisy barrack-room banter when suddenly the room went quiet. One young man was kneeling by his bed with hands together saying his prayers. Most fellows pretended not to notice and quietly went on with what they were doing. One joker, however, seeking to extract some humour from the situation, shouted some ribald remarks towards the prayerful one. Those nearest to the comic shook their fists in his face and whispered threats so he shut up. The lad saying his prayers gained our immediate respect, not only for his faith but for his courage in showing it. In six years of barrack-room living it was the only time I saw anyone carry out his devotions publicly.'

For every three fatalities one man was wounded or injured. Brilliant surgery and dedicated nursing saved many lives. The fire hazard inherent in aircraft of the time meant that many survivors of crashes or airborne conflagrations were badly burned, some horrifically. The fortitude of those who faced many painful skin grafts left a lasting impression on those they encountered. John Wray:

'Arriving as a new boy, or rather, new patient at the Palace Hotel Hospital, Torquay, about lunch time, I made my way to the dining-room and there he was.

Sitting by himself, no hair on his face or head, no ears, no nose, just two holes for his eyes, two holes for his ears and the hole that was his mouth. He had two fingers missing from one hand and one from the other. I believe the worst case of burning there had been up to that time. I was so sickened by the sight that I had to leave the dining-room immediately, having no further stomach for food. But what a marvellous person he turned out be be. One soon didn't notice his burns and treated him as a normal person. He loved playing tennis and if someone hit the ball hard at him the racket would fly out of his hand because he had only three fingers left on that hand, and he would roar with laughter. He was the life and soul of any party and if at any time anybody was down in the dumps, as was likely to be the case in a hospital, he would use his enormous enthusiasm to cheer them up.

'One night he, with others, went up to the Imperial Hotel, which was occupied chiefly by rich people who had left London, and we went into the bar. So far as we were concerned there was nothing wrong with him, but two women who were sitting at a table said in a loud voice. "It's disgusting to allow somebody like that out into a public place." Before we could gather our wits a young VAD who was sitting by herself, leapt to her feet and tore into those two women, causing them to retire in disarray with red faces and very red ears. He spent his time commuting between East Grinstead and Torquay for a considerable time and I don't know what happened to him. But he taught me a thing or two about courage and humility. If anybody deserved to be restored to normality, it was him.'

How then did others – citizens of other nations – view the ethos of the wartime Royal Air Force? The habitual character and disposition evoked by those who served under the banner *per ardua ad astra*? Opinions inevitably ranged from the commendatory to the adverse via an extensive and varied middle ground of prejudice and indecisive judgements, all no doubt coloured by national outlook. Whatever views were held they were rarely expressed to RAF personnel directly. Frank Cheesman tells of a notable exception:

'Surprisingly, soon after the United States entered the war, a USAAF captain was attached to our squadron for the purpose of getting the hang of the night-fighting business in the ensuing weeks. Mel, as he became known, was a regular or "career" officer, having entered aviation by way of West Point and the US Army and had done spells of duty in Central and South American countries. It was soon evident that he was a pilot of considerable experience, having flown most of the aircraft types on the current USAAF inventory, not to mention a good quota of civilian machines. He could also speak authoritatively on such accoutrements as fan markers, radio ranges and the like, things about which the average fighter pilot did not know his As from his Ns. It was not surprising, therefore, that Mel converted readily to our Beaufighters and was shortly not only flying the beast to the manner born, but with sufficient expertise to be included on the duty rosters. A career officer he may have been, but it was obvious he was also a "professional" pilot and an avid type-hunter to boot. Any spare time found him at the ASR squadron or the Gunnery Flight cajoling them into letting him fly their Ansons, Lysanders, Defiants and – joy of joys – their Walrus. Socially he fitted in well, was quiet and clean around the house and took part in most activities except the more outrageous. Reserved by nature – one might say taciturn – he was not given to idle chat and the utterances he did make were often droll, sometimes pungent and always to the point. Like all true soldiers he had a cynical philosophy and anyone misguided enough to voice a complaint about some injustice was drily reminded, "Waal, nobody said anything about fair play!"

'Mel's transition from the fleshpots of the USA to the atmosphere of a somewhat remote and stark RAF camp must have been a traumatic experience though he showed no signs that this was so. The new environment, the unfamiliar routines and perhaps most of all the mish-mash of nationalities he was now living and working amongst were all taken in his stride as he merged readily into the set-up. The time arrived when his attachment was over and that morning he arrived at the dispersal, looking very snappy in his olive and fawn uniform, to clear his locker and say his farewells. Well-wishers from the other flight and elsewhere swelled the throng. Occasions like this were normally marked by an exchange of ribaldry and mutual expressions of a derogatory nature – the RAF way of demonstrating regard – but it seemed not quite appropriate here and a comparative hush prevailed. His luggage having been loaded, Mel got to the car door, stopped and took a long searching look over the length of the airfield. Dropping his gaze he ran his eyes along the assembled faces by now full of expectancy of a memorable pronouncement. It came. With the faintest grin and in ringing tones tinged with disbelief Mel opined, "Jesus H. Christ. If this isn't the Goddamndest air force I've ever seen!" – shut the door and was gone.'

CLOSE ENCOUNTERS

Understandably, an individual's most prominent memories of service life are those when he or she was faced with possible extinction or personal catastrophe. This did not necessarily involve a brush with the enemy, for there were risks enough in flying during wartime. Cyril Clifford:

'As a qualified navigator recently returned to Britain from Canada, I did an advanced flying course on Ansons to get used to European wartime conditions such as the blackout and the presence of balloon barrages, and to use the few navigational aids available. This took place at Llandwrog, an airfield only nine miles from Snowdon. As a safety measure we were told that if we had to descend through cloud and were approaching over the sea we should knock five minutes from the ETA and come in at low level. Conversely, if approaching from the land side we should add on five minutes to the ETA to be sure we had cleared Snowdonia. One night, coming in overland, the pilot said he could see the sea and would start descending. I said our instructions were clear and we should stick to them. So he agreed and we maintained height for another five minutes. We descended right into the airfield circuit and the pilot realized with a shock that what he thought was the sea was actually snow on the mountains! So we escaped being yet another aircraft wreck added to the large total of crashes in Snowdonia.'

Albert Benest:

'At Westcott near Aylesbury, there were a number of ATC boys who were often on the airfield trying to get flights. Because these lads would be joining the RAF when old enough we were instructed to give them encouragement whenever possible, particularly air experience. One weekend we were asked to take a few of these cadets on a cross-country, when for some reason – probably weather – this was cancelled. So as not to disappoint the cadets my pilot said he would take them up for a flight around the local area. He said that in the circumstances there would be no need for me to go along so I went off for a snooze. Around five that afternoon I walked into the officers' mess for a cup of tea to be greeted with some strange looks followed by a few exclamations. Everyone thought I was dead! I then received the bad news that the Wellington had lost its starboard wing in flight and all in the aircraft had been killed. It had been supposed that I was on board too.'

Len Barcham of No. 404 (RCAF) Squadron:

'In August 1943 we had detached from Wick to train for practice firing the rocket projectiles for which our Beaufighters had just been fitted. At the mouth of the Dornoch Firth a target had been set up out on the beach and we were doing circuits and bumps all day trying to find out the best way to aim the rockets. Normally they had HE, incendiary or armour-piercing warheads, but for these trials we were using practice concrete heads. No navigation being necessary, we had agreed to give a ground erk a flip – his first ever – putting him in the navigator's seat under the rear cupola. I was standing astride the well behind the pilot, F/O J. H. Symons, thus not strapped in at all, while calling out and checking various speeds, angles of attack, etc., while he concentrated on the target. One engine suddenly lost all its oil, seized up solid with a dreadful scream, wouldn't feather and from then on we went more or less where the Beau' took us, which happened to be downwards towards Clashmore Wood and Evelix.

'The Beau' was a very strong aircraft indeed; our expression was "built like a brick shithouse". We finished up in a clearing in the woods where the trees had been cut down to 2-foot stumps. These literally tore the Beau' to bits each time we bounced. With rockets and cannon now firing of their own accord, it was indeed something of a panic. When we eventually came to a stop, only about the first 10 feet of fuselage was left in one piece. Though badly bruised and shaken, we got out a bit smartly and looked round for our passenger. He had apparently been catapulted out before the remains of the aircraft came to a stop and we caught sight of him just disappearing over a nearby hill at a great rate of knots. I never ever set eyes on him again. Before the trip he had told us he had been accepted for flying training. It would be interesting to know if he carried on with that idea!'

George Irving of No. 406 (RCAF) Squadron:

'In May 1943 I was taking off on a normal air test, travelling down the runway at about 100mph, when, without warning, the constant speed regulator packed up on my starboard engine throwing the propeller into coarse pitch. This caused the Beaufighter to swing violently to starboard, off the runway. We raced across the grass and just got airborne in time to clear a Wellington taxi-ing across towards its bay. I then cleared the hedge and roofs of a housing estate by a few feet. Gradually gaining height, I was able to make an emergency landing on the first circuit. There were several complaints from the housing estate residents about low flying over Exeter.'

Bill Dickinson:

'My first solo trip in a Beaufighter at No. 2 OTU, Catfoss, was quite an experience. After take-off I discovered my radio was u/s. Everything else was fine so I flew around enjoying the new experience. After about three-quarters of an hour I came back to the airfield to land, noticing things were rather quiet and there was no one else in the circuit. When I touched down the aircraft swung violently, so much so that I couldn't control it. The Beau' veered off the runway, swung across the grass, hit the edge of another runway, ground looped and the undercarriage collapsed. The ambulance and fire engine came streaming out but I was only shaken and worried what was going to be said. We had been warned about the Beau's tendency to swing on take-off and landing. "I made a mess of that," I said apologetically to the first blokes to arrive. To my great relief they told me that I had a tyre burst on take-off and that this had been seen flapping about before the wheels were retracted. An instructor had taken off in another Beaufighter with the intention of communicating with me but couldn't establish radio contact. Flying had been suspended while they waited for me to come in and crash – they say ignorance is bliss!'

Roy Larkins:

'We took off from Charmy Down, near Bath, on what was supposed to be a training flight. The instructor said, "Let's forget about the exercises today. Let's take the old kite up, as high as we can." It was an Oxford aircraft and certainly not designed to fly at any great height. At 10,000 feet, or perhaps a bit more, it stopped climbing and just hung there, in the rarified air. We were very much in a "nose-up" position and although the propellers were spinning, they were not pulling us forward or up, but rather, just holding us there. The instructor was flying the aircraft and I was there, simply enjoying the ride, until I glanced along the wing. A small feather of flame was coming from the engine cowling. "Port engine's on fire," I shouted. "What shall we do?" shouted back the instructor, more for moral support than anything else because he had practised this manoeuvre many, many times. "Let's dive and hope that the wind puts it out," I replied. "At least we'll be nearer the ground that way."

'I was not frightened in the least – nothing to the apprehension I suffered when I practised this manoeuvre. Also, this was the second time that I had lost an engine, but perhaps it was the instructor's first. The aircraft dived at a speed that I had never encountered before (or since) and the sensation to the body was like that of the deepest part of the Big Dipper in a fairground. At the commencement of the dive the flame had grown a little and as we screamed earthwards it tried to grow larger still, but the wind was blowing it out. I don't know for how many seconds we were diving, but the battle between flame and wind was an absorbing one. First, the flame gained and then retreated. Then it gained again and similarly retreated. And so it went on. Luckily, just as the plane came out of its dive, the flame went out. The instructor trimmed the aircraft to fly on one engine and we went back to base. As I was not captain of the aircraft in this incident, I did not have to attend the inquiry concerned with this engine fire. I learned later that moisture on the plane at that height had frozen near to where the exhaust gases leave the engine. This restricted the flow of outgoing gases, which in turn caused the engine to overheat and eventually to catch fire. The final comment on the accident report stated, "Cause of fire . . . block of ice!" '

James Donson of No. 2 Armament Practice Camp:

'At the time of the cross-Channel invasion, June 1944, it was feared that the dispatch-rider system of communication between the stations of No. 16 Group Coastal Command and their HQ might be interrupted by enemy parachutists. To counter this risk, air delivery was ordered and our unit at Docking in Norfolk given the task of the daily round trip, landing at all the Group airfields and carrying mail to Detling in Kent from where it was transported by road to HQ at Chatham. We carried out our "Pony Express" programme, as we called it, from early June until the end of August.

'During the early weeks after the June invasion the V-1 attacks on the southeast began and increased in intensity. Balloon defences around London increased, so that we could no longer fly directly to Detling. We used a route to Watford and turned east in the area of Guildford and on to Maidstone where we made another turn and flew on to Detling. One day in a Martinet I was on the Guildford-Detling leg at about 2,000 feet, just under the cloud base, when a V-1 appeared to my right and passed at right-angles close in front of me. It all happened so quickly; I felt a blast of hot air and was rolled almost upside down. Realizing the aircraft had half rolled, I put on more throttle and continued to roll. On regaining level and stable flight I saw a mast a few feet below my starboard wing. Checking my position I found I had just missed Crowborough beacon – a tall radio mast along our normal route.'

Some 'close shaves' were nothing short of traumatic. Tom Minta:

'Because there were more pilots than needed at the time, we returned from training in South Africa to be sent down to South Cerney to keep our hand in by flying Oxfords. We had to do quite a bit of formation flying and one of the exercises involved three Oxfords in a vee formation, with each taking it in turn to be leader. The position change took place over the airfield. The drill was for No. 3 on the starboard side to move forward, No. 1 to stay where he was, while No. 2 slid along the back from the left to take up the position previously held by No. 3. One day I had been flying No. 2 and was in the process of moving across to make the change. Just as I got astern of the other two I saw them coming together. The next thing the complete tail unit of one came hurtling back and knocked my aerial off, it was that close. The Oxford which had lost its tail dropped out of sight, but the other one started to flip over right in front of me. I expected his wing to go into my belly as I tried to miss him; how it didn't I'll never know. My Oxford was holed in several places by bits of debris but all that remained of the others was a couple of smoking wrecks on the aerodrome. The instructor came out and asked how I was feeling. "Bloody awful really," was my reply. "Well get another aircraft and up you go right away," he ordered, and I did. It was sound advice.'

Being mistaken for the enemy and attacked by your own side happened on a number of occasions with tragic results. Few people could match Tony Reid's experience of this:

'On 21 December 1939 I was in a Hampden of No. 44 Squadron returning from a sortie along the coast of Norway and flying at around 1,000 feet. The weather was cloudy with a slight haze and we were supposed to come in at Lossiemouth before continuing down to our base at Waddington. Instead we made a shocking landfall, some 130 miles to the south at Dunbar. Hurricanes of

No. 111 Squadron were sent to investigate and this regular squadron saw we were Hampdens and sheered off. Not so the former auxiliaries of No. 602 Squadron who intercepted us with their Spitfires. They apparently identified us as Do 17s and attacked. Two members of our crew were shot, one fatally. The pilot managed to ditch into the approaches of the Firth of Forth where, with the other survivors, I escaped with a ducking – but it was cold! A second Hampden was also shot down but all four crew escaped without injury.

'A couple of months after recovering from this ordeal, on 3 March 1940, I was co-pilot in a Hudson of the Photographic Development Unit with an assignment to take vertical photographs from 7,000 feet of selected airfields in the south-east for the benefit of the French Air Force. The weather was perfect and our first objective after leaving Heston was Gravesend. Arriving at this location we were suddenly attacked from the rear by Hurricanes and the Hudson became a blazing inferno in seconds. I managed to bale out by squeezing through my cockpit side window, the sole survivor out of four. *Mais – c'est la guerre!* By chance, a year or so later, I met the flight leader of the three No. 32 Squadron Hurricanes that shot us down. When I asked for an explanation he insisted we had fired on them first! But our only armament was two fixed Brownings in the nose! The only theory we could evolve to explain this illusion was that our trailing aerial was glinting in the sunlight and that this was mistaken for tracer.'

Another man with Lady Luck on his shoulder was Arthur Anthony:

'Early summer 1942 found me at Ford, Sussex, a flight mechanic/engineer just out of training school. I was serving with No. 605 Squadron which had been wiped out in Java and was being re-formed as a night intruder unit flying twin-engined Douglas Havocs and Bostons. Although learning about the engineering tasks with these aircraft, I was keen to have a flight. As the pilots spent a lot of time practising interceptions it wasn't necessary for other crew members to go along, so ground men were often allowed to go in their place. I did not have to wait many days before one of the pilots said I could come on one of his training sorties. For a 19-year-old who had never been in the air before, this was a very exciting prospect. The pilot was a very energetic type and engaged in a series of climbs, dives and turns. One moment I was looking out of my position in the nose at fields, the next there was nothing to see but blue sky. It wasn't long before all this throwing about made me violently airsick; by the time we had landed and taxied back to the dispersal I was feeling dreadful. Somehow I dragged myself out of the nose compartment but accidentally pulled the emergency exit panel as I left. This didn't make me very popular as it was a tricky thing to reinstate. Then in my agony I picked up my parachute by the release handle and the whole lot spilt out on the ground. For all this I had to take a lot of stick from my mates plus having to pay one of them a half-crown to clear up the mess in the nose. "You'll never be any good for aircrew," was the cry from many of them.

'However, I was still determined and waited my chance to get airborne again. I didn't have many days to wait and this time I flew in the back compartment. The training exercise consisted of making dummy attacks on another Havoc which took evasive action. This time I managed not to part with my dinner. After landing to refuel I was all set to go up again when the pilot continued the exercise. While waiting, three Canadian soldiers appeared and wanted to know if they could have a trip up. It didn't rest with me, of course, and I advised them to see the two pilots and ask. I said I'd be quite prepared to stand down as there would be lots more chances for me to fly. The Canadians returned, all smiles, and I gave one of them my 'chute and harness. The other two flew in the second plane. Off they all went while the "Chiefy" gave instructions that I was to remain until the two Havocs returned and then refuel them. This meant I would be having a late tea. It was a beautiful afternoon so it was pleasant to while away the time lying on the grass. I'd been idly lounging there on my own for perhaps a half-hour when Chiefy came pedalling up on his bike: "Go and get your tea Anthony." "But Chiefy, you said I had . . ." He cut me short.

' "You lucky little sod! I've just had a phone message; those two Havocs have collided in mid-air and all six are dead. It happened over Banstead."

'For a few seconds I thought he was having me on; I couldn't believe it. Then the realization that this was true enveloped me in a dread sinking feeling; as if I had been responsible for those Canadians' deaths. But neither was it lost on me that if they had not come on to the airfield I would have been one of the fatalities. A morning or so later the rigger and I were doing a duty inspection on a Havoc. We pulled the port prop through and then crossed in front of the aircraft to the starboard engine prior to engine run up. As I went to get hold of a prop blade there was a loud blast of gunfire. Under the nose lay 21 ejected bullet cases. Had I moved across in front of the nose a couple of seconds later. . . . Armourers were testing the electric solenoids but were unaware that the four machine-guns were cocked. No one could tell me about luck.'

If your side didn't get you, the enemy could still make life risky on home ground. Alan Staines:

'I was called up as a Reserve in June 1944 and sent to the ACRC in Regent's Park right in the middle of London. We were billeted in blocks of flats, but at the time the Flying Bomb campaign was at its height. One Friday afternoon we were supposed to go out for rifle drill in the road by our billet in St. James's Terrace. Our corporal appeared dressed up in his best blues, which puzzled us at first. "I'll give you a quarter of an hour of my time," he confided, "and then you can go back to your billet and lie low until 4 o'clock when your next lecture is due. I'm off to meet a bird in the West End. Should someone want to know where I am, just tell them I got took ill." We were quite happy to go along with this if it got us out of drilling on a hot afternoon. We did fifteen minutes and while the Corporal crept off to see his girl, we went back to our billet, which was on the top floor of a block of flats. We were taking it easy when some of the chaps who had been out sun-bathing on the roof came hurtling down the stairs shouting that a flying-bomb, engine still running, was diving straight for us. All we could do was throw ourselves on the floor and hope. There was a hell of an explosion, a shock wave and lots of dust. When we picked ourselves up and looked out, we could see that the bomb had struck in the street outside, partly demolishing a house on the other side and caving in the lower part of our building. Three RAF chaps down below had been killed and about 30 injured, but all on the top floor escaped. It didn't take long to realize that our squad of 35 should have been marching up and down that road had our corporal not gone AWOL to see a girl. Was my life saved through a bit of illicit romance? I'm sure it was.'

It could happen that a man who had experienced several 'near things' in the course of combat operations was more impressed by traumas encountered in what should have been more peaceful surroundings. Harold Southgate, a veteran Bomber Command pilot, is unlikely to forget the occasion he went to collect his second 'gong':

'With my wife and baby daughter, I set out in my Ford 8 from Worcestershire to attend an Investiture at Buckingham Palace to receive a Bar to my DFC. The first stage of the journey, to Coulsdon in Surrey where we were staying the night, was completed without event. However, next morning when I went to start the car it would not. No joy whatsoever. Took out the plugs, pulled out this and that, tightened anything that looked as if it was loose, but still no joy. It was now getting late so the car – which had by this time been pushed down hills in an effort to generate life – was abandoned in Coulsdon High Street. A taxi was ordered and, after cleaning up as quickly as possible and suffering some anxious moments, we arrived at Buckingham Palace with just ten minutes to spare. The Investiture went without hitch and it was an honour to meet the King for the second time. It was not without problems for my wife, as the daughter in arms cried throughout the ceremony and was eventually taken in charge by Buckingham Palace staff.

'Having returned to Coulsdon by train I found, of course, that the car started first time. So we set off back to RAF Defford. Leaving Marlow up a slight incline, a small boy on a bike decided to turn right – having given no signals – just as we were overtaking. The boy managed to make it safely to the other side of the road and sped away, presumably very happy with life. We were not so fortunate as, in taking avoiding action, the Ford went up a bank, turned over on its side, ending up partly in a ditch. My wife and I were able to crawl out through a window, having passed out our daughter like a piece of luggage. Help soon arrived in the form of the police and an ambulance. A hospital check-up found we were all okay. Arrangements were made for the car to be collected and made roadworthy again while we continued the journey to Defford by train. The car was collected a month later with repair costs of £5. All quite an adventure. But I was convinced it was safer to fly.'

Bomber Types

RAF Bomber Command's campaign of wreaking destruction in the enemy homeland became a controversial issue in post-war years. With the benefit of hindsight the morality of aerial bombing, with the huge casualties and the manufacturing effort and money expended for debatable achievements, was questioned in many quarters. Judgements vary, for it remains a campaign without clear answers in several areas, particularly the true worth of destruction and disruption caused by the bombing – plus contesting these raids – had on the German war effort. With in excess of a million persons engaged in air raid defence and associated work, this alone must have imposed a heavy burden on the Reich's war economy.

The visionaries' belief that strategic bombing could defeat an enemy without need for bloody land battles was never realized. In the first instance the RAF chose to operate principally under cover of darkness, to minimize losses from enemy fighters and anti-aircraft artillery, but the development of radar devices by the Germans eventually made the night sky very dangerous. Meanwhile, the development of the long-range escort fighter was the salvation of the day bombing undertaken by the USAAF. Moreover, while night operation may have afforded the RAF bombers some protection, it also made targets more difficult to locate. During the first two years of Bomber Command's operations only a small percentage of bombs dropped fell on the targets for which they were intended. Bomber Command did not possess the technical means of accurately hitting factories and similar strategic targets of limited size in darkness. Not until the final months of the war in Europe were the equipment and technique readily available to do this work successfully.

To meet the situation whereby most bombs dropped at night were going astray, Bomber Command leaders turned to so-called 'area bombing', attacking cities to disrupt industry and communications by causing worker casualties even if war plants in the area survived. The concept that in total war the factory worker was as much a legitimate target as the soldier was not universally supported, even if the Luftwaffe had apparently tried the same tactics over Britain. 'Innocent' civilians inevitably suffered. There was, allied to this doctrine, the belief that sustained bombardment would break civilian moral and precipitate a collapse of the national economy. British morale had held in the London *Blitz*; so why should enemy morale succumb to bombing? Perhaps the instigators had been conditioned into believing the propaganda that the German was an inferior being. Only on a few occasions were Bomber Command's attacks heavy and concentrated enough to bring about a complete breakdown of order in an enemy city.

However, that Bomber Command's effort made a contribution to victory is without question. The degree is in question as is justification of the cost. A total of 55,358 aircrew are listed as killed in both operations and accidents, which is almost four-fifths of the total RAF war dead. It has been said that no other service command suffered such a high percentage of loss in the Second World War apart from the German U-boat crews. The strategy that brought such attrition to comrades has in no way mellowed the pride of survivors. To them it was duty, well performed in the face of grim odds. There is perhaps no greater camaraderie than among the men of an individual bomber crew.

AIRCRAFT, EQUIPMENT AND EXPERIENCE

In wartime aircrew were subordinate to the aircraft they flew in official reports and Press releases to newspapers and radio. It was not '5,000 men of Bomber Command attacked Essen last night' but '700 Halifaxes and Lancasters'. The bomber was the tool of trade and the hallmark of the aircrew – 'I was in Lancs . . .', 'I was a Halybag mid-upper . . .', and the like. Loyalty to the aircraft type that had seen you successfully through an operational tour was unshakeable, as demonstrated by opinions such as Bill Coote's:

'I first became associated with the Wellington bomber at 21 OTU, Moreton-in-Marsh, and from that time no other aeroplane captured my affections in quite the same way. Designed by Barnes Wallis, there can be little doubt that it was the finest British bomber taking part in World War 2. Of course there were varying opinions about its handling, stability and ability to fly on one motor, although it must be said that much depended upon the Mark of the aircraft and its engines. Naturally, the early Wellington ICs, equipped with Bristol Pegasus engines developing 1,050hp, used at Operational Training Units, did not have the same performance as the later Mk Xs, powered by Bristol Hercules developing 1,700hp, in which we operated with No. 70 Squadron in North Africa. Nevertheless, the one aspect of the Wimpy, universally acknowledged and agreed by all who flew in them, was the extraordinary strength that existed in its geodetic construction. It was unique in its ability to soak up punishment, far beyond that of any other aeroplane, and still continue to fly!

'There are numerous instances of its toughness on record, typical of that experienced by my colleague, W/O Custance, who while flying over Budapest in July 1944 collided with another aircraft, losing 10 feet off his port wing in the process! We were based at that time on Tortorella, a satellite of Foggia Main, and I remember walking over to dispersal the following morning to witness the result of the collision. I shall never understand how old Cuss managed to fly that aeroplane back to base in such a condition, since he was quite short in stature and the task must have presented him with many problems.'

Perhaps others who had a wider experience of RAF bombers would be less laudatory about the Wimpy, but the fact remains that this alone of the three medium bomber types in squadron service in September 1939 endured in operational squadron service until the end of the war, which gives an indication of its worth. The Wellington was a reliable performer, until 1942 the most numerous medium type in Bomber Command. Along with the Whitleys and Hampdens it gradually gave way to the new four-engined heavies. The first of these, the Short Stirling, was generally viewed as anything but reliable. William Drinkell on an experience while at No. 14 OTU:

'On my first solo in a Stirling I lost an engine due to oil pressure failure and had to feather. Then the Gee navigation set burnt out, filling the cockpit area with smoke. On top of that, the undercarriage wouldn't lower hydraulically and had to be wound down – 960 turns by hand of the emergency lever. Finally I made my approach only to have the rear of the aircraft shimmy as soon as the tailwheels were on the ground. I cleared the runway, notified the control tower I was going to check the tailwheels, applied the parking brake, took off my helmet and placed it on the control column, unstrapped and went back to have a look. There was a chain linking the dual tailwheels and I thought that might have broken, but the investigation didn't locate the trouble.

'So back to the cockpit to continue taxi-ing to a dispersal point. When I replaced my helmet I was told to report to the watch tower once the aircraft was parked. When I got there I was reprimanded for bad language and asked to apologise to the WAAF operators present. Not given to swearing, I was a bit taken aback. It was explained that following the request to park on the perimeter to inspect the tail wheels, our radio had continued to broadcast the intercom conversation. I realized that in placing my helmet on the control column the "Transmit" switch had been moved to "on". In my absence the bomb-aimer had asked the others what they thought of this Stirling and the rest of the crew responded in no uncertain terms, including a few cryptic comments as to what the Chief Instructor could do with it. It would have been very painful.'

George Smith was another unimpressed member of Stirling aircrew:

'A cumbersome giant, some pilots had difficulty getting the hang of the Stirling. We had several mishaps in 1651 Heavy Conversion Unit at Waterbeach. A lot of the time was spent doing night cross-countries. After one such flight we were finishing our landing roll when there was a hell of a bang and the Stirling nosed over. I cut my knee in the haste to get out of the navigator's seat. There was no fire and none of the other crew members were badly injured. Not until out of the aircraft did I discover we had collided with a steam roller! The pilot had landed too far down the runway, crossed the perimeter track and ended up in some construction work. The next night we spent two hours doing circuits and bumps at Tempsford with the same pilot. On the last bump before returning to Waterbeach the port tyre burst and the Stirling slewed off the runway and chewed up a parked Halifax with its props. Our pilot was distraught, "This is it. This is the end for me." It wasn't. He may have been unlucky enough to wreck three four-engined bombers in a few days, but the RAF weren't going to waste a trained pilot.'

The trouble remembered by Stanley Tomlinson was not – to be fair – a fault in the aircraft:

'The Stirling was a horrible aircraft to land and always having undercarriage problems. There was a spate of brake failures while I was with No. 149 Squadron and some of this was found to be due to corrosion of components. This puzzled the authorities for a while until the realization that it was due to the "nervous pee". The last thing the crew of seven did before going on an operational trip was to relieve themselves. And out on a bleak airfield where there is no cover the only substantial object to hide their modesty was a main wheel. Under this repeated shower, followed by heat generated in taxi-ing, all sorts of chemical changes occurred. We were told that the nervous pee had to be directed elsewhere.'

Nevertheless, there were many aircrew who became very fond of the Stirling, having mastered its idiosyncracies. Roy Ellis-Brown, a US national, was a veteran of 30 operations in the type:

'When I joined No. 7 Squadron they had only recently commenced operations with Stirlings. Some of the early aircraft were none too reliable and beset with mechanical problems. Then we started getting those built by Short & Harland and the Austin Motor Company with even more troubles. One of the biggest worries was the efficiency of the throttle exactor controls. The lines to the engines from the throttle controls were so long the designers decided to use an hydraulic system. Before starting engines the system had to be primed and this was achieved by pushing all four throttle levers right forward, which opened valves in the oil reservoir. Unfortunately these hydraulic lines were given to leaking like blazes at the many connections and this allowed the throttle levers to creep. As this was common it was necessary to keep a hand on the throttles during take-off – usually the Second Dicky got this job. On one occasion after take-off, as we passed 200 feet, I told my Second Dicky to set the rpm for climb. When he took his hand off the throttles all four levers shot back and the engines started to die. There was a wild scramble by both of us to push the levers forward again, but only two engines caught. Such happenings were not good for the nerves. They never really cured this problem in my time.

'The design of the undercarriage was terrible and crumpled undercarts were a frequent event. Each landing was an adventure as the airfield was not large and the Stirling was a very heavy aircraft. You didn't want to overshoot and you had to guard against swinging off. When I arrived at Oakington there were no concrete runways and it was easy to get bogged down. The drill was to taxi with the throttles well open to keep her moving. Even then you would often slip and slide. It was a worthy old bird in the air but a brute to handle on the ground.'

The Stirling was withdrawn from bomber squadrons by late 1944 and the heavy effort was carried out by Halifaxes and Lancasters. Early Halifaxes suffered hefty teething troubles, a few only becoming evident when the type was well into squadron service. Later Halifaxes had a better reputation as Derek Waterman proclaims:

'The Halifax Mk IIs with Merlin engines and triangular fins were pretty hopeless in my opinion. They had a tail imbalance at certain flight attitudes which could lead to an uncontrolled spin. Quite a few were lost this way. I only flew them during type conversion and, happily, when I reached No. 158 Squadron at Lissett they had the Mk III which was a completely different kettle of fish. The Hercules XVI radial engines were more battleworthy and enabled the Mk III to outclimb the Lanc as well as giving a faster speed in level flight. Also most Mk IIIs had the revised rectangular-shaped tail fins and rudders giving greater stability.

Apart from a rather nasty swing on take-off, that had to be guarded against – and was a characteristic of most powerful multi-engined aircraft – I found the Mk III an excellent bomber. My first trips with 158 were in several different Halifaxes, but then my crew was given a veteran which carried the nickname Friday The 13th. This embellishment was derived from the fact that the aircraft was received by the Squadron on Friday, 13 March 1944. Some of my crew may have been a bit uneasy about the name, but I wasn't particularly superstitious, having been on course Number 13 during my pilot training in America. I flew most of my tour in this aircraft, 26 trips to be precise, and apart from the flak fragments that were almost inevitably collected on visits to the Ruhr, we came out practically unscathed. Friday The 13th went on to survive 128 raids, a record for a Halifax, confirming my view that it was a marvellous aircraft.'

This again reflects the individual view of an aircraft that brought a flier through a tour of ops. Such loyalty was not expressed for the obsolescent Fairey Battle, which equipped the squadrons of No. 1 Group in the early months of hostilities. A single-engined monoplane of poor performance and light armament, it stood little chance against enemy interceptors. The Battle squadrons were decimated during the 1940 Battle of France, but the type had to continue in service until better bombers were available. Eddie Wheeler, who survived two tours totalling 66 sorties with Bomber Command, started his operations on No. 150 Squadron Battles and describes the puny effort of those days:

'Ginger took up his position as navigator in the well of the aircraft, a most unenviable position, and sorted out his route maps. Rocky, our pilot, ran up the engine to full power, checked that we were all satisfactory, and then said, "Here we go chaps, good luck." We bounded across the grass field and took off for the first of our affrays against enemy-held Europe. Of the three squadron aircraft assigned to attack Hingene airfield near Antwerp, one had to return to base within half an hour with engine trouble. My brief was to keep a listening watch on the Command frequency at half-hourly intervals for possible recalls or diversions, and at my position in the rear of the aircraft, with cupola open, to man the Vickers Gas Operated gun against possible fighter intervention. It was very cold but at the same time sweat was very evident under my flying-helmet. Many times I thought that I had sighted interceptors, but then realized it was the shadow of our own plane on the clouds. It was a constant switch from "safe" to "fire" on the VGO gun but I was determined not to be caught napping. The thoughts that went through my mind varied from, "Have the armourers correctly set the interrupter gear on the gun?" – this enabled the gunner to sweep the area of fire to the rear and quarters without shooting off the tail – to "How near is my parachute in case I need it in a hurry!" Happily, the flight in effect was "uneventful" and we dropped our four 250lb bombs on the target with 7/10ths cloud obscuring results. After we landed back at Newton. I thought, "One down and 29 to go; if they were to be as easy as this perhaps I would see my 21st birthday." Ginger emerged with his maps and logs smothered in glycol and this was to be a persistent feature on all flights; the Battle was notorious for its glycol leaks.

'Four nights later, on 29 July 1940, we were briefed to attack Waalhaven with our usual "magnificent" load of four 250lb bombs. In my anxiety to scour the sky for enemy fighters I was guilty of missing the first group broadcast cancelling the operation and instructing all aircraft to return to base. As a consequence we landed long after the other Battles. We were met by the CO, Wing Commander Hesketh, who said, "Do you know you were the only aircraft over enemy territory tonight?" Nevertheless he was glad to see our safe return and handed me my first pint of beer, which was to be the first of very, very many over ensuing years.'

Like aircraft, the navigational and bombing aids improved as the war progressed. Personal equipment too. In the early days this left much to be desired when flying in the bitter cold at 15,000 feet. Steve Challen, a gunner in No. 40 Squadron:

'Our first operational sortie scheduled for 27 December 1940, the target Le Havre, take-off 16.30. Just before we made our way out to Wellington T2515 we were issued with a flask and a bar of green foil-wrapped plain chocolate – the best ever issued! No escape aid package, benzedrine pills, silk map, no flying-boots that could be separated at the ankle leaving the bottoms looking like civilian shoes. None of these helpful items for us. I had just the stuff that was issued me at Manston a year before; Sidcot brown-padded inner suit, long silk gloves, light leather gauntlets, black sheepskin calf-length flying-boots, helmet with earphones, oxygen mask with microphone and goggles. Over the top of the Sidcot came a parachute harness suit known as the Goon Suit which had the clips to attach the chest-type 'chute. What a job to get into the turret the first few times, especially if the 'chute had been clipped up to the upper starboard curved-in side of the turret. It was easier to get in, then lean back and bring the 'chute over the top of your bulk. All this exertion usually made for heavy breathing causing the perspex to steam up, more sweat trying to clear it.

'During the next two weeks we were issued with sheepskin flying-suits that had plugs for heated gloves and boots. I could only just get my Goon Suit over the top and the zips under the chin were hard to start. Wilhelmshaven, 16 January 1941, was a try out for the gloves and boots, which seemed to get too hot. The only way to control the heat on the extremity, which was too hot, was to unplug. Not an easy thing to do, especially reaching your ankles where the connections for your boots were located. Another most important extremity was very hard to reach when you wanted to pee in that empty bottle! What a struggle, sheepskin trousered flap, parachute harness straps in the way and the centrepiece of the Goon Suit (about three to four inches wide) which came between the legs from the back up to the front under your chin where the zips connected: zipping downward making a tight fit around your legs. Not a situation for urgency! Removing your gloves to use the bottle, your hands soon became cold enough not to know when you returned them into the heated gloves whether they were hot, warm or cold. I suffered blisters on occasions through not feeling how hot the gloves had become.'

The rear-gunner's perch was the coldest and loneliest position in Wellingtons and Whitleys although few could have had such an uncomfortable operational début as Tom Imrie:

'After completing my training on Whitley Vs at No. 10 OTU, Abingdon, as a Wireless Operator/Air Gunner, I reported to No. 51 Squadron, RAF Dishforth, on 1 September 1940. I was assigned to rear turret duties for my first night operation on 9 September to bomb the naval base at Bremen. Those who knew the rear turret on the Whitley with its four Browning .303s had been suitably impressed that it was essential to make sure the double doors were securely locked before the turret was operated. This required the pulling of one door towards your back by a strap and, having got yourself into position, closing and locking the other door with your spare hand. On this first trip all seemed well until the "skipper" ordered gun testing and turret movement. I dutifully swung my turret through 45 degrees to be greeted by a loud bang – a door had opened and I was jammed with my backside out over the North Sea and my parachute out of reach in the fuselage. An unpleasant couple of hours followed while we bombed secondary targets on the Dutch coast and returned to base where I was suitably chastised. Not a good way to start one's squadron service, but perhaps a blessing in disguise. I was, from that night on, confined to the comparative comfort of the wireless operator's position adjacent to the navigator.'

Not to fully heed the directions or warnings of others is a common failing of the self-confident. Personal experience is a far more effective cautioner as Harold Southgate, a No. 50 Squadron pilot, discovered:

'Having raided Rostock on 24 April 1942 with comparative comfort and with very little opposition, another raid two nights later was regarded as "a piece of cake". Although a long trip of some four hours and on a more or less direct route, the flight to the target was uneventful. The Manchester was loaded with one 4,000lb bomb plus several canisters of incendiaries, and feeling – stupidly – rather brave, I decided to bomb from 4,000 feet, the minimum altitude from which a "cookie" could be dropped safely. Having started the bombing run, all hell was suddenly let loose from below with Flak bursting all around us and shrapnel hitting the aircraft. In an effort to avoid this surprise reception the bombing run was continued in a dive – contrary to Bomber Command's laid down procedure – and the load was eventually released from about 2,000 feet.

'Our Manchester was nearly blown out of the sky by the detonation of our own bomb plus sundry others which had been released correctly by other aircraft from far above. We took hits in several places and the controls were becoming unmanageable, particularly the rudder. Fortunately, on board for a familiarization trip was a young Flight Sergeant pilot. He really had to earn his keep on the way home, as both of us had to push hard on the rudder controls to keep the Manchester on a straight course. This was a really hard struggle for more than three hours. Approaching our base we received a priority for landing and with a great deal of effort got the Manchester down safely. It taught me two lessons: always obey orders, and never underestimate the Germans – who had completely reorganized the defence of Rostock in two days.'

The confined, noise-ridden and vision-restricted world of the bomber crew in the night sky invited error, particularly from the adventurous. Continually finding one's way with a degree of accuracy was in itself a demanding task. As the war progressed, so new electronic navigational aids, Gee, H2S, etc., gave outstanding improvements, but even then it was easy to blunder. Ivan Mulley of No 432 Squadron:

'Our first operation took place on 17 September 1944, a daylight mission to Boulogne in support of First Canadian Army who were investing the port. The aiming-point in France was at the end of a timed run on a specified heading from a defined point on the Kent coast. In Halifax aircraft the bomb-aimer operated the H2S set situated in the navigator's compartment, which was forward of the pilot's cockpit and blacked out so that readings could be taken from both the H2S set and "Gee". Both instruments had been used in our journey down England and shortly after crossing the coast in the vicinity of Clacton and while traversing the wide mouth of the Thames estuary, Walter, our bomb-aimer, moved forward from the darkened navigator's compartment to the nose in order to set up his bomb-aiming instruments. He saw the Thameside coast of Kent coming into view, and panicked, declaring he could see the French coast, and requested that bomb-doors be opened. The pilot and engineer, who had been studying the scene below with interest as we passed over the flight path of the aerial armada which was *en route* to Arnhem and the other areas in Holland, and who knew where our aircraft was flying, refused the request. Eventually Walter settled down and made a successful bombing run – on France!'

THE DEMANDS OF BATTLE

The whole Command learned lessons the hard way, but as its technique and strength improved so did the enemy's counter-measures. Losses over Germany almost doubled for a not much greater number of sorties in 1942 when, under a new commander, Air Marshal Sir Arthur Harris, a new urgency was adopted. A typical scenario for a bomber 'trip' during that year is given by Alan Haworth, a navigator with No. 214 Squadron:

'The pattern of a night raid on one of the industrial cities of the Ruhr varied little. From Stradishall to Cromer, climbing to 7,000 feet, Cromer to the Dutch coast, climbing to 15,000 feet. Avoid cities like Rotterdam where the anti-aircraft guns (flak) were formidable. I usually sought to cross the coast at the small island of Over Flakkee where, ironically, there was no Flak. As you approached the target you saw two or three independent searchlights sweeping the sky, apparently aimlessly. But let one of them catch you and you were immediately the centre of a cone of five or six. Getting out of that demanded immediate and very strenuous action of cork-screwing, weaving and diving, anything to escape those lights and their attendant guns and fighters. Many seasoned crews were known to wait around the target until the cones of searchlights were busy with some other unfortunate. During the summer nights of 1942 the German night fighters were especially menacing. A moonlit night, with vapour trails forming at the height you were flying, made you a sitting target. There was some safety in the numbers of other bombers which were around and about you but sooner or later a fighter was sure to pick on you. On three trips in July and August our Stirling was attacked and on each occasion our gunners managed to fight the enemy off claiming two destroyed and one damaged.'

With more resources, better aircraft and equipment, the number of sorties rose steadily in 1943, but so did aircraft losses and the survival rate was little improved. In 1942 on average one aircraft was missing for every 24 sorties and in 1943 one for every 27. With these odds, the chances of surviving the 30-raid tour were slim. Despite attrition, morale was generally good among aircrew, with a stoic acceptance of the situation; and while they nicknamed Harris 'Butch' – the Butcher – his leadership was accepted. An entry in the diary of Harry Quick of No. 101 Squadron reveals this confidence:

'After such a long period of inactivity, we were very glad of a visit from him on 17 Sept, to inform us that without a doubt we were winning the war, and should win the war if we could keep going as we had been doing during the last few months. It was mentioned that since April – the month of our joining the squadron – had been the best time for the RAF. Give us the planes and bombs and good weather and we will keep it up. By this visit he proved himself a grand chap, and by his reference to air-gunners' pay, being – "If I had my way you would all get £10,000 a year." '

Those aircrew who survived their tour had by then become the veterans of their station. The crew on which Ralph Harrington served as a WOP/AG, in No. 78 Squadron Halifaxes, was one in this category, and also had the unusual distinction of all members collecting the DFC or its NCO equivalent of DFM:

'Our crew must have been one of the youngest in Bomber Command. We flew all 30 ops of the tour together, except on one occasion when we had a different rear-gunner as ours was sick. We started with Milan, Italy, on 12 August 1943 and finished with Lens, Belgium, on 10 May 1944, taking in most of the tough targets during this period. At the start we were seven sergeants and by the time we finished six had become officers. We had also collected six DFCs and one DFM. The rapid promotion was the result of the misfortune of others – during hostilities our squadron had over a thousand aircrew members missing, nearly three-quarters fatalities. Our pilot started out as a sergeant and had four promotions in five months, becoming a Flight Lieutenant in January 1944.'

The belief that Bomber Command was performing a war-winning job was the chief motivating factor for aircrew. Even so, the prospect of being shot down prompted many captains of aircraft to encourage their men to practise emergency drills. William Drinkell, a No. 50 Squadron pilot, believed in being prepared and his account also highlights crew superstition:

'We had a good idea of the attrition in Bomber Command, but one believed it always happened to the other chap. Even so, you could not help thinking about your chances and taking measures to better them. My crew regularly practised dinghy drill and also clearing the aircraft on the ground. We had it down to 11 seconds from the word "go". As the captain I was the last one to leave. Before an operation you made sure you had your best bib and tucker on, clean underclothes and were well shaved. Firstly to aid escaping if shot down; secondly, to be well clad if ending up in a prison camp. There was a pecking order for climbing into our Lancaster on every raid. I was first and then the others always in the same order. Nobody decreed that this should be so, but it was adhered to rigidly, a kind of ritual I suppose. Some of the crew had personal superstitions. The mid-upper always carried a medallion that had been given him. The navigator made a point of never looking out at any target, he always drew his curtain. He had another superstitious practice: if we were going across the North Sea he wore water boots; if it was only a short crossing of the Channel he wore shoes. But he was an excellent navigator and looked after us well. The bomb-aimer always placed his

Above: *Halifax II J-Jig of No. 35 Squadron. Fuselage letters were the usual means of reference used by RAF personnel to identify individual aircraft. The pair of letters were the unit code marking. (Megura)*

Below: *No. 90 Squadron Stirlings on dispersal at new and muddy Ridgewell, early 1943.*

Above: *Tour-expired aircrew of Lancaster LM241, GI:Q at Mildenhall, 12 August 1944. Sitting on the Wing (l. to r.): Bernard Dye (mid-upper), Arthur Horton (pilot), Ken Monether (navigator) and Dave Parsons (flight engineer). At back: ground crew member, Jock White (wireless operator), Brian Grant (rear-gunner), Brian Gray (bomb-aimer) and the other two members of ground crew.*

Left: *Gerhard Heilig of No. 214 Squadron. Note whistle attached to left lapel of jacket, which was for use in drawing attention if disabled in a crash or parachute landing. It also served as an unofficial mark that the wearer was 'on ops'.*

Right: Powerful, but initially troublesome Sabre engine as exposed in Typhoon SA:L of No. 486 Squadron at Raydon, early 1944. (M. Olmsted)

Below: A Whirlwind of No. 137 Squadron, one of only two squadrons to be fully equipped with the type.

Right: The immortal Spitfire came in many models. A Mark IX of No. 66 Squadron with two-stage supercharged Merlin engine, usually considered the best all-rounder.

Right: A clipped-wing Mark XII of No. 41 Squadron, with powerful Griffon engine. It excelled at low altitude.

Left: A Spitfire Mark VII of No. 154 Squadron, Merlin powered with pressurized cockpit for very high-altitude work. (M. Olmsted and P. Knowles)

Bottom left: A formation of Mustang IIIs of No. 309 Squadron clutching 75-US gallon 'drop tanks' which gave this excellent fighter a combat radius of more than 600 miles. Fighter pilots with ranks of Wing Commander and above were permitted to identify their personal aircraft with initials. The Mustang marked ZW is that of the Andrews Field Polish Wing CO, flown on this occasion by Tony Murkowski.

Below: High jinks at Biggin Hill, January 1945. Snowball fight team are, left to right: Flying Officers 'Bluey' Hargraves, 'Junior' Newell and Philip Knowles. (P. Knowles)

Left: More high jinks at Biggin Hill, January 1945. Flying Officer Ron Palmer and baby Austin leaving the Officers' Mess. Actually, the car had been man-handled up the steps by fellow-officers. (P. Knowles)

Above: George Irving (left) and his radar operator 'Wee Georgie' Millington with ground crew after bagging a Do 217 in Beaufighter VA:A.

Below: George Irving flying Mosquito NF 30 of No. 125 Squadron at 25,000 feet over Church Fenton, May 1945. (G. Irving)

Left: Even the tapering rear fuselage of the Sunderland had plenty of room to move around. Note the workbench behind the navigator who is checking Dead Reckoning Compass master unit. (Official)

Right: A Sunderland of No. 201 Squadron in Coastal Command's white dress, flying near Lough Erne, Northern Ireland. (Official)

Below: Flight Lieutenant Tom Minta, second from right, and the crew of No. 58 Squadron's Whitley Z-Zebra.

Above: Flight Lieutenant Len Barcham, second from right, and a No. 404 Squadron group beside Beaufighter EE:C at Davidstow Moor, June 1944. Deputy Squadron Leader Schoales (with white scarf) flew back from Norway on three occasions with one engine stopped.

Top right: A photograph taken from Beaufighter EE:Q by Flight Lieutenant Barcham shows rocket attacks on a German destroyer (just visible above tailplane) beached on D-Day plus one at Ile de Batz. The crew were trying to re-float the vessel when the Beaufighters arrived. In contrast to the usual successful report on a vessel destroyed, this one read that 'the captain went up with his ship'.

Right: Familiar to all who served at Shallufa, Egypt; the popular haunt of off-duty hours. (H. Kidney)

SHALLUFA R.A.F. CINEMA

Left: A tin can served for erks' washing-day in the Western Desert. 'Twitch', 'Hyme' and Harry Kidney (right) at Gambut, 1941.

Below: Desert breakfast, Libya 1941. Charlie and crew beside their No. 37 Squadron Wimpy B-Beer, serial number R1033. (H. Kidney)

Right: Disaster at Shallufa, 1941. A 20lb anti-personnel bomb explodes in a Wellington. (H. Kidney)

Below right: The new and the old. A Douglas Boston light bomber and a Vickers Valentia at Hurehada on the Red Sea. The ageing biplane was used to transport personnel around the Middle East. (H. Berry)

Left: Steve Challen nurses a neck wound caused by a splinter from the shell burst that blasted the tail of No. 108 Squadron's Z-Zebra. (S. Challen)

Below: A Marauder of No. 14 Squadron ready to roll.

parachute pack under his thighs during the bombing run – but that was more for self-protection!'

There were many instances of an act begun that had always to be repeated. Vernon Wilkes:

'When our crew started ops the rear-gunner, Danny Driscoll, made a habit of spitting on the tail for luck before climbing aboard for a raid. No one thought much about it at first, just a bit of a joke. Then one day as we were on the peri' track just about to turn on to the runway, the brakes went on and I heard the skipper, Gordon Markes, came on intercom and ask, "Danny, did you spit on the rudder before we boarded?" "No, I forgot." "Well get out and do it now," the skipper commanded. There followed a lot of cursing from Danny but the skipper said he wasn't moving until the usual ritual had been performed. Finally Danny got out of his turret, opened the rear fuselage door, and dropped out. By this time there were ten or so other Lancs lined up behind us, no doubt wondering what our rear-gunner was doing round the tail. Flying Control must also have been concerned as we ignored their repeated "greens" to start on to the runway. Danny wasn't very happy as the slipstream from the props kept taking his spit off target. He only achieved his aim by cupping his hands and almost kissing the rudder. He then had the problem of clambering back into the aircraft as the doorway was about four feet from the ground. What with his bulky flying-clothes and slipstream blast from the engines, Danny was somewhat hot and out of breath when he finally struggled aboard. By which time the skipper, impatient to be off, had started to taxi our IQ:B on to the runway. From then on we made sure Danny always greeted the rudder before a raid. I wouldn't like to say it was responsible for getting us through 36 ops unhurt, but at the time no one was going to let him break the pattern just in case!'

Perhaps belief in acts and articles being lucky helped an individual's confidence; for even some of the most brave and intelligent airmen took comfort from a secret talisman or rite. Equally, anything that had associations with misfortune would be tagged unlucky and avoided if at all possible. This even included people. Bernard Dye:

'In 1944, when not on duty with the lads from No. 622 Squadron, I would spend many happy hours drinking and singing in the Bird 'N Hand just outside Mildenhall 'drome. Behind the bar was a very attractive young blonde, the object of much male attention. Three young officers who each fancied the girl made a pact that each in turn would take her out. Our gunnery officer was the first and soon afterwards he was shot down. The second to take her out was also shot down and so was the third. From thenceforth the young lady was known – behind her back – as "The Chop Blonde".'

Good aircrew discipline was another factor that improved the chances of survival, an immediate response to intercom messages being one facet. John Studd of No. 101 Squadron describes what could happen if one didn't get it right:

'There probably wasn't greater comradeship than that of a bomber crew. We seven depended upon one another and no one wanted to let the side down. We were drawn from all walks of life and two were Australians, including Frank our skipper. Frank was a bit of a rough diamond and quite a character, but an ice cool disciplinarian in the air. We had set procedures for instructions and requests over the intercom and it was essential that we all adhered to these: a misinterpretation might cost us our lives. Human nature being what it is, in a dicey situation apprehension could cause a lapse. When an enemy fighter was seen, the rule was for the gunner spotting it to warn the pilot in which direction to evade. We were going over Essen one night; it was on the last leg into the target and as bomb-aimer I was busy in the nose. Suddenly over the intercom I heard the gunners shout "Dive!" A fighter must have been making an overture, but we kept on our course. "Dive," the call was repeated and still no action from Frank. A third time the alarmed gunners yelled "Dive," and received the exasperated roar from Frank: "Which fuckin' way?!" He got his answer, he dived and we lived to fly another day.'

Immediate evasion manoeuvres were generally acknowledged to be the best means of escape from fighter interception. However, there could be a deterrent to such action, as Vernon Wilkes discovered:

'Our flight engineer, Ken Brotherhood, unfortunately suffered from airsickness and was frequently sick on ops. Normally he suffered in silence as he was keen to continue flying with us. This showed courage because had he so wished he could have been medically grounded. One night we were over the target with Flak and numerous searchlights when, as I was sighting the target through the bombsight, the Skipper's peeved tone came over the intercom to the crew, "If we're attacked by a fighter you've all had it! Ken's been sick on the throttles and I'm not going to touch them!" Fortunately his threat was not put to the test so once again our Lancaster returned home to Hemswell unscathed!'

In 1944 the survival position improved with a loss for every 42 sorties, with Germany remaining more dangerous with a one in 30 rate. In the final six months of hostilities the position improved to better than one in a hundred sorties. Not that this was generally known or would have been of much consolation to aircrews. They still preferred to put their trust foremost in fellow crew members; being part of a good crew gave some sense of security. Ken Doughty of No. 101 Squadron was one who recognized this:

'I was 19 and didn't think all that deeply; somebody had to go and it was me. People got killed or didn't come back, but when I started my tour in the latter part of 1944 the losses weren't that bad. Perhaps I had a cushy time on my 31 trips compared to some. To a chap of my age it was exciting and I don't ever recall worrying about getting the chop. For one thing, the fact that there were six others up there with you, each one depending on the other, made for a special kind of comradeship that gave you confidence. There were only two occasions when I was really scared. The first was when we were caught in searchlights; the black of night suddenly turning white with the expectation that any moment cannon-shells would come crashing into the 'plane. The other occasion was on take-off with a full bomb-load when, just as we reached the speed of no return, an engine faltered. The pilot had to feather the prop and there were some worrying moments wondering if we were going to clear the row of houses beyond the end of the runway. Somehow we struggled over them and gained enough height to jettison the bombs in the sea. Take-offs were always anxious.

'People who had been through some harrowing experience probably had more trouble with fear. The pilot and myself – the engineer – teamed up with five chaps who had managed to bale out of a stricken Lancaster over England. Their original pilot and engineer couldn't get out and were killed. After our first trip with them the rear-gunner went LMF; he could no longer take it. I didn't realize how the experience had affected some of the others until one night when over Germany, two engines cut out. It was only a momentary failure due to a fuel or ignition switching, perhaps no more than a second or so, but two of the crew panicked, picked up their parachutes and started for the exits.'

LMF – Lack of Moral Fibre – was the official classification for those men whose nerve broke. This could be levelled at a man who quit at the outset of his tour or a veteran of many raids succumbing through horrific experience and battle stress. The lumping together of all cases as LMF, regardless of individual circumstances, caused considerable resentment among aircrew. Little sympathy was shown for the obvious collusion that caused the break-up of Bernard Dye's original crew.

'The target was Stuttgart, our first trip. After arriving at the Lancaster we did our pre-flying checks and then smoked and chatted with the ground crew until it was time to board. As we taxied round the peri' track for take-off the two Canadians on the crew, the bomb-aimer and navigator, came on the intercom and said they had destroyed their maps and refused to fly. Our pilot called the tower and reported we had to return to our dispersal point. The Wingco was awaiting us and, after questioning, the two Canadians were arrested and taken to the guardroom. The rest of us were completely shocked by all this as we had trained well together and there had been no indication that anything like this was going to happen. Next day our crew was again on the night's "Battle Order" and the bomb-aimer and navigator were released from detention. We all ate together, attended briefing and it seemed that all was now well and we would soon be on our way. The target was again Stuttgart. As we taxied out exactly the same thing happened as on the previous night, the two men came on intercom to say they had destroyed the maps. Once back at dispersal they were both re-arrested and taken to the guardroom, eventually facing a court-martial. The last I heard they were sent to an Air Crew Correction Centre.'

If a man did not have the fortitude to face the bombers' war he would usually succumb to his fear after the first operation or so. Ralph Harrington:

'On one of the Berlin raids we were asked to take along a new pilot for his first operational trip. As was the practice with newly arrived crews, the captain flew his first as second dickey with an experienced crew. It was a fairly hairy operation but we got back safe and sound, ours being one of the first Halifaxes down. The new pilot was the first chap out of the aircraft and found himself surrounded by a group of newspaper reporters who had been sent to our airfield. They were asking him about the raid and as he seemed willing to shoot his mouth off, our crew left him to it. Next day there he was spread all over one of the national dailies with quotes of how we clobbered the target and fought our way through heavy enemy defences. A real line-shoot and it read as if he was an experienced bomber pilot rather than a rookie on his first outing. The irony of the episode was that this chap never flew another operation. He left the squadron and we never saw him again.'

Gerry Hatt recalls an instance deserving of more sympathetic treatment:

'One day I noticed that a sergeant, a much older bloke than the rest of us, about 30, was missing from our section but the rest of his crew were there. The story I was told was that on the previous night's raid they had been attacked by a fighter but got away. The pilot noticed that the mid-upper turret hadn't fired so he sent this sergeant, the flight engineer, back to have a look. When he reached the turret the gunner was sitting in his saddle but didn't answer. So the engineer unhooked the saddle and swung the gunner down. When he shone his torch in the gunner's face there wasn't one; it had taken a direct hit from a cannon-shell. You can imagine the shock and the sheer horror of such a sight. It was too much for the engineer. He was made LMF, which wasn't really fair as he'd previously done five trips and it was simply this ghastly experience that made him quit.'

There is no doubt that the stigma of LMF was considerable and one suspects that this classification was instituted with some thought of its deterrent nature. The majority, however concerned for personal safety, avoided any action that might be construed as looking for a way out by fellow airmen. Sometimes this thought would induce men to try too hard, as in the incident described by Morgan Hewinson:

'The unofficial motto of No. 9 Squadron was "There's Always Bloody Something!" And there was. One evening in the summer of 1942, our third operational trip. Sprogs then! In a Mark III Wellington we taxied to the end of the runway, revved-up and started to take off. About halfway, realizing there was something amiss with the starboard engine, braked hard and pulled up at the far end of the Honington strip. Pilot to crew: "We'll go around and have another shot at it. Our last two trips were scrubbed because of faults. They will think we don't want to go."

'The second attempt seemed to be going better, the wheels left the grass. I switched off my intercom to tune my radio for the half-hourly broadcast, then realized that something was wrong. Switched on my intercom and heard the navigator say in an urgent voice: "Jim, your starboard revs are dropping back." We were clear of married quarters and just above the trees; luckily we missed hitting them on the way down. I heard the pilot say: "Right, here we go chaps." Braced myself between the radio equipment and the back of my seat. There was a bump and violent vibration and shuddering. The radio equipment broke away from its moorings and swung around to the left with my forearm. This probably saved me serious injury, leaving me with nothing worse than a small cut above the left eye.

'The rest of the crew were leaving via the pilot's cabin. I looked back, intending to escape by the astrodome in the fuselage, but the incendiary bombs were already burning. I thought that this would be a write-off, so everything I could take would be mine! Strange how cool and mercenary one can be on these occasions. I collected my watch from its container on the table, log-book and parachute. The door between the radio operator's and pilot's cabins was jammed. A heave from my side and a kick from the other and the door came off its hinges. A climb on to the wing and we were out. A walk or run across the field and shelter behind a hayrick. By this time ammunition was exploding, pyrotechnics flying and the incendiary bombs (our load for the raid) well and truly burning, and eventually an explosion as the full petrol tanks blew up. Fire engine, ambulance and crews arrived, but any effort to extinguish the blaze would have been useless, so none was made. Later, walking into the mess, there sat the very glum looking reserve crew, old colleagues of ours from OTU, eating their "Ops" meal of bacon and egg. Everyone stood and greeted the rear-gunner and myself. The drinks flowed. This and six days survivor's leave made it all worthwhile.'

The effect of combat stress on aircrew did not go unnoticed by the ground staff who could soon distinguish the suspect malingerers. Roy Browne:

'Occasionally, when the aircrew were ready in the aircraft, an op was scrubbed for a few hours for some reason or other. The crews would then go to the flight huts the ground staff had near the dispersals. Here they'd sharp cards and play up merry hell until it was time to go. Joking and laughing, you'd think they were going to a football match rather than a possible date with death. Some of this was undoubtedly due to tension – and there was a lot of chain-smoking too. But I never saw any fear displayed. At breakfast, after a raid, you'd hear someone say, "So-and-so boomeranged last night." That meant he had abandoned the raid because of some supposed mechanical problem, a mag' drop or something. Of course, there were genuine cases but a few pilots made a habit of doubtful failures. On the other hand, I've known pilots who came back because of a mechanical fault, had it seen to and went off again, an hour behind the rest of the squadron.'

But the men who were deemed LMF were very few, a mere 0.9 per cent one study concluded. The vast majority of aircrew suppressed fear and did their job.

A NEAR THING – FOR SOME

Often the four to eight hours spent in a thundering, vibrating bomber was fraught with fatigue as much as apprehension, although most men had moments when their worst fears seemed about to be realized. There follow three examples of such experience. Harry Robinson, a No. 101 Squadron wireless operator:

'As a wireless operator in a Lancaster you were tucked down in the fuselage behind the pilot, flight engineer and navigator. Apart from on the bombing run, when it was duty to observe from the astrodome to provide another pair of eyes, you couldn't see much of what was going on. The occasional searchlight beam and the odd flash if you looked up through the canopy, but for the most part all was dark, the only illumination being the shaded lights over the radio set. You concentrated on listening out for broadcasts and only knew what was going on around through the talk of other members of the crew that could be heard on the intercom. All this against a background of constant engine roar and vibration.

'In an emergency you felt rather helpless; it was a case of sit there and take it. On one of my trips – 4 April 1945 – I was listening at the set when the gunner called out "Corkscrew! Corkscrew!" As we dived and turned with engines screaming, my log and everything loose went flying. The smell of cordite filled the cabin, I didn't know if it was from our guns or from hits we might have taken from the night fighter. Neither did I know whether we were out of control or what was going on. A few seconds of terror and confusion and then we were flying level again. I began to sort myself out and pick up the scattered equipment. I found my log under the navigator's foot. As we had been shot up the pilot decided to land at Juvincourt in France. There we found holes in the Lanc but the damage was not serious and we were able to fly home next day. At Juvincourt they had been unable to notify our station that we were safe so we were still thought missing when we arrived at Ludford Magna. I suppose after this bit of excitement for a 20-year-old I felt quite important. Until I turned in my log to the signals officer. He took one look at the print of the navigator's boot and proceeded to tell me off: "What a state to bring a log back in." My explanation was no excuse; he was making it plain that standards had to be maintained, even if you were being shot at.'

Ken Brotherhood, No. 150 Squadron flight engineer:

'We were 15 minutes from our target in the Ruhr with plenty of anti-aircraft fire and searchlight activity all around. Vernon Wilkes, the bomb-aimer, was checking his bombsight and selector switches when we heard him cry out over the intercom, "I've been hit!" Pausing just long enough to grab a portable oxygen bottle from its stowage, I leapt from my flight engineer's seat and went down into the nose. All sorts of things flashed through my mind – "How bad is he? How do I get him back up into the main cabin? Who will do the bombing?" By the time I reached him Vernon had discovered the hefty blow to the chest and back he had received was not due to enemy action but his having accidentally inflated his Mae West. The lever of his life-jacket had caught on something as he moved about in the confined nose compartment. The immediate inflation under his tight parachute harness felt like a mighty whack.'

Gerry Hatt, a No. 426 (RCAF) Squadron flight engineer:

'The Jerry night fighters could home on our H2S ground scanning radar sets so the procedure was to turn off the modulator as soon as we had bombed. As engineer, it was my job to do this. On one occasion when we were at 20,000 feet it was time to go back to the H2S set. I got myself a portable oxygen bottle and strapped it on to my parachute harness. It tended to make you top-heavy and with everything else you were like a walking teddy bear. I set off climbing over equipment and had just reached the wing spars when I heard the rear gunner open fire. Bad news, followed by being sent crashing face first on to the wing spar as the pilot put the Halifax into a dive. Although badly shaken my first aim was to get back up front to keep an eye on the fuel tank gauges. If one was holed and losing fuel the procedure was to bang all four engines on to it and use what you could before all was lost. Apart from being frightened in that I didn't know what was happening, I was trying desperately to keep my oxygen mask in place even though my face was cut and bleeding. After much effort I struggled back up front to find I was the only man in the crew still using oxygen. We were down to 2,000 feet!'

Reg Fayers of No. 76 Squadron:

'He seemed too young, a schoolboy masquerading in battledress as a sergeant-pilot, and now, for a Jolly Jape, inserting himself somehow into our company-at-arms as a Second Dicky – or conversely perhaps it was that we seven had been unconsciously aged by our fifteen trips. Anyway, he came, a stranger, with us to Mannheim one night. Next day, liking the boy, we laughed easily together, bestowed a nickname on him, played snooker in the mess, drank tea –

and prepared for Nuremberg that night. He stayed by Steve, standing watchfully by the controls, I suppose learning the bomber trade, while I kept my head down over my charts as usual, concentrating my mind, holding my water until after we'd bombed and set course for Yorkshire and eggs and bacon. I smile with hindsight's incredulity to think that, still over Germany, I should have unplugged and gone back to the Elsan down near the tail merely to pee. But, seduced by the hubris from which young men in particular suffer, I went back. I really did.

'Even as I was still back there, fiddling about, we ran into trouble. Steve started throwing the Halifax all over the sky, engines screaming as we dived and twisted about through the great night skies in a frenzy to escape the searchlights and Flak. Stumbling and crawling and being flung from North Star to Nowhere and back, I lurched in my own private chaos of gravity back up from the tail to rejoin my crew. The port inner engine was on fire and heavy Flak was still exploding all around. They had us. Still the Halifax was flung about. I stumbled against a body, prostrate in the darkness, before I reached my table and plugged back into the intercom, but it was all part of the vast bewilderment that encased us all in the confusion of attack. Skipper and engineer between them conquered the engine-fire and somehow we slowly escaped back into the relief of the straight-and-level way homeward. "Has somebody been hit, Steve?" I ventured. "Where the hell have you been, navigator?" he stormed and tore me off my well-earned strip. Soon through the intercom mush terse bulletins issued from Phil and Lew as they struggled to tend the wounded Second Dicky – until the final one. "He's gone, Steve." "Are you sure?" with some disbelief. "Yes." "OK. Back to work."

'We landed at Ford, just into Sussex. Next morning, totally subdued, we went out to inspect our aircraft. The picture was entitled 'The Morning After the Battle'. The great stricken Halifax stood nose-in-air in silent suffering on the tarmac. Inside it was drenched and spattered everywhere with the congealed life-blood of Witt, the dead schoolboy Second Dicky. He had said, "I think I've been hit, Skip . . ." and merely lowered himself away from Steve's presence. The aircraft had been pierced time and again by shrapnel but there, in the unbelievable peace of an August morning in lovely Sussex countryside, we were able to trace clearly the tragic trajectory of that single significant lump of German metal, no more than a couple of inches across, that had shot up through the bottom of the aircraft capriciously to sever the main artery in Witt's thigh. And on its way upward, we plainly saw, it had torn a neat hole in the canvas of the seat – my seat – upon which I should have dutifully been sitting had not the chance wisdom sent me back down to the aircraft to the Elsan to pee.

'As we left our desolate aircraft reflectively, we were accosted by a young sprog MO. Did we realize, he demanded, that we ought to have saved Witt's life last night? Within that first silence of our indignant anger, I kept hearing not that cruelly unnecessary lecture on the application of tourniquets – for did we not have desperate practical experience of the attempted application of tourniquets under battle conditions, which he did not – but only the sound of his leather gloves continually slapping against his own left palm. He too was very young, still "wet behind the ears", beautifully kitted-out in his brand-new Bond Street uniform, although his new cap was already pressed fashionably into an "old sweat" shape. One or two of us began to storm at him, about did he have the remotest notion what it was like up there over Saarbrucken, the chaos, the darkness, the long moments of not-knowing, of those great demons of gravity, the confusion of an aircraft on fire. He had started to apologize and cringe a bit under the fury of the crew's anger even as I deserted them all and walked off to cogitate on the odds of living or dying. If He chose to move in ways so mysterious His wonders to perform as to appear a nonsense, then I'd henceforth be placing my bets with a different bookie.'

By and large, aircrew considered Flak the most intimidating part of the German defences but, naturally, individuals' reactions varied. Freddie Brown's fears were not untypical of mid-upper gunners:

'By the time you'd seen a Flak shell explode, if you hadn't been hit then there was nothing to fear from that burst. You didn't consider the next, if there was going to be one in your vicinity; that was the unknown. Running up to a target there would be comment about the Flak from the crew up front and I'd sometimes ease the mid-upper turret round for a brief look. Often there appeared to be a solid wall of shell explosions ahead and an exclamation of "Bloody Hell!" was appropriate. It looked worse than it was as you were seeing bursts over a large area. Once amongst the barrage you saw it was actually well spread out and your chances of getting through seemed much better. Although your firepower was inferior to that of enemy fighters, being behind a pair of guns did give that "him or me" feeling. If your vigilance was good and you saw him first or he missed with his first burst, there was a chance. Searchlights gave me my greatest anxiety. On one occasion, over Essen, a big blue light found us and immediately many others caught us in a perfect cone. The vivid brightness took away what little security the turret offered, I felt exposed to the whole of the German defences; absolutely naked! I had one foot out of the turret on the step as I cowered from the blinding light. Somehow words came from my mouth telling the pilot to dive starboard through the main concentration and luckily we quickly escaped into the lovely black sky. We were free.'

The majority of Bomber Command losses were from night fighters, the fatal blast of enemy fire being the first the bomber crew knew of the enemy presence. When a night fighter approach was seen, evasive action could be taken while the rear and upper gunners engaged the interceptor in a duel. The rifle calibre machine-guns of the British bombers were no match for the heavy cannon in the German fighters; but the outcome was not always in the enemy's favour. Bernard Dye witnessed a particularly successful air battle:

'We took off in Q-Queenie at 23.48 hours, 14 June 1944, and set course for Le Havre. Cheshire had marked the target, we dropped with no problems, turned away and headed home. It was a beautiful night, clear skies, stars shining and a full moon coming up behind us. All around I could see many Lancs heading back to their bases. My thoughts turned to the bacon and eggs and the issue of rum to be enjoyed when we landed. All at once I saw a Ju 88 open up at a Lancaster on our port side. Excitedly I reported this to Arthur Horton, our pilot, with the suggestion we pull over and give the Lanc support. "No bloody fear," Arthur retorted. Of course, he was right; his duty was to get his aircraft and crew safely home. Then I saw that good shooting by the other Lanc's gunners had set the Ju 88 on fire. It broke off the attack and I watched it go into the sea below. Almost immediately a second Ju 88 appeared and started to fire at the same bomber. The gunners returned the fire and again the enemy caught fire and spun down in a mass of flames. Back at Mildenhall our Wingco, Ian Swales, was taking an interest in our debriefing when suddenly in burst an excited Flt Lt Hargraves and crew shouting that they had destroyed two enemy night-fighters. Quite a feat.'

There were other very real dangers in the Command's war. Aircraft stacked in the bomber stream heading to and from the target, each hidden from the others in a veil of darkness, except when in very close proximity. Vernon Wilkes recounts one hazard that was not an uncommon occurrence:

'We were on a night trip to Munich flying through pretty murky weather. As usual I was in my bomb-aimer's compartment keeping an eye open as we could feel the slipstreams of invisible aircraft ahead. Suddenly the alarmed voice of Ken Brotherhood, our flight engineer, came over the intercom shouting "Climb Skip!" Without hesitation the skipper pulled the nose up making the aircraft feel as if it was going to stall. I leaned forward into the transparent nose cone and saw a Lancaster pass from left to right about fifteen feet or so below our nose. It was close enough for me to distinguish the illuminated instruments in its cockpit for that fleeting moment. As I thought what a narrow escape we'd just had, there was an explosion about a quarter of a mile to starboard as the other bomber hit someone else. Two burning masses cascaded down. No one in our crew said a word about this incident until we'd bombed the target and safely landed back at Hemswell after a nine-and-a-half-hour trip. Collisions were fairly common, but this was the nearest we'd been to having one. Gordon Markes, our skipper, aged just 20, always refused to fly with George (the automatic pilot) engaged and never queried spontaneous directions given him by the crew members. If he had hesitated on this occasion our Lancaster would have been a gonner.'

Dick Enfield's experience was an even closer 'near thing':

'Our first trip to Kiel, a piece of cake. The skipper said, "If they are all like that we've got no worries." We had more worries than we wanted on our second. We were on our way to Stuttgart. Over France I was idly pushing out "Window" (anti-radar foil), sitting on the lowest of the steps from the flight deck to the bomb-aimer's position, when there was a sharp ripping sound. My immediate thought was that we'd been raked by fire from a night fighter. I bounded back up to the flight deck just in time to see a four-engine bomber going down in flames below us. From its proximity I realized it had collided with our kite. A scan of my flight engineer's instrument panel revealed the starboard inner engine oil pressure had dropped to zero. "Shut down starboard inner," I yelled to the skipper and while he closed the throttle and cut off the fuel, I moved to press the prop feathering button. At this instant the engine burst into flames which streamed back past the tailplane.

'The skipper called: "Prepare to abandon aircraft!" but at the same time decided to put the Lanc into a dive which snuffed out the fire. When he levelled off there was a definite vibration from the port side. Another look at the engineer's panel and the needles on the port engine gauges were oscillating like metronomes. It was obvious the props had been bent in the collision – our props had cut into him and his had ripped along our underside. The skipper wanted to know if we could carry on to the target. I informed him we had only one good engine and were going to need a lot of luck to get home from where we were. So he gently turned the Lanc out of the bomber stream and took a heading for home. Because of intercom noise it was apparent that one member of the crew had left his transmit switch on. The skipper called us individually but got no response from the rear gunner. Our WOP/AG was sent to investigate. After a couple of minutes he came on the intercom and said "He's gone Skip." I suppose the gunner saw the flames going by his turret, thought the aircraft was doomed and baled out. All this time we were losing altitude. The intention had been to jettison the bombs when we reached the Channel, but at 4,500 feet it was obvious we'd never make it so we had to let them go over France. At least we could now maintain height although the port engines had to be run at reduced revs.

'We made it safely to southern England where it was decided to test the undercart. When I selected "down" the port wheel didn't budge and the starboard only came halfway, enough for us to see the tyre was flapping in the breeze. As our radio was dead we decided to make for Woodbridge which had a special long runway to handle aircraft in distress. Once in the circuit a red Very cartridge was fired to signify we had an emergency and the skipper then ordered us to take up crash positions behind the wing spars. He put her down so gently we hardly felt a bump. It didn't even crack the bomb-aimer's perspex nosepiece. We got out in double-quick time but there was no fire.'

In addition to collisions, aircraft were in danger of being struck by bombs from higher aircraft – even in daylight. William Drinkell of No. 50 Squadron:

'Our daylight trip to Duren on 16 November 1944 should have been an easy trip with fighter escorts there and back. We had settled down on our run at 165 IAS, the optimum speed for a Lancaster's bomb-sight, when the rear-gunner reported another Lancaster approaching from the rear with his bomb doors open. I had a quick glance back but wasn't concerned as he would be doing the same speed as we were. I returned my attention to the instruments when the next thing there was a terrific thud and the aircraft dipped violently to the right. For a moment I thought it was going to invert. There was some frantic action at the controls and a fleeting glance at the starboard wing revealed a large hole right between the two engines and what appeared to be a trail of flame behind the wing. After hitting the feathering switch on for both engines, the crew were called and told to stand by for abandoning the aircraft. Out went the escape hatches and the draught created whipped up the strips of Window anti-radar foil we carried. It really was a dog's dinner inside the cockpit.

'Part of the drill was to take your helmet off in case you strangled yourself while baling out. Having done this, I managed to bring the aircraft level so we could jump and was about to give the order when I realized I could hold this flight altitude. So I kicked the engineer with my foot, as he was off intercom as well, and gave him the thumbs up sign when he looked round. He stopped the navigator going out and he in turn yelled back to the gunners who had the rear door open and were ready to go. Although I could keep her on an even keel I couldn't understand why we were going down so fast, then suddenly realized we still had all our bombs on board. A pull on the emergency toggle to jettison them solved that problem and stopped our descent. Then there was time to assess the damage. A 1,000-pound bomb had gone clean through the main fuel tank between the two starboard engines, fortunately missing the main spar. The escaping fuel had apparently been ignited aft of the trailing edge by engine exhaust but had not burned the wing. The mid-upper turret gunner had seen another bomb pass between the wing and the tailplane on the starboard side. We had been extremely lucky. Having lost so much altitude – we were down to around 3,000 feet – and alone with two engines out, our concern was being picked up by an enemy fighter. There was no sign of our own escort all the way home. When we landed at base our aircraft, T-Tommy, became the object of much attention. Its ground crew were horrified.'

A less fortunate episode was experienced by William Reid of No. 617 Squadron, this also on a daylight raid:

'On the last day of July 1944, 617 Squadron was sent to Rilly-la-Montage in France to block up a railway tunnel that was being used to store flying-bombs. We were to go in at 12,000 feet to obtain a precision drop with our Tallboys while a following higher formation of Lancasters was briefed to complete the job with 1,000-pounders. Just after I had dropped our bomb and was starting to turn off, there was a bang – we had been struck by bombs from an aircraft above. One knocked out our port outer engine and the other must have come down through the rear fuselage severing cables, as the control column went sloppy. What followed occurred in a few seconds of time, far quicker than it can be told. The Lanc was literally knocked down and it was beyond control. I shouted for the crew to bale out, got my parachute from the engineer and tried to force my way out of the side window despite the likelihood of going into the props. Centrifugal force made movement almost impossible and I then turned attention to the top hatch. At this moment there was an almighty crash and the aircraft broke up. The next thing I was falling free and pulling the release on the 'chute, but also keeping an iron grip on the pack as I was not sure if I had attached it to the harness properly. After the jolt of the opening I just had time to transfer my grip to the shrouds before crashing through the top branches of an oak. My next concern was the likelihood of being clobbered by a piece of the falling wreckage.

'My right hand and face had been badly cut when the cockpit disintegrated and after getting free from the 'chute a dressing was taken from the personal first-aid kit in an effort to stop the bleeding. My face also had several nasty cuts. I pushed my Mae West under a bush and did the same with a .38 revolver as I had lost the small box of ammunition carried in my hip pocket. Then I picked a way through the wood to get away from the place where I had landed, then sat down to adjust the dressing on my hand. On looking up, the barrels of three machine-guns were pointing at me. The Germans were from a nearby Flak installation and had watched my fall into the wood. Ordered to march, the crumpled tail section of my Lancaster was seen. I persuaded the guards to let me take a look. The rear-gunner was dead, half out of his turret. In another piece of wreckage lay the body of the mid-upper gunner. Neither man had a chance to use his parachute and had probably been trapped by centrifugal force as the bomber spun down. The only other member of the crew to survive was the wireless operator, who was nursing a swollen ankle when brought in by the Germans.'

William Reid was one of the nineteen Bomber Command aircrew to receive the Victoria Cross during the Second World War. This, the highest of the nation's decorations for valour, was awarded for his conduct on the night of 3/4 November 1943, when he was captain of No. 61 Squadron's Lancaster O-Orange. The following is his personal account of that operation, together with his observations on the reasons for the Award:

'We were over Holland at around 20,000 feet on our way to Düsseldorf when I received an almighty thump on my left shoulder. At the same time there was a blast of cold air and fragments of perspex peppered my face as the windscreen panels shattered. The night fighter didn't attack again – he was either driven off by the gunners or lost us when the kite started skidding around. The elevator trim had obviously been hit, but I could not get any information from the rest of the crew as the intercom was out. Eventually Jim Norris, the flight engineer, came up to me and indicated that everyone else was all right. To protect my eyes from the grains of perspex coming off the shattered windscreen I put on a pair of flying-goggles. The silk gloves I usually wore were no longer sufficient to keep my hands warm and the heavy leather pair kept in the cockpit were used to lessen the effects of the icy blast. The compass was u/s but as I could remember the briefed course changes there was no reason not to go on to the target. My shoulder was a bit sore but I wasn't really aware of any injuries at that busy time. Then, crash, we were riddled with cannon-shells and bullets again. I dived the Lancaster in an effort to evade, but the enemy fighter gave us a second burst before he lost us. My hands had been hit by shell fragments and the oxygen supply was failing. After a minute or two the flight engineer came back from the navigator's cabin and spread his arms out, meaning that Jeff was out; I didn't realize he was dead and that the wireless operator was wounded. I made signs for Norris to get me a portable oxygen bottle which I connected to my mask.

'Despite the mauling the Lancaster had received, all engines were operating satisfactorily and although we had no port elevator it was possible to keep the plane straight and level by holding the stick back hard. So I decided to continue to the target, an estimated 45 minutes' away. To turn back now and fly a reciprocal course in the midst of the bomber stream presented a high risk of collision, while without communications or compass, guessing a new course away from the bomber stream might get us hopelessly lost and make us even more vulnerable to night fighters. In my mind, continuing to the target was the right action to take. I was now becoming conscious of my wounds; blood kept trickling down my face from under my helmet. My memory of course changes was proved correct and there was no difficulty in finding the target. After Les Rolton, the bomb-aimer, released our load I used the Pole Star and moon as direction guides to help in getting home.

'As the flight progressed I began to lose my concentration and felt I might lapse into unconsciousness. Norris and Rolton had been helping with the controls all along and now that the bombs had gone Les stayed at a position where he could help hold the stick back. As the intercom had been out the bomb-aimer had been unaware that there were casualties among the crew. We received the attention of the Flak batteries before leaving the Dutch coast. After crossing the North Sea, landfall was made over Norfolk and we prepared to land at the first airfield we saw that was big enough for us to get down on. Morning mist shrouded the runway, making it difficult to see the lights, and what with the blood still getting in my eyes and my own weakened state, it required both the flight engineer and bomb-aimer to put all their strength on the control column to counter the lack of an elevator on the approach. We made it, but one leg of the undercart started to fold and we ended up on our belly about fifty yards along the runway. Only after being removed from the aircraft did I learn that our navigator had died of his wounds.

'I was carted off to hospital to have metal and perspex removed from wounds that I had not realized were so extensive. There was a hole in the left shoulder and my hands were skinned on the surface like a gravel rash. My head had a bad cut just above the hairline and my face had been peppered with perspex fragments. Minute pieces of perspex appeared on my skin for weeks afterwards whenever I shaved. While in hospital I received a visit from AVM Cochrane who commanded No. 5 Group. He was full of praise for my determination to carry on to the target and said this would be an example to others. I think they felt there were too many turn-backs on raids, and that some were not for genuine reasons. I got the impression that was why they made such a big fuss about my experience. It was not for me to say so at that time, but had I known the navigator was badly wounded – which I did not – and that there had been any hope of saving him, or if I had not felt the aircraft was still capable of reaching the target and bringing us home, then I would have turned back without hesitation. There was no intended act of bravado on my part; I did what I thought the right thing to do in the situation.'

In the winter of 1943-4 Bomber Command took some of its highest losses, largely in a sustained series of raids on Berlin. These raids were made at long range, often in severe weather, and in the face of well organized and effective defences. The losses were most grievous in squadrons equipped with Stirlings and early marks of Halifax; aircraft which could not operate with a load at the higher, safer altitudes of 20,000 feet plus where Lancasters and newer-model Halifaxes flew. These squadrons were eventually given less vulnerable work, but this simply had the effect of adding to the concentration of Luftwaffe night fighters attacking those bombers engaged in the Berlin raids. Fortunate indeed were those crews that finished a tour during this period. The combat stress involved is evident in the final mission entry of Harry Quick's diary – for the night of 2/3 December 1943 – which saw the heaviest loss of aircraft attacking the enemy capital, 41 bombers. This was also the fifth Berlin raid in two weeks:

'Number thirty, on Berlin, with the Wingco and a new 'U', on her maiden voyage; so was not feeling very happy and did not feel very happy till we got back. He seemed to have finger-trouble and, I think, it turned out the worst trip I have had. I brought back a bit of Flak in my turret that made a hole in the perspex the size of a half-crown, being deflected by an armoured stay. Bags of other holes as well as mine, two in the petrol tank, from which we lost a little fuel; a good job we had two hours' spare, as all this happened before we reached the target. We had been caught by searchlights and held for several minutes, but why we were not shot at then I fail to understand. Perhaps we were being held for a fighter which did not turn up, thank God. Met boobed with their wind direction predictions, which were all round the clock, making the navigator's job very hard and making other crews late bombing, breaking up the concentration. More fighter flares than I have seen before were evident, but no fighters seen. The moon showed up plenty of ours going in to bomb.'

LAUGHS AND SURPRISES

It would be wrong to imply that the grim statistics of the bomber airmen's war sapped youthful spirits. Indeed, the dangers faced appeared to have had the effect of accentuating play; parties were wild, pranks were many, the outrageous remembered with delight by veterans. Such famous occasions as when the adjutant of No. 101 Squadron swept down the grand staircase of the mansion serving as officers' mess to greet distinguished party guests. He was naked but for toilet roll swathed in strategic places and a tin hat on his head. A few drinks had aided this display. Perhaps a case of drink and be merry for tomorrow we die, except, as has been already noted, each individual believed it would be the other fellow and not himself. The 'who gives a damn' antics could sometimes lead to remorse, as Stanley Tomlinson of No. 149 Squadron experienced:

'At the back of our frying-pan (aircraft dispersal point) at Lakenheath – or Foresakenheath as we called it – there was a small pit and bank of earth. Before you took off for a raid the rear-gunner depressed his four .303 Brownings and fired a burst into the pit to test the guns. Behind this particular frying-pan, about 200 yards away, was a wooden hut that had been used by the Forestry Commission before the airfield was constructed. There was still pine forest beyond this side of the airfield, but the hut was now derelict and abandoned. One winter's afternoon when we were preparing to go out on a raid and I was about to test fire the guns, the mid-upper gunner calls out over the intercom: "Tomo, why don't you try and knock that soddin' window out of that old hut." He only said it for a laugh. But I was 22 years old and as silly as they come, so what the hell. Without thinking, I lined the ring-and-bead sight up on the one unbroken pane of the four frames in the hut window and let fly with a short burst – around 300 rounds I reckon. To my amazement the door flew open and a bloke belts away like I've never seen anyone run before or since. He looked as if he was wearing three overcoats, he had on a battered old hat and hanging from a belt round his middle were several tin pots. Now this really shook me I can tell you; I could not believe anybody would be in that broken-down hut. Of course there was nothing I could do, but I worried all during the trip and when we got back. After interrogation and supper I went to bed but couldn't get it out of my mind. Was there someone else in the shed who I'd killed? I couldn't sleep and eventually got up, cycled the three miles out to the frying-pan and went over to the hut. Apart from some straw and some lavatory leavings in a corner, the place was deserted. The Gentleman of the Road must have been laid out having a kip when I put all that lead through the hut a few inches over his head. I bet he never forgot it. I didn't.'

Nor were aircrew slow to exploit opportunities afforded by an operational mission to enhance their future entertainment. Harold Southgate:

'Both Nos. 50 and 617 Squadrons had selected crews for a special mission to Italy and after bombing were to fly on to land at Blida airfield near Algiers. The raid was launched on 15 July 1943. The attack on the target, a power-station at Reggio, was not very successful but we enjoyed a lovely flight out over the Alps and across the Mediterranean. We had to remain in Algiers for nine days owing to bad weather back in England. Much of the time was spent in nearby Arab markets buying things that were in short supply or unobtainable in the UK, such as wine and exotic fruit, although a good deal of the fruit went bad before it could be flown home. One bright spark in 617 Squadron decided that as they were having a mess party in the near future they would take a very, very large flagon of wine back with them. It took all the aircrew and most of the ground crew to manhandle this flagon into a Lancaster which, with the rest, was expected to bomb a target at Leghorn on the journey to England. We completed the trip without incident, but I later learned that the large flagon of wine blew up as the Lancaster carrying it was forced to increase altitude to cross the Alps. Fortunately no damage was done except to mess funds, from which a fair amount of cash was recovered to pay for the wine that had flushed out the fuselage of a Lancaster.'

Eddie Wheeler, a No. 97 Squadron WOP/AG, was another who was deprived of his investment:

'After our flak-damaged Lanc was written off on landing in North Africa, we hitched a flight back to England on another aircraft. At Gibraltar I purchased a whole bunch of bananas which were practically unheard of in the UK. As we emerged from the Lancaster at Scampton we were greeted by the Station CO and when he saw my branch of bananas he said how nice it was that I should think to bring them back. He peeled off six and handed them to me and said the remainder would be sent to the children in a local hospital. I stood dumbfounded, but then agreed totally with the CO that it was my intention to do just that! Never did taste one banana as even the six I had were entered as prizes in a raffle!'

Wisecracks in the face of adversity were a common veil for courage and concern. There were instances when verbal bravado was heard in the most surprising circumstances. John Sampson:

'During the latter part of 1944 Oboe ground stations were positioned on the Continent and, being moved forward as the Allied armies advanced, eventually provided facilities to reach as far as Berlin, although it necessitated taking the Pathfinder Mosquitoes to 34,000 feet to receive the signals. The last raid on the German capital by RAF heavy bombers was on 24/25 March 1944, but the city was subsequently bombed on many occasions by the Mosquitoes of the Light Night Striking Force, the last being on the night of 20/21 April 1945. I always seemed to miss out on the notable events, but had flown to this target the previous night with a force of 79 Mossies. Our load was four Target Indicators (T/Is). As the Germans sometimes tried to confuse the situation by using false target markers it had become the accepted procedure to announce over the VHF radio when we had made the drop. On this occasion my pilot, Derek James, DFC, called out "Pathfinder F – Freddie – Markers going down," to be greeted by a chorus from the pilots of some of the other Mossies (listening in for the signal) of "Lookie, lookie, lookie, here comes Cookie" – "cookie" being RAF slang for the 4,000-pound bomb.'

John Sampson flew with No. 105 Squadron, then part of the special Pathfinder group that marked targets for the main force of bombers. Pathfinder crews were selected from experienced men who had successfully completed a tour in bombers. Precise navigation was the foundation of good pathfinder work, but there were lapses as Alan Haworth – also of 105 – tells against himself:

'Despite having completed an operational tour on Stirlings, one of my first in Pathfinder Mosquitoes of 105 Squadron was not a distinguished piece of navigation. The target was Aachen and our task was to light the aiming-point with flares from 31,000 feet. On the way in I worked out that the wind-speed at that height was 125mph as forecast, but from north-north-west, not west as the Met boys had said. After dropping our flares and seeing the start of the raid, we were hit by Flak in the port wing. The port engine packed up and with it all the electrics and radar equipment. We had the task of returning to base in Norfolk on one engine with this considerable wind blowing against us. And instead of using new courses based on the winds I had worked out on the way to the target, I made the error of relying on those based on the Met forecast. As a result, instead of crossing the coast at Great Yarmouth, we came in over Southend. Having no electrics we were unable to send out the normal identification signal required when returning home and as a consequence the Thames Valley guns opened fire on us. Luckily they missed. I gave my pilot, Ian McPherson (who played outside-right for Arsenal before and after the war), a new course for about an hour's flying to Marham, our base. I sat back content that my job was done and started eating my currants and barley-sugars with which you were issued on each raid. The pilot was less pleased because we had lost a lot of fuel and he was scared that we would have insufficient to get us to Marham. He reached across me, tapped the fuel gauges on my side of the cockpit and said with feeling: "And what do you think we will get home on – piss?" '

While No. 8 Pathfinder Group aided bombing performance, No. 100 Group was set up late in 1943 to reduce losses by counter-measures against the enemy's defences. This work took many forms, but much was connected with the burgeoning electronics technology for detection and disruption, all highly secret. Gerhard Heilig:

'Because of my ability to speak German, I was sent to No. 100 Group which was engaged in counter-measures against enemy night defences. Flying in No. 214 Squadron Fortresses, my job was chiefly jamming. The control unit in the aircraft had a cathode-ray tube scanning the German fighter frequency band. Any transmissions would show up as blips on the screen. We would then tune our receiver to the transmission by moving a strobe spot on to it, identifying the transmission as genuine (this was where our knowledge of the language came in as the Germans were expected to come up with phoney instructions in order to divert our jammers), then tune our transmitter to the frequency and blast off with a cacophony of sound which in retrospect would put today's pop music to utter shame.

'On one of my leaves I had lunch with my father at a Czech emigrées' club in Bayswater. Among a group of his friends there was a WAAF sergeant and I made polite conversation with her. To my opening question she replied that her work was so secret that she could not even tell me where she was stationed. However, before many minutes had passed, I knew that her job was my own counterpart on the ground with 100 Group. When I started to grin, she told me indignantly that it was nothing to laugh about, it was all terribly important. She was mollified when I told her that I was in the same racket. She then told me the following story.

'Receiver operators pass Luftwaffe radio traffic to a controller who then issue co-ordinated false instructions to transmitter operators designed to cause confusion to the enemy. One night there was nothing happening whatsoever. Then the controller was roused from his torpor by repeated calls for a homing which obviously remained unanswered. Mainly in order to relieve the utter boredom he decided to give the lost sheep a course to steer to – Woodbridge airfield in Suffolk. The German pilot had been faced with the prospect of having to abandon his aircraft and was going to buy everyone concerned a beer on his safe return to base. He came down safely – to find himself a prisoner, and could hardly be expected to keep his promise to stand drinks all round. The aircraft was a Ju 88, stuffed with the latest German equipment, quite a catch for Intelligence. The capture of this aircraft was made public at the time, but not how it had all come about.'

VIEW FROM THE GROUND

On a heavy bomber station there was an average of eight to ten ground personnel for every aircrew member. Most fitters, riggers, armourers and other specialists remained with one squadron for the duration, becoming more the squadron than the aircrew – whose association was generally only a few months, if fortunate enough to complete a tour. Ground staff personnel were often in a better position to assess morale and status of their squadron. Roy Browne reflects a mechanic's view:

'*Esprit de corps* at Skellingthorpe was very good despite the heavy losses. In the six months I served as a rigger in "B" Flight of No. 50 Squadron, four of my Lancasters went missing – and this was the final period of operations when overall losses were lower. None of these Lancs survived more than a dozen trips; one never completed any. This was W-Willie. A new crew under a sergeant pilot arriving in the squadron was given this aircraft. That afternoon, 20 March 1945, they took it out for a practice bombing over a range and that night went on their first operation – against an oil plant at Bohlen. I never saw them again. You couldn't be indifferent to losses, but in cases like this it didn't have the effect that the loss of old hands had. Unless it was your own aircraft or one from a nearby dispersal, you didn't know the night's losses until you went to breakfast. Then you'd hear another erk say "so-and-so went for a Burton last night." If it was a crew that had nearly finished a tour everyone felt a bit down. There was a Canadian crew who we got to know well. They lived in the next hut on the squadron site and when we were working and they weren't flying at night they would light the fire in our hut. Conversely, if they were on ops, when we got back from the 'drome we'd light their fire so the place would be warm when they returned. This crew completed a tour of 31 ops just as a tour was raised to 32. On 14 March 1945 they went out on number 32 with a force of 244 Lancs to hit an oil-refinery at Lutzendorf and didn't come back. Such rotten luck, really upset me; just hoped they'd all survived.'

John Everett of No. 102 Squadron expresses similar sentiments:

'Ground staff mechanics on bombers did not usually have a lot of contact with aircrew apart from when they came to check the aircraft or were going on a raid. I was an engine fitter on D-Donald, a 102 Squadron Whitley, and although the same crew usually flew this aircraft on ops there was not much opportunity to get to know any of them very well. However, one morning the pilot came out to take the plane on a test flight after engine overhaul. He asked if I would like to go on this local flight and I jumped at the opportunity. We took off with me in the 2nd pilot's seat and climbed several thousand feet and circled the Vale of York. The pilot then motioned for me to take over the controls, a great thrill. This pleasure was short-lived for the wireless operator appeared and shouted he had just received a signal that an enemy intruder aircraft was somewhere in the clouds. The pilot quickly took over again and brought the Whitley back to Topcliffe. It was nice to be appreciated in this way, for ground people rarely got a chance to fly. While one became hardened to the losses the squadron regularly sustained, it was particularly sad for me when this crew didn't come back.'

Ordnance and highly inflammable material were part of everyday life on a bomber airfield. Roy Browne again:

'The RAF did more damage at Skellingthorpe than ever the enemy did. In August 1944 a WAAF was driving a tractor towing several bomb trailers round the perimeter track when the train started to snake and the last bomb was flung off. There was a hell of an explosion as the lot went up, demolishing a nearby Lanc and killing the WAAF. On 1 February 1945 a No. 61 Squadron Lanc was taking off for a raid when the starboard outer engine cut out. The pilot got it off the ground and after flying the circuit, brought the bomber down again. There should have been no problems; his approach was okay, but he hit hard and then proceeded to run all the way down the runway, off the other end, where the undercart folded and the whole thing went up with a tremendous explosion. There was nothing much left. A little while later a Corporal was cycling round the perimeter track over a quarter of a mile away, when he saw something lying off to one side. He went over and found it was the rear-gunner, alive but in a bad state. They got him to hospital and although just about every bone in his body was fractured he recovered. What probably helped was the absence of perspex in the rear of his turret. No. 5 Group Lancasters had this panel removed as it reflected glare at night. Open to the elements it was a cold perch for the rear-gunner but in this case it saved his life. In the same month our Squadrons attacked the Dortmund-Ems Canal, but weather interfered and the kites returned with some bombs. E-Easy, with four left in the bay, taxied to a dispersal near the Repair and Inspection hangar where the crew departed and a bowser came to refuel. Half-an-hour later the Lanc suddenly exploded, killing three of the ground staff and making a mess of the hangar. A Court of Inquiry later decided the bomb doors had not been closed properly and the combination of wind speed and a heavy landing severed the wire securing the arming device of one of the half-hour delayed-action bombs.'

John Everett tells of another miraculous escape:

'One evening in the summer of 1941 a No. 102 Squadron Whitley blew up on its dispersal at Topcliffe. Presumably one of the delayed-action bombs in the bay had some fault – the aircraft had been bombed-up for a forthcoming raid. At the time of the explosion an armourer had been putting protective canvas covers over gun turrets but his remains could not be found. It was assumed he had been blown to bits. Then word came that the missing man had been found in his bed, bruised and suffering from shock but otherwise okay. Apparently, arms outstretched, he had been in the act of placing the canvas cover over the rear gun turret when the explosion occurred. The canvas caught the full force of the explosion and, acting like a parachute, deposited the shocked man a considerable distance from the wrecked Whitley. Dazed, he picked himself up and staggered back to his billet unnoticed.'

Ground staff engaged in servicing and arming aircraft frequently worked long hours, often in trying conditions. The bomber dispersal points dotted around the 3-mile perimeter track were exposed to the vagaries of the weather and mechanics often worked in wind, rain, frost or snow to prepare their charges for operations. Maintenance equipment was basic and some tasks performed would never have survived safety regulations of later years. Albert Heald can testify to this:

'There was a strong gale blowing with torrents of rain. Everyone was busy getting the kites ready as evidently good weather had been forecast come the night – which did nothing to help us. Apart from getting wet there was the usual "duff gen" going around that ops had been cancelled, when in fact they hadn't. It transpired that what had happened was that the target had been changed for some reason or another which, in turn, created extra work, particularly for the armourers who had to change the bomb load. During all the on-off duff gen that was going around the rain gradually stopped, making life a little easier. It was necessary to get to one of the engines and to do so I clambered up on to the wing of our Stirling via a trestle. As I stood up my feet slipped on the wet surface and the next moment I had slid off the wing. It must have been my lucky day, for the 18-foot drop to the ground ended on a pile of canvas engine covers. As I picked myself up, unhurt, I did not appreciate "What do you do for an encore?" and the various remarks made by my mates.'

Apart from falls there was another danger for ground staff which claimed several lives. John Everett:

'Carrying out an engine run-up with other members of the ground staff, we noticed that a wheel cover that might be damaged by the slipstream was still in place. One of the men went down to remove it. I was looking out of the pilot's window and saw this chap approach from the side and remove the guard. Then he must have forgotten himself for he suddenly started to move forward towards the propeller arc. To my horror I saw what was going to happen and dashed my hand against the throttles to cut them; the engine had been running quite fast. For a moment I dared not look out, expecting to see a bloody mess on the ground. Fortunately, my cutting the throttles and the instant change in noise had brought the bloke to his senses. He had stopped only a foot or so away from those lethal blades.'

Propeller blades became invisible when engines were running and the noise tended to have a soporific effect, making people drop their guard. Notably, there were a number of accidents through people walking into propellers in those squadrons which converted from Stirlings to Lancasters, there having been no risk with the former bomber as the blades at their lowest point were some ten feet above the ground. In Jim Swale's squadron there was a rhyme to remind one of this danger:

'On a Stirling, props a-whirling will miss your head. But on a Lanc you'll get a spank, and then you're dead.'

Sabotage of aircraft was an oft heard rumour but there were true incidents of this, albeit rare. Roy Ellis-Brown:

'Before I made any test flights in my Stirling I used to do a very thorough walk-around examining tyres, control surfaces and essential parts of the aircraft. On one occasion I climbed up on to a main wheel to take a look at the undercarriage locks. The Stirling's undercarriage weighed a ton each side, a tremendous thing that folded up in two sections; it was the only way they could get that long undercarriage into the wing. The height was necessary because of the length of the aircraft. When she was standing on both feet the cockpit was 23 feet off the ground. Well, I was up there looking around when I saw a strange wire coming down through the gear: I couldn't see where it went to or understand its purpose. So I got hold of my chief mechanic, Sgt 'Rosie' Fuller, a very fine man. I said: "Rosie, what in blazes have you got hung up here. What's this jury rig here?" He climbed up with me and said it was nothing that he had put there. I said, "Well, how about shaking this out and finding what it is. It doesn't look like part of the aircraft to me." So he said, "Okay, I'll do that." I got down while he rigged up a stand to get right beneath the wing for an examination. After several minutes he came down; his face was white. He said, "Skipper, it's a good job you looked up there," and opened his fist which held a Mills hand-grenade! "This was taped up to the struts. The wire that you saw was leading to the safety-pin. When you next retracted the undercarriage that pin was going to come out. The grenade was right under No. 6 tank which holds 481 gallons of petrol and you would have gone up in smoke."

'We were a bit perturbed about this and there was a very quiet but thorough investigation of all the Stirlings on the field. However, I had the dubious honour of being the sole recipient of this particular piece of felony; it may have been that the perpetrator didn't get around to doing any more. The first thought was an enemy saboteur, but I later learned that suspicion fell elsewhere. At the time a permanent concrete runway was being installed at Oakington and we had a large number of Irish labourers around. Labour was so short in Britain that they were bringing these Irish boys over. There was strong evidence that an IRA extremist had got in amongst them and decided it might be fun to blow up a British aircraft. We heared a search was made and one of these workmen was led away by the police. The whole episode was kept well hushed-up.'

The maintenance effort required on bombers was considerable. Many items of equipment were prone to failure, and improved versions were long in being introduced into production. There were often parts shortages which meant that make-do and mend was the usual policy. This was particularly so with second-line aircraft where wear and tear could try the patience of the gods. Martin Mason recalls a particular example:

'Being detailed for a 24-hour spell of Duty Crew with an engine fitter, our job was attending to visiting aircraft that arrived on our station at Binbrook. One of these was a Wellington which should have given us no bother as our squadron, No. 12, was equipped with this aircraft. Unlike our Wellingtons, which were Mk IIs with liquid-cooled Merlin engines, the visitor had air-cooled radials and try as we might we could not get these to start. The engine fitter was in the cockpit operating the switches while I was on the ground pushing the button on the mobile starter accumulator. After some perplexing minutes wondering why our efforts failed, my colleague noticed "Tired Tim" painted on the side of one of the engine cowlings. On the other side of the aircraft he found the engine called "Weary Willie". Comments which indicated to us that we were not the only fitters who had experienced trouble starting these.'

Fighter Types

KITES

An interest in aircraft or the desire to fly were the paramount motivations for joining the 'Raf'. If you were going to fly you wanted to be a pilot; and if successful in that aim, fighters were the first choice. The appeal of duelling in the sky in a fast interceptor held the imagination of many young men, but achieving this particular ambition was not easy. Only one in five of those gaining their wings were required for fighters and these were men who, during the various phases of training, had measured up to the medical and character assessments deemed necessary for the occupation of a fighter cockpit.

The type that most aspired to fly was the Spitfire, the beauteous and nimble craft which the public believed far superior to enemy contemporaries. In fact, the Spitfire's performance was in some important respects inferior to that of its main antagonists, the Me 109 and Fw 190, and while the later marks gave the required advantages, not until the closing months of hostilities were versions in service capable of better acceleration in a dive than the enemy types. Being able to attain higher altitude than your adversary and out-dive him were the two most advantageous factors in fighter-fighter combat during the Second World War where surprise attack and swift escape were the main tactics for success. For too long British fighter pilots had to fight at a tactical disadvantage. That they more than held their own acknowledges their tenacity and skill. The Spitfire was the chief vehicle of this achievement for it became the most numerous type in RAF squadrons. Antoni Murkowski was a Polish pilot with considerable experience in 'Spits':

'As with most pilots who had experience in different fighters, the Spitfire was a favourite. It was very manoeuvrable and enjoyable to fly. I liked the clipped wing Spit' V best as it didn't have the tendency to fly one wing down like those with the original wing design had at low altitudes. There were no aileron tabs so you had to hold the stick slightly over all the time to keep level flight at low altitudes. I never found this necessary with the clipped wing V. The Spit II could be a bit tricky until you got used to its controls. The undercarriage had to be pumped up by hand and it was awkward because the selector was on the right-hand side of the cockpit and the hand pump lever on the left. To work this you had to change hands after take-off; it was awkward. When you see a formation of Spit IIs taking off they go bobbing up and down, up and down because the pilots are all pumping away like mad. The Spit' IX gave us the extra power we needed; it was a very good kite at high altitude. Our squadron, No. 316 (Polish), got the IX when at Northolt in March 1943. It had the Merlin 63 engine, early models having an automatically engaged supercharger when you reached 18,000 feet. Sometimes, instead of engaging the engine conked. You could re-start but it was not a nice thing to happen. Once the squadron was jumped by Focke-Wulfs near Abbeville and as we were at a disadvantage we went into a slow vertical spiral climb to out-manoeuvre them. I was Tail-End Charlie following Sgt Stuka. We went up through some thin cloud at 16,000 feet and had just emerged when Stuka's engine suddenly conked – the supercharger hadn't cut in. He immediately nosed down and spun. Like a good No. 2, I followed. We came out of the cloud right into the middle of a large formation of Focke-Wulfs. They must have thought the whole Royal Air Force was attacking them for they broke away in all directions. Just like a shoal of little fish, flicking over and diving. There were only the two of us and we didn't even have time to shoot.'

Fred Pawsey was another enthusiast for the lively steed, although with some reservations about attachments it was sometimes required to carry:

'The Spitfire IX, with its slightly longer nose, was to me and everyone else who flew them the most beautiful aircraft ever. Even on the ground it epitomized the grace of a bird. However, when it had a 90-gallon overload tank slung between the undercarriage legs it was transformed into something more like a pregnant duck, making taxi-ing, take-off and flying much more difficult. On one occasion in April 1944 my squadron, No. 253, was detailed for an escort of Marauders and Mitchells bombing Rome marshalling yards. My section was top cover and the round trip from our base at Borgo Bastia, Corsica, required 90-gallon overload tanks – the first occasion we had used them. We were the last section to take off and as we were delayed coolant temperatures were high when the green was fired. I swung straight on to the runway and opened the throttle immediately.

'We had been instructed that with the 90-gallon tank extra forward pressure was required on the stick to get the tail up, but care was necessary as the pressure could cause the tyres to blow out – especially on the metal plank surfacing. As the Spitfire gathered speed I found that much more pressure had to be applied than was anticipated – I kept forward pressure on the stick but the tail wouldn't budge. Concerned, I increased the pressure. All at once the tail rose and kept rising and for one frightening moment I thought the aircraft was going to nose over. Pulling the stick back countered this tendency and the Spit eventually staggered into the air off the end of the strip. Now the nose kept rising and I could not get enough force on the stick with one hand to bring it down. The pressure of two hands prevented the oncoming loop and stall, but to add to my alarm the nose was now going down again and wanted to keep going down. Once more both hands were required to pull the nose up. This see-sawing continued three or four times until I managed to hold a more or less steady climb.

'This fight for control had been an unnerving experience for the prospect of a crash had been very real. As I went into a gentle turn I saw the rest of the section cutting corners to catch up and no doubt wondering what my strange manoeuvres were all about. As we headed for the rendezvous over Monte Cristo I asked my No. 2, Jack Finnie, to have a look at my tail unit as I felt something must be wrong. He assured me he could see nothing adrift so as we were now climbing steadily I decided to continue. Throughout the trip the nagging fear persisted that something was broken or loose and that if I entered combat and had to engage in violent manoeuvres the aircraft tail might come away. However, the escort proceeded without incident and the handling seemed to improve. In any event I was able to make a normal landing on return to base. The Engineering Officer was somewhat sceptical of my report, but the next day he called me over to the flight lines. He had two empty 90-gallon tanks lying on the ground and he asked me to try and lift each of them. The difference in weight was very obvious and it provided the explanation for my two or three minutes of take-off terror. The lighter tank had been fitted to my aircraft and was found to have too few baffles in it to prevent fuel movement. As a result that near half-ton of extra fuel had been slopping backwards and forwards accentuating each change of flight attitude. It could easily have induced a crash with almost certain death for me. The initial fault was in manufacture. Had the ground crew had previous experience of the weight of these tanks they would have queried the weight of the empty tank before fixing it to my aircraft. That was a really close shave.'

The sturdy, able, if less technically advanced, Hurricane predominated in fighter squadrons during the first two years of war and was expected to be replaced by an advanced design from the same manufacturer, Hawker. In the event, the Typhoon proved unsuitable as a fighter to contest the 109s and 190s on their own terms. George Aldridge:

'I was posted to No. 198 Squadron at Ouston while it was working-up on Typhoons in January 1943. At the time there were still a lot of problems with the aircraft which Hawker's didn't seem to know how to solve. To start with, because of the possibility of carbon monoxide fumes penetrating the cockpit from the engine compartment, we used oxygen immediately the engine was started. There were stories going around of what happened to pilots in other squadrons and I didn't have a lot of confidence in the type. Several Typhoons had lost their tails in tight turns and it was found they were coming apart at the fuselage joint where the tail section was attached. They did a bodge strengthening job, riveting patch plates all around this join. The work was carried out by an MU at Henlow. With others from our squadron I was sent to collect a batch that had been doctored and on the way home we put down at Church Fenton to refuel. When I selected "wheels-down" only one leg of the undercarriage lowered. I tried everything to budge the leg that was stuck up, but finally had to retract the other and make a wheels-up landing on the grass. While at Church Fenton, waiting for transport back to home station, a Typhoon from the resident squadron that was being brought back from Henlow also had an undercarriage leg fail to lower and was brought in with one wheel down. There were other incidences of undercarriage failure on modified Typhoons returning from Henlow. An investigation found that a WAAF with a tractor was the cause. The attaching chains she used to tow Typhoons around the Henlow grass were not taking up the strain evenly and often twisting part of the undercarriage assembly.

'The 2,200hp Napier Sabre was also troublesome. There was plenty of power but it dropped off rapidly at higher altitudes. Most of my operational flying was spent skimming over the Channel waves patrolling for hit-and-run raiders and at this height we could overtake most other aircraft we came across. Of course, the Typhoon really came into its own as a ground-attack aircraft after D-Day.'

The Typhoon certainly made good in a ground-attack role, doing sterling work supporting ground forces following the invasion of Normandy. Its successor, the Tempest, had a superior performance to most of its contemporaries at the lower altitudes and left a favourable impression on most pilots. There were two indigenous fighters that never really made the grade. The two-seat Defiant with power turret armament, based on a misguided concept of air fighting; and the Whirlwind, a beautiful single-seat twin-engined interceptor that could offer little tactical advantage over the less costly Spitfire. Nevertheless, those who flew Whirlwinds had a great fondness for the type. John Wray:

'It had a big tear-drop canopy which gave excellent all-round visibility, when others were still peering through bubble-type hoods. It was easy to fly by day and by night despite its higher than average "over the fence" speed [110 mph]. It had the big Fowler flaps which allowed one to land shorter than the Spitfire. It was faster at sea level (where we mainly operated) than any other aircraft apart from the Fw 190. However, this speed was reduced by some 20mph with bombs on. It had two very reliable Peregrine engines which were slightly hotted-up Kestrels, as used in the old Hart variants. This was very helpful in operations where one was likely to receive a hit in the engine doing low-level attacks. In a Spit or a Hurricane you'd have had it, but many times we came home on one engine. It was very manoeuvrable and in the hands of an experienced "Whirly" pilot could see off a 109 or 190 provided it weren't being flown by Galland, Nowotny or someone of that calibre.

'The Whirlwind did have some shortcomings; no fuel crossfeed for example. So, if you lost an engine you couldn't transfer the fuel from its tank to the good engine. It had drum-fed cannon with only 60 rounds per gun. However, the pilot looked straight down the guns, mounted in the nose, which was ideal for ground attack. It had the exactor system of controls for throttle and airscrew. This used oil under pressure as opposed to linkage. Both throttle and airscrew controls had to be primed from time to time. This involved going to full throttle for the power and to fully coarse for the aircrew controls. At altitude the engines were frequently getting out of synchronization and so one was constantly priming them; not always convenient if you had a 190 up your backside! However, we did not have any problems at sea level where we mainly operated. We did, however, always prime for landing in case we had to go around again, in which case one would want the engines to pick up together.

'Because there were only two squadrons, Nos. 137 and 263, few people had the chance to fly Whirlwinds. Pilots tended to go from one squadron to the other! On promotion to Flight Commander, for example. Moreover, the pilots tended to stay, unless they weren't good enough. So we had a lot of experienced Whirlwind pilots. Therefore pilot error accidents were rare. I think it is fair to say that all who flew the aeroplane for any length of time came to regard it with affection. Those of us who operated fairly extensively with it can think of occasions when, if we had been in another fighter-bomber, we would not have got back. One can remember those occasions leaving the French coast, bombs gone, throttles hard against the instrument panel, the 109s gradually dropping back. Or on a moonlight night low-level over France or Belgium, happily listening to the busy buzz of the two Peregrines and feeling much safer as a result. As one of our Canadian pilots said, "She was a great little bird".'

Of the American-designed and built fighters acquired by Britain, only one, the Mustang, was considered worthy of extensive employment in Europe. The version fitted with a US-built Merlin engine became one of the most successful fighters of the war, having all-round versatility and possessing those two essential capabilities, high-altitude performance and high diving speed. The Mustang's unique attribute for a single-engine, single-seat fighter was inbuilt fuel capacity which gave a 400-mile radius of action and made it ideal for escort duties. The early Mustangs received by the RAF had low-altitude rated Allison engines and these aircraft served in a fighter/reconnaissance role. They proved redoubtable in a war where the average life of a fighter plane was about six weeks. Rex Croger:

'Funnily enough, the first thing that I recall about the Mustang is its cigarette-lighter. I was astonished when I first saw this, but I'm told most of the early aircraft supplied to the RAF by America had this fixture. The cockpit was roomy and comfortable, far more so than contemporary British fighters. A pilot's opinion of an aircraft type must, to a large extent, be based on a comparison with other similar types he has flown. In my case the only other experience of fighters was with Hurricanes and late marks of Spitfire. Both these British types, being lighter, left one with an impression of being more manoeuvrable than the Mustang. All the same, I never found the Mustang lacking in this respect. It was fast, had no real vices that I recall, and could be flown rock-steady for photographic work. There was a speed restriction of 505mph when diving as the acceleration was surprising and pilots were warned that they could quickly get into difficulties if exceeding that figure. The Allison engine was smooth and responsive, even if it lacked power at high altitudes. This was not important in our job which, when I joined the squadron, was spotting targets for naval guns in Channel coast German strongholds, and looking for V-2 sites in Holland, all at altitudes below 5,000 feet – the ideal height to get yourself shot at by light Flak. Although I did not know it at the time, the Mustang assigned to me for the majority of my sorties, XC:Y, serial number AG361, was the 17th Mustang off the production line in 1941 and had already seen three years of service when I became its pilot. That was an exceptionally long operational life for a wartime aircraft. I flew it on the last operation undertaken by our 26 Squadron; on 12 May 1945, to check that the German gunners in Jersey had dismantled their artillery guns as ordered.'

THE FEW

The Battle of Britain dominates any review of Royal Air Force fighter action. This crucial victory has captured the imagination of succeeding generations of Britons. It was won by a narrow margin, and the grim reality of that time is captured here by accounts of men on the ground. William Drinkell:

'On Tuesday 12 August 1940, the ground staff of No. 266 Squadron moved south from Wittering to Eastchurch to support our Spitfires. The next morning I was up bright and early. While happily making my way to the ablutions from our wooden hut with other members of the maintenance crew, an Irish aircrafthand remarked, "See all them Ansons up there." I looked and started to run; my aircraft recognition being more accurate – they were Dorniers. Small bombs could be seen coming down so we threw ourselves on the ground as these burst quite near. Fortunately the surface was so soft the bombs penetrated deeply before exploding and there was little shrapnel. Our squadron's hangar was set on fire, but all aircraft were pushed out and only one was damaged. Other units were not so lucky, with 16 airmen killed and 48 injured and five Blenheims written off by No. 53 Squadron. The whole airfield was devastated and we were forced to move to Hornchurch next day. No. 266 was in the thick of the air fighting during the next week and we worked day and night to keep the Spitfires serviceable. Although an engine fitter, I found myself doing everything: riveting, changing wheels, harmonizing guns and many tasks I had not been trained to handle. We didn't have to be told the seriousness of the situation and Spitfires were repaired, modified and serviced one after another. The turnround of aircraft was such that we often only had time to chalk the squadron identification letters "UO" on the fuselage sides before replacements were sent into battle. On the 21st we were withdrawn to Wittering. In ten days' fighting half the squadron's pilots had become casualties, eight Spitfires had been destroyed and a dozen damaged.'

Alfred Pyner:

'In June 1940 I was sent to the small grass airfield at West Malling, formerly Maidstone Airport. It was occupied by Lysanders of No. 26 Squadron recently back from France. After a few days in general stores I was put in charge of fuel, about 50,000 gallons of aviation petrol in an underground store tank, as well as that for motor transport. Visiting aircraft were serviced with a tractor and towed bowser operated by a small group of personnel who also did duty as ground gunners. But I often had to pitch in and help them. At first things were all very peaceful, but early in August we received our first bombing which caused a few casualties and made a mess of a couple of Lysanders. From then on we had a number of bombing attacks. We began to get used to a lot of activity overhead; vapour trails, smoking aircraft and occasionally the nastiest noise of all – which seemed to fill the sky – an aircraft coming down vertically out of control. On the afternoon of 15 September I was on my way back from the fuel store when suddenly a whole crowd of aircraft came over the field, seemingly from all directions, some of them firing and in the middle was a Heinkel He 111. With the Intelligence Officer, who was coming from the other direction, I ducked down. When the row stopped we looked up to see the Heinkel on the ground no more than 50 yards away. We reached the plane as ambulances came up. One of the Germans climbed out and the ambulance people removed four more, one dead. I put out a small fire under an engine and saw that several of the fighters engaged in the fight were coming in to land. The German who had climbed out of the Heinkel was complaining bitterly in English to the Intelligence Officer about our fighters still shooting at him when he had his wheels down. Two RAF fighter pilots were arguing over who shot the Heinkel down, while six or seven Hurricanes and Spitfires stood in a cluster, a perfect target for an enemy plane that might make a strafing run. Luckily none did. I remember thinking: this is chaos, not an air force engaged in modern warfare.'

Hugh Berry of No. 249 Squadron:

'Our squadron was on a "recce". It was a beautiful sunny October afternoon in 1940 when, without warning, a crowd of Me 109s swept over North Weald dropping high-explosive bombs. I was outside the cookhouse at this time and dived for the only bit of cover that I could see nearby – a trestle-table! As one bomb struck a few yards away, I vividly remember screaming as débris rained down on top of the table. This particular bomb caught a hut, half of which was the orderly room and the other half consisted of toilets. One poor airman was actually on the throne at the time and a large piece of bomb splinter sliced him almost in half. While I was still in position under the table, Hurricanes of No. 257 Squadron were taking off to intercept. One had barely got off the deck when a bomb caught him and he pancaked only yards from me. It was a blazing wreck with ammunition going off in all directions. The Station Fire Crew eventually foamed it out and when Jerry had departed I decided to go over and have a look at what remained of the aircraft. In the cockpit, hunched over the controls, was what looked like a hunk of charred wood in the shape of a human being . . . the only relief in colour was a yellowish excretion oozing from the skull remains of that young pilot. This ghastly sight – my first corpse – made the realities of war very clear to me that day.'

THE PRIDE AND THE PITCH

Horrific sights were inevitable on the battlefield or as a result of accidents. The unexpectedly gruesome embedded itself in memory. Peter Hearne:

'In August 1944 I was at Boulmer, Northumberland, giving advanced trainee pilots the benefit of my operational experience. One day I was walking near the control tower with the station commander, Squadron Leader Stonham, when a Spitfire made a shallow dive at the runway trying, it seemed, to land. The pilot opened the throttle, retracted the undercarriage and flaps and went round again. His second attempt was also abortive and Stonham, sensing an emergency, dashed up to the control tower and established communication with the pilot. The barely coherent and agitated pilot was calmed sufficiently by the authoritative voice of the Squadron Leader who, with consummate skill, talked him down safely to a safe landing.

'The pilot taxied the Spitfire round the perimeter track and parked close to Flying Control. A crowd of curious airmen gathered round as Stonham came out of the tower and strode purposefully towards the aircraft. His annoyance that a fully trained pilot should act in this manner could be contained no longer. He mounted the wing of the Spitfire and launched into a verbal inquisition of the pilot, who was still in the cockpit. He had hardly commenced his tirade when there was a sudden stillness – an eerie silence which seemed to transmit itself to all around the aircraft. Even Stonham paused to see what was the matter. All eyes had focused on a large hole in the leading edge of the port wing, about half way down its length around which were splashes of blood. One airman moved forward, looked into the hole, stretched an arm right into the wing and pulled out a human head. The Squadron Leader's reaction was immediate and compassionate. As gently as he could he helped the pilot out of his cockpit and, with his arm around him, walked quietly to the mess. It transpired that the pilot had been authorized to perform some army co-operation, carrying out dummy low-flying attacks on soldiers training nearby. The enthusiasm of a soldier on spotting duty had taken him to the topmost spindle of a tree and this tree had been in the line of flight of an ill-judged low pass by the Spitfire.'

Attrition in fighter squadrons varied considerably, generally being highest in units engaged in ground attack where light Flak and small-arms fire had to be faced. While overall casualties were but a tenth of those suffered in bombers, it was nearer one to two when only pilots are taken into consideration. The nature of most fighter operations was such that the mood of aircrew was more eager, a 'let's go and get 'em' attitude pervaded many units. This is not to suggest that the average fighter pilot was fearless or less concerned with fate. Rather the mood of concealed apprehension engendered among bomber aircrew through having to 'sit there and take it' was not found in a fighter squadron. For the average fighter pilot fear came only in a moment of crisis and with the pace of action might not even be recognized. John Wray:

'We were the first squadron to become operational on the Hurricane IV, carrying eight 3-inch rockets with 60lb explosive heads or, as an alternative armament, two 40mm guns. We opted for the rockets as our principal armament because they were so devastating. However, we were not allowed to take the rockets overland into enemy territory because the Air Ministry wanted to keep them as a surprise for the Invasion when it came, so we were confined to attacking only shipping targets. This, of course, meant that we could not carry out "Rhubarbs", something we had enjoyed a great deal in our beloved Whirlwinds. So we kept six aircraft armed with the 40mm cannon, just for "Rhubarbs". These weapons were very accurate when correctly harmonized, and really sorted out trains. Whereas the 20mm and .303 would cause steam to rise from the punctured boiler of the engine, the 40mm blew the boiler right off.

'Four of us set off on a "Rhubarb" in an area just behind Le Touquet. The Hurricane IV had no defensive armament, the two remaining Brownings being used to "keep heads down" when attacking ground targets with our primary weapons, to which the gunsight was harmonized. Moreover, with all the weight we now carried, the poor old Hurricane, never the quickest climber, had a pretty poor rate of climb. On the instrument panel was the boost override toggle, a red knob that could be pulled out an inch or so which gave emergency boost if required. However, if you used it for more than about two minutes the engine was liable to blow up. The red toggle had a piece of wire which extended through the instrument panel to the boost control on the engine.

'We had just attacked a train when the air was suddenly full of Fw 190s. One would like to say there were a hundred, that is what it seemed, but there was probably only a squadron. We had a big turning match, the Hurricane still retaining its amazing manoeuvrability, and then one by one we managed to make cloud cover. We landed back at base individually, but more or less at the same time. As we walked in I said, "That was a dicey do, by God." A Canadian said, "I wasn't the least bit worried, I didn't see any problem." I noticed he was clutching something in his hand and asked what he was concealing. Unknown to himself, he was clutching the red toggle of the boost override, with a couple of feet of wire attached. He had pulled it right out of the instrument panel!'

Cool nerve and clear thinking in a dangerous situation enhanced survival for the fighter pilot – characteristics common to the majority of those who survived three or four years of combat flying. Such attributes are discernible in this account from Peter Hearne, a No. 65 Squadron pilot, of extracting himself from a 'spot of bother' on 8 April 1943:

'We were above cloud and in the vicinity of Brest when three Fw 190s bounced us going straight through the squadron and carrying on down through the cloud. No one was hit. We were flying Spitfire Vs, each with a 30-gallon slipper under the belly. My immediate reaction to the attack was to jettison my slipper tank and follow the Fws down. Visibility was misty below the cloud and there was difficulty in adjusting to the low light conditions after the brightness above. I looked round for my No. 2 who should have followed me, but I was on my own. Two Fw 190s were seen heading towards the French coast and I gave the rear aircraft a long steady burst at 30 degrees deflection. There appeared to be some strikes, but I knew I was somewhat out of range. Worse still, all my 20mm cannon rounds were exhausted, leaving only the .303s. About five minutes after I had turned for home, flying low, I noticed I was being chased by two Focke-Wulfs in line abreast. I opened the throttle to the gate but they still gained on me. Waiting until they were just outside effective firing range, I turned steeply to port, then came back on to my course for home. This simple manoeuvre, executed at the right moment, outwitted both aircraft and I knew then that I was not dealing with very experienced pilots. However, once again they were behind, catching me up, but this time they were in long line astern. The second man was too far behind and instead of being in position to pick me off as I turned sharply to port, he found himself head-on with me at 300 feet above the sea. Overland I would have accepted a head-on attack, but with no No. 2 to report my position if an unlucky hit put me into the sea, I quickly decided my tactics. With 300 feet to spare I had no qualms in flipping the Spitfire on to its back, righting it again as I passed underneath, to climb steeply immediately and confront the Fw wherever I found him. Possibly bemused by my manoeuvre and expecting to find me in the sea, he had tamely pulled up straight ahead and I was now behind him in perfect position to open fire. Alas, when I pressed the firing button the guns fell silent after only a few rounds. I was mortified; but had been taught an important lesson – not to waste ammunition firing out of range. I broke away and turned once more for home. After a while I knew I was no longer being followed so could relax somewhat, looking around the cockpit, checking my fuel, air speed, etc. I did not think the aircraft was travelling fast enough bearing in mind my throttle setting. I reached down for my slipper tank release toggle and pulled it again. The Spitfire seemed to leap forward and I knew then the reason those Fw 190s caught me so easily.'

The night fighter squadrons were mostly equipped with twin-engined aircraft; at first the Blenheim, then American Havocs, followed by the versatile Beaufighter and the even better Mosquito. A two-man crew was the norm, the companion being the radar operator who gazed at a cathode-ray tube screen for 'blips' and directed the pilot towards the quarry. Mostly the quarry was an enemy bomber unless sent on offensive operations to hunt Luftwaffe night fighters over enemy-held territory. Even in enemy airspace this sparring in the dark came to depend largely on electronic aids, as indicated in the account of an interception made by George Irving of No. 125 Squadron:

'When operating from Bradwell Bay we were able to use a forward ground control station near Arnhem. This unit was actually in a specially fitted-out glider which had taken part in the recent airborne landings but had fortunately landed on the Allied-held side of the Rhine. We were notified by Bomber Command of the time and place of bombing missions and would go out on the edge of the bomber stream to protect it from the attacks of German night fighters. On the night of 14 October 1944, more than a thousand bombers went to Duisburg and on the way out I made contact on several bogies which, on closer inspection, turned out to be bombers straying slightly off course. Coming into the range of the forward "glider control", called Milkway, they directed me towards a bogie which was following a Lancaster. This was probably a German night fighter under their ground control because as I closed in he suddenly dived away from the Lancaster, no doubt having been warned by his GC that he was being followed. Almost at once George found another contact at about 15,000 feet and on closing in I identified it as a German by the markings on its fuselage. But I could not identify the type. It was a twin-engine aircraft with tailplane dihedral, the engine nacelles extended behind the wings and it rather resembled a Dornier 217. I dropped back and opened fire from about 150 yards and the starboard engine exploded. My second burst hit the cockpit and wing tanks. The aircraft spiralled into a slow dive to starboard in flames while I followed it down and saw it explode on the ground.

'After watching our bombers reduce Duisburg to a huge bonfire, I turned east. George informed me he had picked up a signal on his rear-seeking radar and almost at once Milkway informed me we were being followed by a bogie, probably a German night fighter. I commenced a slow dive and orbited to port on to a reciprocal course, hoping to get a contact on the follower. Milkway then informed me that it had dived rapidly away towards Münster. Back at base, on reporting in to complete my combat report, our Intelligence Officer was unable to identify the aircraft that I had shot down. Later it was found to be a Heinkel 219, a new type recently brought into use as a night fighter. It carried a crew of three and was equipped with their latest radar and infra-red equipment designed to home on aircraft exhaust emissions. I was informed that this was the first sighting and destruction of an He 219.'

In the summer of 1944 fighter squadrons in England turned their guns on a new type of hostile invader. 'Tony' Murkowski of No. 316 (Polish) Squadron:

'We were at Coltishall on Mustangs. One evening a big team arrived from Rolls-Royce with special fuel, special oil and bits and pieces to put on our engines to give us more boost. They warn that if you run at full power for more than ten minutes the engine will be ruined and have to be changed. The fuel, of purple colour, blistered your skin if you got it on your hands. All this is to let us catch the flying-bombs that had just started to come over. First thing next morning six of us are sent to West Malling and take it in turn to be at readiness. It was one of those hot and humid days and a little bit foggy. There were no flying-bombs reported and West Malling is being inspected by a party of high-ups. When I returned from my lunch my flight commander said I was to take over Red Section on readiness so he and the others who hadn't eaten could go. I put my parachute on the wing and got myself a chair and was going to sit down near my aircraft and amuse myself by playing spit in the ring with pips and watching the cavalcade of air force VIPs. I had only just sat down when the telephone rang in the Readiness Hut. I thought it is the officers' mess wanting to know when the pilots I and my No. 2 had relieved were coming to lunch. It wasn't that, but "Red Section, Scramble!" When we got airborne, control advised: "Red Leader, Witchcraft 5 miles east of Hastings." Witchcraft was the code-name for flying-bombs at that time. I was just coming up to the coast when suddenly there was a puff of white smoke ahead, a flare fired by the Royal Observer Corps, a signal to indicate where the flying-bomb was crossing the coast. Looking down I saw it flying just below me. Well, it was a piece of cake. I opened the throttle, turned into a shallow dive to gain more speed and quickly took an accurate sighting. It hardly seemed that I had touched the firing trigger before the flying bomb exploded. The force lifted the Mustang about a thousand feet – just as if someone had given me a big kick in the arse. I heard my No. 2 say "Cor!" I had hardly time to recover from the surprise when Control came over the radio, "Good show Red Leader. You may return now to base and pancake." I say, "How do you know? I didn't tell you I shot down that thing." It was the first flying-bomb shot down by a Mustang.'

Officially frowned upon because of the general policy to encourage teamwork and not the individual, the distinction of being an 'ace' (shooting down five or more enemy aircraft) was well publicized by the contemporary Press. Those with large 'bags' were individuals with courage, skill and more than a little of what passed as luck. There were, inevitably, outstanding fighter aces for whom luck ran out and who left an indelible impression on the memories of compatriots, like the pilot John Wray recalls:

'He was a loner, much older than we his contemporaries, and much more experienced as he had been a commercial pilot before the war, flying newspapers to Paris at one time, often in bad weather. He was a devotee of Lawrence of Arabia and had his own personal reasons for hating the Germans. Few knew him well, this rather older Pilot Officer. His squadron of Defiants also had four Hurricanes which had been given to them to operate with the Turbinlite Flight. However, this particular form of night fighting had not been too successful and so the squadron commander flew one of the Hurricanes, the flight commanders the other two, and he flew the fourth. They were Hurricane IICs with four 20mm cannon. These Defiants had no radar aids, and therefore were not much use as night fighters. Although the Hurricane was also without radar it gave the pilot a rather better chance, particularly on Fighter Nights. The Pilot Officer was a law unto himself. He would take off at night, sometimes in quite nasty weather, and once airborne would clear himself with Sector Operations before switching off his R/T and disappearing into the night. Mind you, he would switch on his R/T from time to time to pick up useful information, but he did not want all the other chatter. He was a good shot and often attacked his target from the side, which was unusual in night fighting at that time. He said that one of his greatest aids was the British anti-aircraft fire. "They can't hit anything," he would say, "but their tracking is superb. When I follow a line of AA bursts I know that there is a Hun out in front."

'He would often wander about the country, using all his R/T frequencies to get information. He would land at any airfield when he was short of fuel then take off again and resume his wanderings. At times he shot down more than one aircraft in a night. In the morning he would return to base. He destroyed 14½ aircraft at night, without any onboard aids other than his R/T. All his victims crashed on land and were confirmed, except one that crashed into the Humber, missing a fishing boat by feet, so they confirmed that one. He often went out to inspect the crashed aircraft and on one occasion as he approached he had to dive for cover because of a fusillade of bullets came at him, fired from a pistol by the dying pilot. His flying clothing and equipment was German, taken from his victims. He claimed, with some justification, that it was much lighter and less cumbersome. As a Pilot Officer he was awarded the DSO, DFC and Bar, but those who knew him always feared that if he was posted to where he could operate in Continental air space he might stick his neck out too far in his keeness to get at the enemy. His half victory was awarded to him when he shot down a Ju 88 over Liverpool. In the morning, after a Defiant from the local squadron had also claimed an 88, both .303 and 20mm holes were found in the aircraft, so a half was awarded to each. He was promoted to Acting Flight Lieutenant and posted to a night intruder Hurricane squadron on the south coast. He failed to return from his first sortie. Today, when the names of those who distinguished themselves in the last war are mentioned, his is not one of them. Yet he was unique, and displayed a determination and skill that, probably, has rarely been surpassed.'

PLAY AND STYLE

If RAF operational aircrew had a reputation for extreme behaviour when at play, it seems the most exuberant of all were fighter pilots. Their escapades were legion. Senior officers with appreciation of conventional military conduct attempted to bring order to these situations but appear to have fought a losing battle – and some even succumbed to the merriment, as Peter Hearne observed:

'In October 1942 my squadron, No. 65, moved up to Drem, near Edinburgh. Shortly after arriving we lost a flight commander in an accident. His replacement was a young officer wearing a DFM, which meant we would be led by an experienced operational pilot. The squadron celebrated the occasion with a party in the mess, a prestigious peacetime edifice, built to the highest specification. The party developed as I was to see such functions develop many times during the war. Always there were a few who never knew where to set a limit. Well after most people had retired for the night the festivities continued.

One chap took off his shoes and socks, placed his feet in the dead embers in the fireplace and, by using tables and chairs, was able to leave the imprint of his soles on the very high ceiling of the mess. He then autographed his masterpiece. Others followed suit. The next morning the station commander, Wing Commander Sir Archibald Hope, walked into the mess and, alerted by the disruption still in evidence, his gaze eventually settled on the smears on the ceiling. Apparently he had not hitherto encountered such desecration and was beside himself with rage. Summoning the Orderly Officer of the day to his presence, Sir Archibald ordered a detailed examination of the signatures to establish the identities of the offenders. Unhappily, the only legible signature was that of the newly appointed flight commander. Such behaviour was unheard of among officers in those parts and had to be dealt with in no uncertain terms. The only culprit identified received an immediate posting.

'Two years later I was commanding No. 19 Squadron at Peterhead and who should be the station commander but none other than Sir Archibald Hope. A big party was laid on to mark the end of hostilities and as inhibitions vanished all sorts of madness reigned. Much energy was expended in a trick called the Dooley Dive, named for its originator. This involved climbing on to the mantelpiece and jumping head-first through a burning newspaper held by assistants, to land deftly on an upturned armchair which would right itself through the momentum of the impact, leaving the performer standing on his feet. This was old hat and the merrymakers sought something special to mark the occasion. Suddenly my No. 2 in the air, Jack May, dropped his trousers and his underpants and then proceeded to rub his bare backside in the fireplace ash. The onlookers knew what assistance was required and five or six of us lifted Jack, bottom high, until he left a discernible imprint on the low ceiling of the prefabricated building that served us as a mess. Jack then called out for a pencil. He was a big boy and the strain was telling on us, but I reached out for a pencil offered by one of the other bodies heaving-to and handed it up to Jack. Jack duly scrawled 'Jack's Bum' and handed the pencil back to its owner – Wing Commander Sir Archibald Hope!'

Communal sing-songs and recitations were a common feature of RAF mess and crew room life and more than one impartial observer has opined that the subject matter was decidedly more crude in the realm of Fighter Command. Such ribaldry was often triggered as a response to a commonplace act, for example, if somebody started messing about with the fire:

'If it's warmth that you desire,
Poke your wife and not the fire.
If you lead a single life,
Poke another fellow's wife.
Poke his wife or poke your own,
BUT LEAVE THE BLOODY FIRE ALONE!'

And this was mild in comparison with many ditties which dwelled excessively on acts of excreting and fornicating. However, propriety was exercised in many circumstances; the like was never uttered if a woman were present. Bawdy ballads helped to beat boredom in the air too. Alan Drake:

'During the summer of 1940 our squadron, No. 29, was based at Wittering, Lincolnshire, and flew regular patrols out over the North Sea in Blenheim IFs. These trips were invariably uneventful and to lessen the boredom the two-man crew would frequently engage in the singing of ribald songs over the intercom. Unfortunately, on one occasion my pilot, Bill Campbell, had forgotten to switch the radio transmitter set from "Transmit". As a consequence several RAF stations in Lincolnshire were treated to our duet and no doubt many a WAAF was caused to blush. Needless to say we suffered upon our return to base.'

Unnecessary use of radio transmissions was important as enemy listening-stations could quickly fix the broadcaster's position. On the other hand, radio communication was a vital part of successful fighter operations through the passing of tactical demands and warnings of enemy presence. Towards the end R/T discipline was more lax, particularly on very long-range escort missions undertaken by Mustangs in the final months of the conflict. Bill Fleming, a No. 126 Squadron pilot, recalls some of this radio chat heard nearly 600 miles from home station:

'The longest mission I flew was to Swinemünde, a Baltic port north-east of Berlin, where the pocket battleship *Lützow* was berthed. Our Mustangs escorted eighteen Lancasters of No. 617 Squadron which, despite murderous Flak that downed one, sank the ship. We were operating not far from the Russian front and on nearing the target we picked up a ground radio station in our earphones. A female controller was speaking in what I at first presumed was the German language. However, pilots in the Polish Mustang Wing, who were operating as part of the escort, identified it as Russian and excitedly began to curse and swear in English and Polish over their radios. When a male voice replaced the female one the British response was, "Put the girl back on again." The next day the British Press reported: "Yesterday the RAF and Russians exchanged greetings over the air." Some greetings!'

The assertive nature of the fighter pilot led to a desire to establish visual identity of his profession. The squashed hat, sweater protruding below tunic, silk scarf and – of course – battledress jacket top button undone, were all part of fighter pilot display, a mark of the fraternity. To relieve a fighter pilot of his scarf – a crucial part of flying togs if a chafed neck was to be avoided – became a trophy of some distinction sought by more adventurous young women. This attraction even spread to the Continent, as Philip Knowles discovered in the course of an amusing adventure:

'On 9 April 1945 my squadron, No. 126, was part of the Mustang escort for Lancasters attacking targets in Hamburg. On the way out my engine started to fail over the Zuider Zee, so I broke off and headed for Maldeghem, near Ghent. Although running very intermittently, I was able to maintain a medium height, largely by use of the fuel priming pump. I was getting homings from Maldeghem, but could see little through the 9/10ths cloud layer at 2,000 feet, which I was reluctant to go below. When I thought I had reached Maldeghem I let down through the cloud, to find I had just overshot the airfield. On turning back, the engine stopped completely, so I asked to come in directly. As I approached on a deadstick landing I saw that the airfield, including the runway, was covered with sheep, and realized it was not Maldeghem but Ursel which, we had been warned, was now closed. However, there was no alternative and I pressed on with a wheels-down landing. Full flap, though, seemed rather ineffective and I had difficulty in slipping off surplus height. It was only after getting down – and missing the sheep – that I found an unfamiliar device limiting the movement of the flaps, which had been left in place by the previous user.

'Ursel had a single RAF officer looking after it and he was having a terrible time trying to stop everything being stolen by the local population. Already several unserviceable aircraft on the field had had their tyres cut open and the inner tubes taken, for shoe repairs, I was told. On my arrival he was doing some painting on the front of his office. When he got back, the paint and brush had gone. While he was looking around for that they took his chair as well. When waiting for transport from Maldeghem, the local Police Chief came and I was invited to go with them on a tour of all the known local thieves' premises, but nothing was found.

'The Maldeghem ground crew reckoned the Mustang needed a new engine so I returned with them by road, stopping on the way in Eekloo for refreshment. Here the girl behind the bar offered her favours in exchange for my flying-scarf, to which she had taken a fancy. It seemed a very reasonable proposition, had it not been for the waiting ground crew. After a fairly hectic night at Maldeghem, where all the drinks were free as the mess was closing, I managed to hitch a ride back to England on a Dakota. The subsequent train journey and night in London were interesting, with no money, cap, tie (all left at Bentwaters before the flight) and carrying a parachute.'

Kipper Fleet
and Pickfords

WITH COASTAL

Although usually overshadowed by the actions of fighter and bomber men, the war of those whose task was defensive or offensive flight over the sea was one of great achievement. From its inception Coastal Command was given the roles of friendly shipping protection and enemy shipping harassment. As this involved a good deal of general reconnaissance, the Command was also handed photographic surveillance and meteorological flights. However, the major commitment was protecting convoys and seeking enemy submarines, work for which it was long lacking adequate numbers of aircraft with suitable endurance. Even though wanting in strength and equipment for four years, RAF coastal squadrons were ultimately credited with the destruction of more than 200 U-boats, amounting to more than two-thirds of all German and Italian submarines destroyed at sea by Allied aircraft. Additionally some 150 U-boats were damaged by Coastal Command action and many more caused to abandon their stalking of convoys because of the presence of aircraft. This contribution to victory in the so-called Battle of the Atlantic has been judged the decisive element.

Command units also sunk a considerable tonnage of enemy shipping through torpedo, rocket and bomb attack, operations where most of its own losses were suffered. For the majority of men engaged in ocean patrol, tedium was the common factor. Scanning mile after mile of ocean surface for hour after hour and sortie after sortie. Many completed a tour of 300 hours without once seeing a U-boat. The ocean-searching aircrews were considered to be 'a fairly steady lot', less given to the wild excesses of bomber and fighter types, but proud of their profession. One well-known mark of distinction of being a member of the Kipper Fleet – as Coastal Command was cheekily known in other Air Force circles – is cited by Tom Minta:

'In Coastal Command it was not unusual for flying officers to let their cap badges become tarnished. The greener the better; this being a sign of much low flying through sea spray and the hallmark of an old Atlantic hand. Almost like that old rugby chant, "Go low, boy! Go low!" '

At the outbreak of war the Command had around 400 operational aircraft of which three-quarters were Avro Ansons, a type with a 260-mile radius of action around the British Isles through being limited to a flight of four hours' duration. The only other worthy aircraft were a couple of dozen Lockheed Hudsons and a similar number of Sunderland flying-boats. The Hudson was an adaptation of an

American light passenger aircraft, but had a maximum endurance of six hours. The long-distance ranging rested with the Sunderlands which could keep aloft for 12-14 hours. This large flying-boat served Coastal Command throughout the war, although only in the closing stages were sufficient available to satisfy demand. It was a stalwart aircraft, beloved by all who flew it. James Kernahan:

'The Sunderland was probably the most spacious of all RAF operational aircraft; plenty of room to move around on the long 10 to 12 hours' flights we made on anti-sub or convoy patrols. There were two pilots, a navigator, flight engineer and assistant and also a wireless operator and assistant, the mechanics and WOs doubling as gunners. We would spend two hours in a turret and have four hours off. When you were relieved you'd go into the bomb bay where there were bunks. Even though the two engines were roaring away each side, it was only a matter of a few minutes before you were asleep; the noise was no obstacle. The Sunderland had a nice galley at the rear and we ate well, especially while flying out of West Africa when we had steaks, oranges, bananas, sweets and all those things that were never seen by the general public in the UK. The worst thing was the boredom, continually searching the ocean with your eyes until you'd lose the horizon as sea and sky became one. Even so, there was no chance of becoming disorientated as the turret had to be rotated to and fro all the time, the two bolted doors behind your back rattling away every time you turned them into the slipstream. To try and overcome the boredom I'd have a crafty smoke – which one was not supposed to do in the turret – or scribble notes with my name and address on bits of paper, forcing them out of the rear turret. Watching them flutter away I probably hoped some girl would find them and write me. None ever did!'

Despite the opportunity to catch some rest during patrol, these long flights induced weariness in all crew members. Tedium and incessant noise were paramount in this, and by the time the sortie was completed individuals were not as alert as they should have been, as evidenced in the mishap which befell Steve Challen of No. 201 Squadron:

'After a 14-hour, 15-minute patrol in our Sunderland P9606, ZM:R, we finished very tired at Invergordon. As a newcomer to the crew I had been trying to make myself useful. "Mucking in," I had been doing the odd chore about the boat. On this occasion I went forward with Biggs who usually did the mooring up to the buoy. Winding back the front turret Biggs positioned the bollards and hung the short, shaped ladder over the port side. The system used by this crew was for the pilot to approach the buoy, keeping it on his port, as slowly as possible with inner engines shut down. When the aircraft nudged the buoy Biggs would go over the side on to the ladder; hanging on with the right hand he would push a sliprope through the wire rope vertical loop on top of the buoy. The assistant would then lean over the bow to take the loose end and make a hitch on the bollards. Not an "Advised Procedure" method, especially when the guy on the ladder falls into the water because he had not fixed the ladder securely! Biggs had the foresight to have a safety rope attached to the ladder with which I pulled until I could grab the top of the ladder. Biggs then climbed the ladder and me, taking a grip of my clothes, arms, anything; up and over me into the aircraft. Back in the "saloon" he stood shivering, much to the amusement of the lads. The pilot, F/O Fleming, had his head out of the side window wondering what was going on as it was difficult to keep the aircraft nudged up to the buoy with the tide running out of the Firth. That helpful fellow, myself, fastened the ladder, quickly down, passed the sliprope through the loop, caught the loose end, up the ladder and took a hitch around the bollards, then used the boat-hook to snag the mooring pendant attached to the buoy, dropping the grommet over a bollard. Thumbs-up to Fleming and he shut down the outer engines. The rest of the mooring up could wait until the "swimmer" returned to the job.

'All this panic seemed to have taken a long time but it had actually been a few minutes. I looked at my watch. . . . No watch! Ah yes, Biggs had grabbed my wrist on his way up and over me; thank you very much Mr. Biggs. A frantic search below my feet; no sign of it. I was shattered at the loss. My aunt had presented the self-wind, waterproof, Rolex Oyster to me on my 20th birthday. I never revealed the loss to her, my feelings were that mixed. Since then I've often pondered the thought that the watch is still ticking away at the bottom of the Cromarty Firth, wound up by the action of the tide. What an advertisement for Rolex if it were found still showing the correct time!'

After innumerable trips when there was nothing important to report, contact with a U-boat was an exciting event. Too often the submarine crew were on look-out and submerged before an effective attack could be made. James Kernahan of No. 228 Squadron had reason to remember one such incident:

'Our Sunderland, M for Mother, left Pembroke Dock in the early evening of 6 July 1943 for a 12-hour anti-submarine patrol over the Bay of Biscay. It was uneventful until the sun started to brighten the sky in the east. I saw something on the sea ahead and excitedly told our Skipper, Flt Lt Gordon Lancaster, I could see a submarine. Before we could get within effective range the sub had disappeared but the Skipper decided he would conduct a square search of the area. As we were on the last leg I again caught sight of the submarine on the surface. The skipper called out "Tally Ho!" and we charged in. Sitting in the front turret I opened up with the single Vickers .303 and saw the bullets curving into the conning tower. This fire was only intended to dissuade the crew from getting to their anti-aircraft guns. While I was firing, Flt Lt Lancaster had run the bombs out on their trollies and released them, but the rear-turret gunner reported only splashes and no detonations. Disappointed, we finished our patrol and flew back to Wales. We were greeted by the Intelligence Officer who produced a manual of submarines and asked me to identify the type. I selected what I thought was similar but he said: "No, you're wrong, you attacked a British one like this," and pointed to another picture. This was a demoralizing blow but happily the Navy lads had not taken any harm through either they or us being in the wrong place at the wrong time. Had we been able to find out who the crew were, it was our intention to stand them a dinner. Sadly, Gordon Lancaster was killed in a crash in France the following year while flying Air Chief Marshal Leigh-Mallory out to the Far East, but I've always wanted to fulfil the promise to make amends.'

Accurate identification of a submarine from an aircraft was not easy, even in good conditions. Roy Larkins gives another example:

'What a Heath Robinson Outfit this is, I thought – but it works! I was a Sergeant Pilot at 61 Air School, based at George in South Africa, and on operational training to qualify as a General Reconnaissance Pilot with Coastal Command. The Station was staffed by RAF personnel at night and by South African Blue Army Air Force people during the daytime. The South African Red Army operated anywhere in the world, but their Blue Army only operated from their homes between 9am and 5.30pm, Mondays to Fridays inclusive. Thus, we had a South African pilot during the day and an RAF pilot during the night. Goodness knows what would have happened if we had been scrambled at 8am. Presumably the war would have had to wait until 9 am!

'We had about twenty Avro Ansons, each with a pilot, a pilot/navigator and a wireless operator. Our job was to "protect" the convoys as they passed between Cape Town and Durban and to discourage all enemy craft. The aircraft were not armed in any way, unless you counted the Very pistols. We would go out, to identify passing ships and to photograph neutrals and doubtfuls.

'On my very first trip I learned not to get too close to a convoy because after weeks at sea the sailors tended to fire first and to consult their identification signal manuals later. At least it proved that I was on "Active Service"! On other occasions we went out on anti-submarine patrol using the fan search method. Three, four or five aircraft set out together, each on a course 15 degrees to the right of the aircraft on its port side. In this way we fanned out over a large area. We were so slow that had an enemy submarine been on the surface, it would have heard us coming and been submerged again long before we got there. But this was part of our strategy. The German submarines used in our waters were usually of a fairly old design, needing to come to the surface every 24 hours to replenish their air supply. And so the longer we kept them submerged, the more the advantage swung in our favour. After we had passed over a suspect submarine it waited an hour and then returned to the surface for fresh air. By that time we were on our way back and, hearing us coming from a long way off, the submarine submerged again. Eventually the air in the submarine became so foul that it was forced to surface and remained there for some time taking on fresh air. And it was when we found one of these submarines sitting on the surface that we radioed base. As we had no weapons ourselves, there was at base a Hudson aircraft already bombed up and ready to take off. This Hudson droned out and was usually quite successful in damaging, if not sinking, the "sitting duck" on the surface. Yes. Truly a Heath Robinson outfit, but it worked!

'On 8 May 1944, in Anson aircraft 'O' with Sergeant Lowes as first pilot, we were out on a routine patrol over the sea-lane between Cape Town and Durban. I was the pilot/navigator and up to that moment had seen no sign of the enemy. And then it happened! There on the surface was a small plume of spray leaving a trail of bubbles behind it. The trail spread back some distance and just under the plume was a large submerged object, moving at about five knots. Quickly, I referred to my submarine identification manual and felt that the object was indeed one of the smallest versions of a German sub. The pilot and wireless operator confirmed my opinion and so we immediately radioed base, giving the position of this suspect enemy craft. Base confirmed our signal and we knew the Hudson would soon be airborne. As these signals were being exchanged, I took two or three photographs of the sub, as it proceeded steadily in an easterly direction. Just then it surfaced. It was a very large whale! Consternation reigned in the cockpit and by the time we had radioed base, informing them of our error, the Hudson was on the runway. Luckily, it was prevented from taking off. During the night my photographs were developed and the Commanding Officer readily agreed that the object did indeed closely resemble a small submarine. Later, the photos were used during identification lectures and the class usually thought they showed a U-boat.'

Many Coastal Command crews experienced being shot at by the trigger-happy sailors on the ships being shepherded. Hugh Fisher of No. 233 Squadron had good reason to be dismayed by the circumstances he relates:

'While based at Aldergrove we escorted a convoy leaving Liverpool. Our Hudson was with it for six hours, all the time keeping at the regulation distance. When it was time to leave we closed in on one of the escorts to report our departure and were immediately fired at. Not shots across the bows, but very close bursts indicating that they considered us hostile! The standard of aircraft recognition among naval gunners may have been bad, but we didn't expect them to take six hours to decide we were an enemy plane.'

From 1940 until 1942 Coastal Command received a small number of Whitley bombers with the object of providing increased cover over the Atlantic shipping lanes where most sinkings occurred. A stop-gap until more suitable types were available, the Whitley endeared itself to many pilots, one being Tom Minta of No. 58 Squadron:

'The Whitley was a fairly solid and lumbering machine. It may have been slow, but you could make the thing slide about the sky if attacked by fighters; slap on full rudder and she would skid, beautifully; and his tracer would go way out. If you could judge when the enemy pilot was going to fire you could make it very difficult for him to hit you. Mechanically they weren't too troublesome. The late versions had Rolls-Royce engines with the usual problem in that we had to run them on very weak mixture if we were after maximum range – about 7 to 8 hours' duration. As a result the cylinder liners tended to crinkle a bit which let the coolant get past in the wrong places. If your exhaust colours took a green hue you knew there was a glycol leak and it was probably time to think about going home. They flew nose down and looked like a stick of celery from the side. I became very fond of them and was quite sorry when they were retired.'

But there remained an area in mid-Atlantic that few maritime patrol aircraft could reach from either North America or the United Kingdom. Tom Minta recalls an attempt to stretch the Whitley's range:

'They said we must try to close the mid-Atlantic gap. So they put four extra fuel tanks in the Whitley's fuselage. With the extra 600 gallons of petrol it was an overload. We had a fellow on the squadron named Freddy Fox, a district officer in Africa before the war, who volunteered to undertake the first flight. He took off from St. Eval and disappeared from sight below the cliff edge. According to Freddy the Whitley kept losing height until the air was so squashed between his wings and the sea that it kept him up until he'd used enough petrol to gain some height!'

The extremely long-range Catalina flying-boat from the United States had the necessary duration, but was a type in short supply. The near ideal was the Consolidated Liberator, which although designed as a bomber, had the required range, speed and armament to make it an excellent anti-submarine aircraft. This was also manufactured in the United States and like other types from that source was generally popular with aircrews. Hugh Fisher:

'The thing about an American aircraft was that the designers did appear to have taken count that there was a crew going to fly in it. All those I flew in were reasonably comfortable and thoughtfully laid out. British aircraft were the reverse; in many, provision for a crew seemed to have been an afterthought.'

Liberators were urgently sought by many Allied air forces and Coastal Command did not really obtain the numbers it wanted until 1944. To supplement the few that entered service in 1941, Liberator bombers were sent on detachment to Coastal Command stations. Mick Wood, one of the pilots involved, tells of a trying sortie, revealing the origin of a well-known crew room tale in Coastal messes:

'Although we were part of Bomber Command in the spring of 1942, several Liberators and crews were lent to Coastal Command for the detection of submarines far out in the Atlantic. On 25 May we were airborne at roughly 0800 hrs. The first leg took us out to Rockall, the rocky outcrop in the Atlantic, and from this leg a wind was computed by the navigator. This wind was then used for navigation for the rest of the trip and, if on the homeward leg we found Rockall, the area searched could then be exactly defined for Coastal Command. The search went off in the usual way. A square search over several hundred square miles and eventually the time to return came round. In the meantime the weather had packed up and we were down to two thousand feet searching for Rockall. Failing in this search, we set course for Nutts Corner, but a diversion message was received sending us to Tiree – Nutts Corner being closed by weather. Presently Tiree also closed and we were diverted to Prestwick. *En route*, Prestwick also closed and we were further diverted to Stornaway where we touched down after some 12 hours airborne. Everyone was tired and a bit strained after several diversions. The Operations Room at Stornaway was part RAF and part Naval Western Approaches. It contained a great number of people of both sexes in both services and a number of very senior officers. It must have been a quiet time of the day, for we were debriefed with silent people all around us.

'The Intelligence Officer had his nose well into the job. The trip was recorded in great detail and every one of us was looking for an early end to this business. "On the return trip," asked this busy man, "Did you see Rockall?" "No," said the second pilot, "We saw Fuckall?" The effect in the Ops Room was magical. One very senior Naval man roared with laughter. Some of the others laughed, some blushed, some hid their faces. Best of all the Intelligence Officer went on writing. It was a spontaneous reply from a very tired and sorely tried young airman.'

Inclement weather was without doubt the principal enemy of the long-range patrol aircraft. The fronts that swept westwards over the Atlantic frequently hid home bases in the west of the UK, to say nothing of concealing high ground. Towards the tropics, the weather could be even more treacherous for the unwary. Peter Lee of No. 490 (RNZAF) Squadron:

'To patrol the Atlantic sea lanes off the west coast of Africa, West Africa Command had four Sunderland squadrons, No. 95 at Bathurst, Nos. 204 and 490 at Freetown and No. 270 at Lagos. During my tour – in the last nine months of the war – there were few U-boats in the area except the odd one in transit from Japan with a special cargo. Our biggest hazard was the weather. Coming back from an eight or ten-hour patrol in the early evening, huge tropical storms were often encountered. These would form off the mountains and extend for three or four hundred miles out from the coast. The mass could rise to 40,000 feet above sea level. Approaching this barrier in darkness was a pretty unnerving experience with the constant flashes of lightning along the line of the front. To reach base we could only go under the storm where there was usually only a few hundred feet between the sea and the base of the clouds. The trouble was that once there, the pressure readings dropped away and the altimeter reading might be several hundred feet out. In pitch-darkness it needed extra vigilance to see you didn't fly into the sea. On the other hand, if you were too high the vicious up-currents and down-currents would take the boat up and down like a yo-yo; it was impossible to fly straight and level. A French Sunderland crew from Dakar tried to penetrate too high one night and before they knew what was happening they found themselves upside down at 14,000 feet. They managed to get out of it – a bit shaken, no doubt. The weather also affected reliability. Maintenance was difficult with all the boats moored out on the river. It was either pissing down with rain or scorching hot. Our crew came back four times with one engine stopped. Sometimes the weight of rain was so heavy it was impossible to get enough lift to take off even though the mid-upper turret was removed and the fuel loads reduced to save weight.'

Several squadrons served to locate and attack blockade-runners or submarines passing through the Bay of Biscay to their bases on the French Atlantic coast. These flights had the risk of encountering Luftwaffe Ju 88s operating as long-range fighters, thus demanding extra vigil from fatigued crew men. Hugh Fisher of No. 224 Squadron:

'Sixteen-hour sorties to patrol over the Bay were laid on in November 1943; the longest I did was just coming up to 18 hours. As we were called four hours before take-off and when we got back didn't have a priority for transport, it was at least another three hours before we finally got to bed. This made rather a long day. The Liberator was a noisy aircraft and it was the noise that tired you as much as anything. We may have been young but sometimes, being awake for 24 hours, you did feel a little the worse for wear. It was always a struggle to keep awake during the final hours of the flight. We Wop/AGs used to swap round positions every couple of hours but even so, with the very bright sunlight, it used to make your eyes tingle and you would have given anything to drop off. However much you tried to remain alert the act of continually scanning sea or sky had a mesmerizing effect and the efficiency of your observation declined. That was when you could miss seeing a surface vessel or be jumped by Ju 88s.'

The enterprising discovered one way to add a little variety to these trips. Tom Minta, a No. 58 Squadron Halifax pilot:

'On long hauls down in the Bay, to break the monotony we sometimes did a circuit over the countryside along the Spanish coast. People would wave at us as we passed over at three or four hundred feet. This was quite an entertaining diversion until the beggars started shooting at us. Very unfriendly.'

Coastal Command's offensive arm originally consisted of a few squadrons of Bristol Beaufort torpedo-bombers, periodically despatched against enemy shipping along his Atlantic and North Sea coastal waters. The nature of delivering torpedoes against a target was fraught with dangers and the losses suffered were the highest for any type of RAF combat during the first three years of war. Nevertheless the Beaufort was a popular aircraft whereas a contemporary torpedo-bomber had the distinction of having the worst reputation of any aircraft in the RAF. James Donson's sentiments were not untypical of those encountering the Botha:

'One of the aircraft used at the Coastal Command navigational training station, Squire's Gate, close to Blackpool, was the Botha, probably the least successful of all would-be operational aircraft. It was designed as a torpedo-carrier but its operational endurance with full load was only a little more than twenty minutes. It was a heavy, high-wing monoplane powered, or rather underpowered, by two Perseus 850hp sleeve-valve engines, which really needed to develop double that to perform successfully. Inside it had watertight bulkheads and doors and the outside skin and doors were watertight too. Evidently the designers (if it had any) expected it to ditch quite often, which it did. One which ditched near Arklow Buoy off the coast of Ireland floated for about three weeks until it became obvious that it was not going to sink so an air-rescue launch was despatched and succeeded in towing it to within a few miles of the English shore where it sank in a storm and almost took the rescue boat with it. During one fortnight the Botha caused 27 fatalities, though one must say that fifteen of those were passengers getting off the London express which had just arrived at Blackpool station as a Botha and a Defiant collided over the station. The pilots' opinion of the Botha was summed up by a neat frieze painted round the walls of one of the crew rooms:

"My abject all sublime,
Is to make a Botha climb,
On one engine at a time. . . ."
Later, someone added in pencil, "Done it! – for two seconds." '

Ageing Hampden bombers were impressed as torpedo strike aircraft but these were more vulnerable than the Beauforts. The adaptation of Fighter Command's Beaufighter proved the most successful aircraft for this mission and several squadrons were ultimately formed to harass enemy coastal shipping. Later, air-launched rocket projectiles became the preferred ordnance. Mosquitoes were also used as coastal strike aircraft, but these could not carry torpedoes. Success in shipping strikes was in large measure dependent upon surprise. To achieve this the outward journey was made at a few feet above the waves. Len Barcham of No. 404 (RCAF) Squadron:

'Trips to Norway averaged some 300 miles each way from our base at Wick. The journey out was always done at low level, a mere fifty feet to stay below enemy radar detection. This produced a great sensation of speed as we sped over the wave tops, until sighting our target when we had to climb to 1,500 feet. Immediately one had a contrasting sensation of being about to stall and that the Beaufighter was hardly moving at all. Although this happened scores of times as we prepared for attack, I always had the same fear of stalling which I was never able to suppress. . . . Especially when operating off the Norwegian coast, a long way from home and in range of enemy single-engined fighters, we much preferred bad weather and good cloud cover. At Wick the saying was "we prefer to fly when even the seagulls are walking" – and Wick seagulls were a very large and hardy breed! During 1942 and early 1943 we usually carried a pigeon with us in the Beaufighter on our shipping strikes off the Norwegian coast. The bird was housed in a sawdust and shavings filled tin box which, being loose in the aircraft, sometimes got chucked around, particularly when we were taking violent evasive action. The bird was, of course, intended to be used should we ditch to carry our position home. On return to dispersal after an "op" we were sometimes told to release the pigeon, whereupon it invariably perched on top of the aircraft's rudder and showed no inclination to fly anywhere, not even back to its loft. We decided that "rough rides" must have upset its gyro-compass navigational system and eventually didn't think there was any real point in continuing to carry the bird. This very much upset one of our better navigators, Peter Bassett, who always said that his accuracy was due to the fact that he never gave a course to the pilot to fly until he had shown it to the pigeon who somehow indicated whether the gen was "pukka" or "duff".'

Weather reporting flights were handled night and day by Coastal Command units; sometimes they were the only aircraft airborne around the British Isles when weather conditions grounded all others. These sorties usually involved extremes of flight, as known in those days, and were not just a safe and comfortable joyride, as many envisaged. Peter Catchpole:

'Although trained in meteorology I had no flight experience and was eager to remedy this. The Met Fortresses operated out of Langham, and the crews were allowed, if so disposed, to take up fellows like myself. I finally managed to get accepted for one of these North Sea trips which proved to be an unnerving introduction to flying. A triangular course was flown, so many miles at high level, so many miles at low level, up and down as met readings were taken. All was well until the climb to 20,000 feet over the North Sea and we were told to go on oxygen. It was then discovered that there wasn't the necessary connecting piece to fit between my oxygen mask tube and the outlet on the aircraft's oxygen system. My fears of expiring from anoxia were very real even though a member of the crew told me not to worry and hold the end of my mask tube to the supply outlet. So there I sat, petrified, clasping the oxygen tube to the supply and unable to see out for two or three hours until the Fortress descended to lower altitude. Then we ran into a storm with all the turbulence that means and St. Elmo's Fire round the wings and engine cowlings. I expected the plane to fall out of the sky at any moment. When we were really low, down just above the sea, I was sent up into the nose where I was more than a little apprehensive to see there was only the large plexiglas nosepiece between me and the waves. If they are honest, I suppose most newcomers are a bit scared on their first flight. Mine was certainly a rude introduction. After a few more trips it was all "a piece of cake".'

Coastal Command also controlled a number of Air Sea Rescue squadrons in the UK with their flights deployed to give service all round the coast. Spotter and amphibian aircraft worked in conjunction with rescue launches, saving more than

6,000 airmen during hostilities. Pop Ewins flew Spitfire IIs modified to carry smoke floats and an inflatable dinghy for dropping near airmen down in the sea:

'Our squadron, No. 276, had 300 plus rescues to its credit. One of the most memorable occurred on 19 July 1944, shortly after the cross-Channel invasion. Patrolling with another Spitfire, flown by F/O Lamb, I found a number of dinghies with waving occupants and directed a Walrus to the spot. When the Walrus landed and taxied to the dinghies the crew found to their considerable surprise that the occupants were Germans – a whole U-boat crew totalling 46. The senior German officer was taken aboard the Walrus and gave the bemused crew a couple of bottles of wine as souvenirs. We saw no reason why this 46 should not be added to the Squadron total of successful rescues!'

WITH AIR TRANSPORT

Although air transportation had been a feature of RAF activity in pre-war years, albeit on a minor scale, not until the spring of 1943 was a Transport Command formed. This organization controlled RAF air transport units operating world-wide, together with those engaged in ferrying, air ambulance and airborne forces work. However, there were several units that did not come under the Command. Additionally, a small number of RAF aircrews found themselves flying air transports that were not part of the service. Ray Jones was one of these pilots:

'In January 1944 I was seconded from the RAF to BOAC [British Overseas Airways Corporation] who required crews to operate their Dakotas. It was a peculiar situation in that while being RAF officers and paid by that service, we lived a civilian life. We were not subject to any day-to-day control by the RAF, could live where we chose, and when off-duty could do as we pleased and wear civilian clothes. BOAC uniforms were the norm for flying, but in civvy street nobody recognized these, so if we wanted to pull a few birds we'd put on our RAF blues. Initially we operated from Whitchurch, near Bristol, on a service to Lisbon, every two days. Most of the passengers were diplomats. Lisbon was a spy's paradise and it was not unusual to return to your hotel room and find your case had been gone through. The trips to Portugal also gave us access to all those luxuries that were unavailable in the UK. Lufthansa crews, made up of chaps seconded from the Luftwaffe – as we were from the RAF – were often drinking in the same bars we frequented. Yet elsewhere in Europe the RAF and Luftwaffe were busy killing each other!'

By 1944 the predominant squadrons with transport associations were those trained and equipped for carrying paratroops, towing assault gliders and the re-supply of airborne forces with weapons, ammunition, fuel and food. A few of these squadrons also engaged in operations supporting the resistance forces in occupied countries, activities involving small numbers of aircraft and often drawing the full attention of enemy defences in the area. It was dangerous work, particularly in the lumbering Stirlings often employed. Ernie Edwards of No. 620 Squadron:

'As a crew we completed a full tour of 32 operations, the majority of which were the classical 38 Group ops – dropping supplies to partisans in occupied

Europe, mainly France. After the liberation of France our attention was directed to Norway. It was during one of these latter ops, near the end of our tour, that we had our biggest scare. Having completed an apparently successful drop in northern Norway, we had returned down to the south coast and crossed it somewhere near Kristiansand and out over the Skagerrak. Shortly after leaving the coast I spotted an unidentified aircraft about 1,000 yards astern. It was bright moonlight – these operations were always conducted on moonlit nights. Moments later I positively identified it as a Ju 88, thus giving rise to the eternal dilemma faced by air gunners; what next?, when we were within range of his cannons, whereas he was well outside the range of my .303 machine-guns. Another alarm was ringing in my mind. Was this one a decoy? They often hunted in pairs. In response to the skipper's anxiety I decided I could wait no longer and ordered him to turn to starboard, to the dark side of the sky. The next instant a burst of cannon-shells (which could have come from a second aircraft) crashed into us. We changed the evasive action to weaving and this the skipper maintained for the duration of the action. The ensuing battle lasted some minutes with me catching occasional glimpses of one or other of them and getting the odd burst in here and there. Although shot at several more times, we received no more hits and fortunately the hits suffered in the initial attack had not damaged anything vital. There is no way of knowing whether it was due to any success on my part that they broke off the inconclusive engagement when fuel and ammunition were unlikely to be short. In retrospect, I feel we must have been favoured by the gods in order to have survived when the odds were stacked so heavily against us, but I am conceited enough to believe that we helped ourselves in no small measure by not being taken by surprise. My personal good fortune extended further inasmuch as a cannon-shell from the first blast passed through the bottom of my turret without immobilizing or injuring me.'

In Europe there were three major airborne assaults involving RAF airborne forces support squadrons: the D-Day drops of 6 June 1944, the attempts to secure bridges at Arnhem the following September and the landings on the eastern bank of the Rhine in March 1945. Of these the Arnhem venture was the most costly, claiming 55 of the Stirlings, Halifaxes and RAF Dakotas involved. Hilary Upward:

'After the Arnhem landings the Keevil squadrons were busy over the next few days dropping supplies to the beleaguered paratroopers. I thought it would be a break from my work in Operations to fly on one of these re-supply trips and permission was obtained to go with Flt Lt Rees' crew of No. 299 Squadron. Our Stirling, X9:B, assembled as lead of a three-plane vic and set off line astern behind two other vics. Approaching the drop zone we reduced altitude to the required 800 feet. The Germans let fly with everything they had and while I couldn't hear anything over the din of our Stirling's engines, there were lots of little black puffs sailing past the cockpit windows. Looking down I saw a Stirling on the ground aflame from end to end. Sitting in the navigator's seat the thought came to my mind that it had been foolish to make this flight which I expected any moment, to be my last. We were briefed to make a climbing turn to port as soon as we had dropped our panniers. All at once I heard over the intercom, "Panniers gone" and Rees exclaimed "Bugger me!" The sky ahead was criss-crossed with tracer and exploding shells. Rees immediately pushed the control column forward and dived the aircraft. Looking back as we sped low over the Dutch countryside I saw that several other aircraft had followed our move, diving to tree-top height to escape the Flak. After what seemed an age Rees started to climb and it was a relief to find we had come through the hail of fire without a hit on our aircraft. Rees told us that three of the six aircraft ahead, including the CO's, had been shot down. In total the two Keevil squadrons lost fifteen Stirlings during the Arnhem operations with many damaged and several returning with wounded aircrew.'

Similar grim accounts can be had from most airmen who survived the airborne drop and re-supply trips to Arnhem. However, one published account was not all it appeared to be, as Ernie Edwards relates:

'When we set out for Arnhem we had a newspaper reporter on board. While going through cloud the pilot of the glider we were towing got disorientated and went out to one side causing the tow-rope to break. We were still over England, and had to abort and return to Fairford. While waiting for the crew bus to convey us to debriefing, our skipper turned to the reporter and said, "Sorry you won't get your story, old chap." The reply was, "Oh don't worry on my account. I'll get my story." Lo and behold, when the news of the operation broke in the newspapers there was his account in great detail of how he had been to Arnhem, complete with names of the crew with whom he was purported to have flown. The substituted crew were real enough as were his eye-witness details. The truth is that, like us, he never left England that day. We all had a good laugh at the cheek of the man, but I shall never understand why he thought it necessary to present his report as a personal experience when many people knew it to be a downright lie.'

Above: Dusty Lings v. Old Sweats soccer match at Berka, North Africa, 28th November 1942. Note the varied choice of attire both off and on the field. In the desert correct uniform was a joke. (H. Kidney)

Below: Not a knobbly knees contest, just the mode of dress for well turned-out fighter pilots in warm climes. Like most squadrons in the MTO (Mediterranean Theatre of Operations), No. 253 (Hyderabad) Squadron had pilots from six different Commonwealth countries. Seated on the Spitfire wing are, left to right: Warrant Officer Ken Russom, Sergeant Derek Preece, Lieutenant Ronnie Briggs (SAAF), Warrant Officer Alec Day(NZ), Flight Sergeant Fred Ellis, Flying Officer H. H. Miller (Canada), Warrant Officer Alec Bowman and Flight Lieutenant Fred Pawsey.

Above: Air crew accommodation, Italian style. The main street of No. 70 Squadron's Tortorella encampment after a winter storm. Each tent had a sunken floor covered with steel runway planking to give more headroom. A deep drainage ditch was dug all the way round the outside of the tent to prevent flooding. Heat came from an oil drum stove fed on diesel with the smoke stack running out under the base of the tent. (*J. Heap*)

Top right: Engine fitter at work on the engines of TH:M, one of No. 418 Squadron's most successful Mosquito VI fighters, Hurn, July 1944.

Right: Having successfully extinguished an engine fire on this crash-landed No. 21 Squadron Blenheim at Watton, station fire-fighters – some splashed with foam – are joined by a curious throng of airmen. Fighting aircraft fires was a dangerous job, often with the risk of exploding bombs and ammunition. (*S. Clay*)

Left: *Convoy of RAF signals cabin vehicles (Crossley Type Q in foreground) on a French road in 1944. The RAF always operated many more motor vehicles than aircraft and many more vehicle types than aircraft types. (Official)*

Bottom left: *Q and K sites were given Lewis gun armament with the aim of picking off any lured low-flying enemy aircraft. Ken 'Badger' Baker mans the Cavenham Heath weapon. In the background are three realistic dummy Wellingtons made mainly of canvas and wood. (R. Howlett)*

Right: *A Sergeant pilot down in France on 5 February 1941, surrounded by his captors. Note torn right boot.*

Below: *'A' Flight, No. 277 Squadron at Martlesham Heath. An example of the traditional unit pose with all personnel assembled in front of an aircraft – in this case a Walrus amphibian. Mick Osborne is third from left, front row.*

Top left: *The twice a day head count assembly, common to all major prison camps that held RAF PoWs. This photograph was taken at Stalag Luft I, Barth (R. Armstrong)*

Left: *Backbone of the fighter effort during the early war years was the dependable Hurricane. Outclassed by the Me 109, it was nevertheless the aircraft chiefly responsible for the RAF's success in the Battle of Britain. This is a No. 263 Squadron machine.*

Above: *Flying could be dangerous and crashes were numerous. This Mustang developed mechanical trouble on a non-operational flight and ended up in a field near Gravesend, killing the pilot, victor of many air combats and survivor of several dicey do's with the enemy.*

Below: *Two fingers for two flying-bombs brought down. Squadron Leader Antoni Murkowski climbs from a Mustang's cockpit after another successful sortie. His thirteen confirmed enemy aircraft and seven flying-bombs included the first V-1 destroyed by a Polish pilot and the last Me 262 jet.*

Above: The Polish airmen were renowned for their prowess. This group discussing tactics on a warm spring day at Northolt are members of No. 316 'City of Warsaw' Squadron. Spitfire V in background is that of the CO, Squadron leader A. Gabszewwicz. (A Murkowski)

Left: Few RAF 'regulars' who commenced operations in the first month of the war were still around in May 1945. One such survivor was John Wray, a Pilot Officer flying night reconnaissance sorties over Germany in September 1939 and a Wing Commander with a Tempest Wing on the Continent in 1945.

Right: A commemorative cartoon featuring Goering and Hitler, made available to No. 9 Squadron crews after memorable operations. (M. Hewinson)

Left: Corporal Hugh Berry.

Below: Stirlings of Nos. 295 and 570 Squadrons assembled at Rivenhall for the launch of Rhine airborne crossing.

Right: Vernon Wilkes at the bombsight in Lancaster IQ:B.

Above: *Indian fighter pilot. Pilot Officer D. A. Samant of Bombay in the cockpit of Whirlwind SF:C of No. 137 Squadron, 1943.*

Left: *The 19-year-old rear-gunner of IQ:B, Danny Driscoll, 'christening' the tail before take-off.*

Above: *Wellington crew, off-duty, at Newton, August 1941; l to r: 'Denny' Denman (AG), Eddie Wheeler (WOP/AG), Paul Carlyon (pilot), Bill Bossom (AG), 'Ginger' Thomas (navigator), and Sam Huggett (2nd pilot). The two pilots did not survive the hostilities.*

Right: *AC2 Edwin Wheeler, Yatesbury, Wiltshire, December 1939.*

Left: Tom Wingham, complete with pin-stripe trousers in orchard of his Belgian hosts, 1944.

Right: The Belgian family who sheltered Tom Wingham; l to r: M. Schoofs, Jennie, Audree, Mme Schoofs and Pascal.

Below: Sixty-eight feet long Air/Sea Rescue High Speed Launch and crew photographed at Calshot in August 1944. (B. Robertson Collection)

Above: Parade ground for new recruits, 1940. It took time to get the line straight. (B. Robertson Collection)

Below: Few RAF airfield Watch Towers in the UK were without a strong complement of WAAF operatives by the end of hostilities. All were selected for their suitability and capability and it was just coincidence that this group, serving night operations at No 54 OTO, Charter Hall, Northumberland, have such good looks. (E. F. Cheesman)

Round the Med

At the outbreak of war the RAF presence in the so-called Middle East consisted of some 300 largely out-dated aircraft in a score of squadrons deployed in colonies, dependancies and protectorates taking in Iraq, Aden, Jordan, Palestine, Kenya, Somalia, Egypt and the Sudan. The potential threat was Italian forces in East Africa and Libya, which eventually materialized with the declaration of war on Britain by Mussolini in June 1940. During the following nine months British and Commonwealth forces managed to eliminate the Italians in East Africa, but by that time German forces had joined their Axis partners in Libya and had also moved into the Balkans. With the then critical situation in the UK, little in the way of reinforcements and modern equipment was forthcoming from home. During 1941 the RAF fought in Greece, Crete, Libya and Egypt with mostly inferior aircraft to those of the enemy, and often with fewer numbers.

The Blenheim was the most modern warplane on hand when actions commenced. Before the end of the year, when Axis forces appeared to be about to take Egypt, some Wellingtons and Hurricanes arrived from Britain. Expansion came to depend on production from United States sources, with Boston and Maryland bombers and Tomahawk fighters arming most of the new squadrons, several manned by South African, Canadian and Australian crews. For most of 1941 and early 1942 air superiority over the Western Desert was held by the Luftwaffe's Me 109, largely due to that German fighter's superior performance over the available Allied types. Weight of numbers and improved tactics began to tell and by summer 1942 the advantage moved to the Allies and remained with them. The Allied air forces followed the armies in the North African campaigns, culminating with the German surrender in May 1943. Then on to Sicily and, in the autumn of the same year, southern Italy.

DESERT SQUADRONS

For those RAF personnel arriving from verdant lands, a lasting impression of desert service was climate and terrain, together with the unpleasantries that went with them. William Coote:

'Of course, on first arriving on a desert squadron, it took time to get accustomed to the heat, mosquitoes, snakes, scorpions, dung-beetles, to say nothing of the Arabs! But probably the most irksome was the sand-storm. Lasting for hours, and sometimes days, the sand got everywhere. Despite the risk of being indelicate, in your mouth, eyes and ears, up your nose! You name it! It was present! To be followed often by long hours of digging out and trying to adjust to an entirely altered terrain!

The desert discomforts were borne by officers and men alike. Aircrews were known to declare that they would rather be on operations as flight brought relief. Perhaps just flippancy; but the ground staff certainly had no escape when duty called and the worst conditions prevailed. In the see-saw of advance and retreat across Libya, living and working conditions were always primitive and the enemy often too close for comfort'.

Harry Kidney was one who suddenly found he was in the front line with, for once, reason to be thankful for the harsh desert elements:

'*Circa* March 1941, a small detachment of No. 38 Squadron was based at Gambut, a grim desolate place in the Libyan desert, once occupied by the Italian Air Force. I was one of the privileged few selected to be sent there. Gambut is approximately halfway between Tobruk and Bardia, inland from the sea, with the landing-ground sited on an escarpment with wadies running down from it. Our Wimpeys [Wellingtons] were operating from here subsequent to the land forces' offensive which had come to a halt at El Agheila – some miles west of Benghazi. History shows Erwin Rommel appearing on the scene about this time and commencing to push our forces rapidly back towards Egypt. Orders came for the abandonment of Gambut and retirement eastwards to Sidi Assiz – a landing-ground near Bardia. Four armourers, my best RAF pal, Alec "Chunky" Bell, two others and myself, were instructed to remain behind after all other personnel departed, to deal with armament stores. We were assured that transport would return later to collect us. It was with more than a little apprehension that we watched our colleagues depart in the early morning.

'We completed our assignment swiftly and returned to a derelict corrugated-iron shed located at the base of the escarpment in a wadi. This was a flea-ridden Italian relic. That day our transport failed to materialize and we knew the Afrika Korps was advancing rapidly; visions of Stalags loomed. Nightfall came and our imaginations ran riot as with every slight sound we expected massive blond Aryan types to burst into our shed firing their Mausers. Our thoughts were not entirely without substance as we learned later that enemy armour did traverse the landing-ground while we were hiding in the wadi. Two factors saved us: one was the element we hated and cursed most in the desert, the Khamsin, a scorching hot, soul-destroying sandstorm which blanketed everything out of sight within a few feet. Thus obscured, the Germans had not seen our shed in the wadi. The other factor was that Rommel chose to pursue his offensive deeper in the desert leaving the coastal area for the time being which enabled our belated lorry to reach us the next day, much to our relief. We set off at speed and reached Sidi Assiz, thankful for escape; but this relief was short-lived as enemy elements were reported approaching this vicinity.

'Once again we quickly boarded our lorry and went helter-skelter for the Egyptian border, reaching Fort Capuzzo extremely fatigued. Nightfall came so we decided to rest awhile but no; as soon as we were putting our groundsheets down, again it was panic stations when we learned the enemy was close on our tail. With alacrity we boarded our lorry and continued the flight eastwards, passing the border at Sollum, by which time it was dawn. Having reached a point somewhere near Sidi Barrani, exhausted, particularly the driver, we decided to rest whatever the consequences. Happily the Axis advance was halted at the Libya/Egypt border. So, after a few hours' rest we pressed on until reaching 38 Squadron's base at Shallufa, safe, thankful and in a bedraggled state, to learn that we had been listed "missing". Lady Luck had certainly been on our side.'

Many of the Wellingtons urgently required for bombing operations in the Middle East were flown out from England, staging through Gibraltar and Malta. The refuelling stop in Malta was a hazardous business as Joe Pugh discovered:

'In 1941 I was a member of one of the crews ferrying a batch of Wellingtons out to the Middle East. At Gibraltar we were told that the trip to Malta was more dangerous than operations as the enemy usually knew when aircraft were going to land there and had fighters up from nearby Pantelleria to intercept. We took off in darkness and landed at Luqa airfield, Malta, to learn that the Wellington that had left Gib before us had been shot down. As we were carrying a Wing Commander and an Air Commodore we were given priority on refuelling and took off again after only a brief stay. Our destination in Egypt was reached without any problems, but we later learned that many of the other Wellingtons were bombed at Luqa and their crews spent the next two or three weeks filling bomb holes in the runway before they could get out of Malta.'

The ordinary airman was always kept in the dark as to the purpose behind his duties other than the cause of ultimate victory. Nevertheless, most could figure the broad line of strategy. This was not the case with those who served in the desert during the months prior to the autumn of 1942. Most were simply bewildered by events. 'We staggered from one victory-cum-disaster to another; everything always seemed to be in such a bloody muddle,' recalled one disillusioned erk. Something of the same sentiment is to be found in Australian pilot Mick Wood's account of his arrival in the Middle East:

'I was sure in 1942 that the British would ultimately win the war. They muddled with such finesse. With my No. 159 Squadron Liberator and crew we flew out of Gibraltar to Egypt in June 1942. Before we left we were shown the "hot spots" to avoid and were given strict instructions to "circle Ras El Knias" before we approached Kilo 40 to refuel. Day broke with the delta in sight and we proceeded to lose height to 1,500 feet to carry out the circling and be recognized. While still over the water and out from the coast it seemed that inland from the Cape of Ras El Knias there was a great deal of dust with hundreds of vehicles moving east. I then decided to give the recognition instructions a miss and thus proceeded directly to Kilo 40. On landing there was the usual debriefing during which the Intelligence man announced, "I say, I hope you didn't go to Ras El Knias." We confirmed that we had not. "Good thing," he said, "Rommel's troops passed there two days ago." '

As in western Europe, only the fighters and light bombers normally flew against the enemy in daylight, while the mediums and heavies (when they arrived) bombed under cover of darkness. During 1941 and 1942 Wellingtons ran regular raids on the Libyan ports used by Axis shipping to supply their forces. At that time, the Flak defences deployed around these places were claimed by old hands as fiercer than those at many German cities. Steve Challen of No. 108 Squadron had good reason to subscribe to this view:

'On 24 September 1941 we were briefed for the "milk run", Benghazi. Flight Lieutenant Vare was rather keen to make a good show of our first op in the Middle East so we stooged straight over the town. Our target was supply ships against the harbour moles and quays. There had been a few before us so all kinds of Flak was coming up, the lights making it difficult as usual to pinpoint anything. Around again. Vare decided to alter height and approach from a different direction in a shallow dive, hoping the increased speed would baffle predictors. No chance! The lights clamped on us, the multi-coloured Flak seemed draped around us. I had fired some short bursts on the first run, knowing there wasn't much chance of putting out those lights, but perhaps the bits of spent lead raining down might possibly disrupt their accuracy. This time round even lower, I fired longer, calculated squirts until my port gun jammed. The .303 calibre ammo we were using was First World War vintage. Again "No bombs gone". I stripped my Browning to find out what the stoppage was, putting the parts with names like "Rear seat retainer keeper and pin" (who thought that name up?) on the ledge where the sides and dome of the turret joined. Third time around lower and slower from a different direction which must have been right for the aiming-point because the chant began: "right, right, left a little, steady, steady, bombs gone". The same instant there was a bang, a rattle against the turret and a burnt smell. I put out my hand to feel for the breech-block bits, but felt only breeze. Then a sensation in my throat; I wanted to cough but couldn't. Putting my hand to my throat it was warm, sticky and wet. Switching on my mike I tried to report that I had been hit, but could tell there wasn't much noise coming out of me. Sergeant Gord Murray, 2nd pilot, said "Okay, Steve. Coming back". We were out over the Med by now, in no danger from that "hot spot". The turret wouldn't move with the hydraulics so I engaged the hand gear, which needed two hands to wind the handle to centralize the turret so that I could open the doors and climb out. There was quite a breeze and light shining in on the port side where fabric had been stripped off. The hydraulic pipes supplying the turret had been punctured and oil sprayed everywhere, no mistaking the smell. I thought that maybe the rudder or elevator controls might be damaged, but was unable to see as I continued along the catwalk until meeting Gord on his way back. I sat on the fold-down cot while Gord shone his torch on my damage. Not much to be done other than place a field dressing over the wound holding it in place with my hand as I lay on the cot. Chuck came back for a look as did Gibbo. Paul and Vare were busy up front as the controls were not quite right.

'With dawn coming it was light enough for me to write some questions in a little diary, like: "How big is the hole in my bloody neck?" and, "Where are you dropping me?" Wireless inquiry to base had advised landing at Fuka Main where an ambulance would be waiting. A soft touch-down at 7am. I crawled out of the mid under hatch where at one time in the design there was to have been a "dustbin" turret. While people became a little impatient I produced my little camera and insisted the occasion be recorded as I stood near the damage for snaps to be taken. Taken to 21st Medical Receiving Centre, a tented hospital in the desert, I was operated upon at about 10am by Squadron Leader Wallace, assisted by his medical orderlies. He removed a piece of Flak from my larynx.

Unbeknown to him and me, there were bits embedded in my scalp which some time later were raked out as I combed my hair.'

The light day bombers – Blenheims, Bostons, Marylands – suffered most grievously during this period, despite the presence of fighter escort over the front line. As appears common, personal experience of combat did not necessarily provide the most frightening incident for an individual during an operational tour. Bob Thompson of No. 11 Squadron had no doubts about this:

'We were recalled for some reason while the squadron's Blenheims were on army support ops. When we landed at an advanced landing-ground one of the main wheel tyres went flat and we swept round in a circle with one wingtip trailing in the sand. As soon as we came to a standstill I gathered up my maps, disconnected the camera and got up from my navigator's table in the nose and then noticed the pilot had left. Going into the cockpit and sticking my head out of the hatch in the top of the fuselage, I was surprised to see the pilot and turret gunner running away as fast as their legs would carry them. It was then I remembered the load of bombs and was not long in getting out of that hatch and belting after the others. Later it was my job to go back to the aircraft and replace the safety-pins in the bombs, which had been removed in flight. To my horror I found that some of the extension rods fitted to the nose of the bombs (so that they exploded at surface level rather than penetrate the ground) had been forced up hard against the bulkhead when we had gone down on one wingtip. These bombs might easily have exploded. The diceyest do I ever experienced.'

That one's own bombs could be more threatening than the enemy's was well known to armourers. Accidents when detonating loads, destroying aircraft and claiming lives, were by no means rare in any theatre of war. Removal of bombs from crashed aircraft was a task tackled with apprehension, particularly so if they were fitted with delayed fuses. Ted Scott:

'Our squadron was operating from a landing-ground in North Africa on anti-shipping work. About eighteen Wellingtons of No. 221 and another squadron were lined up awaiting take-off when Jerry found us and played havoc. Ten Wellingtons were destroyed and most of the others damaged. They had been loaded with bombs having delayed-action fuses timed to work within from four to twelve hours. Our Sergeant Armourer, a grand chap, came to our tent for volunteers to remove the bombs from three aircraft that, having undercarriage damage, were lop-sided. But it wasn't a case of volunteering as there were only four armourers present. Although each of us carried on as if it were just another job, I'm sure we were all dead scared. I knew that with delayed-action bombs you could not tell if the fuse capsule had broken and the delay system was already working. Each second felt like an hour as we worked on those bombs. We were lucky – and three Wellingtons were saved for repair.'

After the battle of El Alamein and the Allied invasion of French Morocco and Algeria during the autumn of 1942, the campaign to drive the Axis forces from North Africa intensified. Fresh RAF squadrons arrived, as did new aircraft and equipment. Spitfires, Beaufighters, Bisleys and improved versions of the Hurricane and Wellington. From the United States came Kittyhawks, Baltimores and Marauders. The RAF only had a single squadron of Marauders operating in the Western Desert (although five South African Air Force squadrons later used this Martin bomber in the Mediterranean area). One of the most controversial yet successful Allied warplanes, initially it had a reputation of being dangerous to fly. In view of this it is surprising that some pilots came to Marauders straight from ambling Oxfords and Ansons. Bill Japp was one:

'After my flying training in Rhodesia I went "to the war up north". Without any operational training unit experience whatsoever I was sent with three other pilots from the replacement pool to No. 14 Squadron, the only RAF squadron with the Martin Marauder, a new American twin-engined bomber. At first we flew as second pilots and once familiar with the controls advanced to the left-hand seat. My transition came at Blida, Algeria, where I started by flying a few circuits with my skipper and another experienced Marauder pilot. Then they put an unsuspecting Aussie, George, who had just joined the unit, in the second pilot's seat and told him to keep his hands on the two toggle switches of the manual pitch control mechanism and watch the rev counters in case we had a runaway prop. When the aircraft was lined up on the runway and everything checked, I opened up the throttles to the specified setting but nothing happened. The tension of the occasion probably caused me to forget that there would be a delay in response and the warnings not to advance the throttle levers further, which I did. Suddenly my seat hit me in the back and we were away like a rocket. The flight was without further incident and only after landing did I inform George that his first flight in a Marauder had been my first solo.

'At this time I knew nothing of the Marauder's reputation in America where it had an alarming accident rate. I was only aware that the aircraft had a very high wing loading and didn't suffer fools gladly. Apart from the occasional failure of the electric propeller pitch control mechanism, a known problem and one which was eventually corrected, we found nothing unusually hazardous about take-offs or landings. The high landing speed – 150mph – didn't seem exceptional simply because I had no experience of landing any other combat aircraft. The most advanced type flown in training was the Oxford and as that came in to land at about 80mph there was no comparison. When all the prescribed procedures had been carried out and you were on final approach at 150–155mph, you felt, as the runway came up to meet you, that the aircraft was on rails and would arrive at just the spot you wanted. This was about 10mph faster than advised by the Americans, but it gave that extra margin of stability and safety while really not making much visible difference to your rate of descent towards the runway. The Marauder, like all American aircraft I flew, was beautifully made and comfortable. The knobs and buttons in the cockpit were so neat and well laid out compared with most British types I later flew. However, I didn't really appreciate just how advanced and what a grand aircraft it was until the squadron returned to the UK and converted to Wellingtons.'

With Axis forces driven from Africa, relief came at last to the once beleaguered island of Malta, recipient of countless bombings over three years. The battering claimed many RAF lives, both in the air and on the ground, but Air Force personnel played a major part in the creation of the indomitable spirit that came to be Malta's hallmark. And, as Tony Spooner relates, despite the pounding, that measure of courtesy opposing combatants showed towards each other still flourished – even if his example did indulge a captive to a degree that must have left him completely nonplussed:

'It was unusual for a Ju 88 to be shot down so close to Luqa, Malta, that we could watch the parachutes open and stream downwards. The last to abandon the crippled bomber landed so close that we set forth to investigate. We arrived just in time to prevent the angry Maltese peasants from hacking him to death with their simple tools. We escorted our "prisoner" back to the large flapping tent which served as the officers' mess after the original one – and much else – had been flattened by the Luftwaffe. While someone phoned the Special Police, we were left to entertain our unexpected guest. The difficulty was that he spoke no English and we no German. "The only German I know are the words of *Lilly Marlene*," lamented one. We all knew these words. It was at an early stage of the war when this catchy tune was purely a German one. Later, Vera Lynn and other British song-birds purloined it for our use too. In Malta we were subject to ceaseless German propaganda usually introduced by this haunting refrain sung so seductively in German. With little else to listen to, we had learned the words. Accordingly, until the SPs arrived to take him away, we entertained the astonished visitor as best we could. First we had rescued him. Then we sat him down, gave him a cigarette, a beer and sang him the famous German tune in his own language. I doubt that Dr Goebbels' infamous propaganda machine had prepared him for this "greeting".'

The gleeful atmosphere so often found in a station mess or crew room in the UK was no less evident in and around whatever served a similar purpose in the desert or Mediterranean agrarian patch, as William Coote observed:

'War is not all danger, daring and decorations. Fortunately, when large numbers of men are thrown together in the services there are always the wags, wits and practical jokers. On reflection, one tends to feel thankful for them since they contributed so much at times to making long, monotonous days bearable. One regular "leg-pull" practised among aircrews flying with Nos. 70 and 37 Wellington Squadrons of 231 Wing, 205 Group in North Africa, was to suggest to new or replacement crews that they might like to freshen up with a shower after the long trip out from England. After deciding that a shower would be just what the doctor ordered, the unsuspecting pilot and crew were directed towards the far side of the airfield. Inquiries where the showers were brought the inevitable and serious response. "You've been misinformed! The only showers hereabouts are where you've just come from!"'

As pranks were adapted to the situation and location, so was 'lingo'. A rich air force vocabulary arose, far more varied than that within the home commands, due to the influx of personnel steeped in the language and expressions of many nations where they had previously trained or served. John Heap:

'In Italy and North Africa we used a lot of Arabic and 'gypo expressions in everyday conversation. As many service people had come out of India to the Middle East when things were bad, several Indian expressions were in use too. We had an exclusive squadron war-cry. It started off as something the Arab drivers used to shout to their horses on the streets of Cairo – "Hod hod!" It became our catch-phrase. If you wanted someone to get a move on you'd say "Hod, hod! you so-and-so." We even used it in the air as an identification. You'd hear people call up Control and just say "Hod hod!" Control knew immediately it was a 70 Squadron aircraft.'

ITALY AND THE BALKANS

The Allied armies met stiff resistence in their attempts to drive up the leg of Italy, eventually coming to a virtual halt in the mountains that barred the way north to Rome. The Allies dominated the skies and the Luftwaffe was never again the threat it had been during the fighting on the southern side of the Mediterranean. Farther afield it was a different matter and ranging RAF reconnaissance or attack aircraft still ran a real risk of interception. An individual's reaction to this kind of situation and what appeared to be pending termination is graphically described by Bill Japp:

'We were doing a reccy of the French Mediterranean coast in the vicinity of Cap d'Agde, of which we were very wary as we knew it had radar-controlled Flak batteries. While gingerly approaching the coast at our normal operational altitude of 50 feet, three unidentified aircraft, presumably enemy, were seen at some distance. Our pilot, Merv Hogg, immediately took the Marauder round on a reverse course, the best thing to do in such circumstances. There was always a chance that we had not been seen, but the gunners soon reported that three Me 109Gs were coming after us. Merv reduced height to about 30 feet above the waves and gave us full speed, a little over 300mph. As the 109 had only about a 50mph advantage at low altitude it was some time before they got within firing range and all the time we were drawing them out to sea. Our defensive armament consisted of a single hand-held .50 calibre gun in the tail position and twin .50s in the mid-upper power turret, not much with which to fight off the firepower bearing down on us. No member of our crew needed to be told we were in a very sticky situation. I remember seeing the sea moving just below me and thinking that in that Mediterranean I would probably end my life. All very matter-of-fact; no fear, just tension.

'One Messerschmitt positioned directly astern and the others off each wing tip to catch us if we turned. As the 109 approaching the tail came within firing range our navigator, watching from the astrodome, shouted which way to skid turn to evade. For six minutes the three 109s took turns in pumping 20 millimetres and bullets into us and although we both took turns in throwing the Marauder around she appeared to be hit on every pass. Then the good news that all three 109s had turned back, perhaps low on fuel, out of ammunition or maybe one had been hit by our gunner's fire. We didn't know. Merv Hogg, like all Canadians, was always well supplied with chewing-gum and kept a generous supply available on the throttle pedestal. I was not, and never became, a chewing-gum addict, but it seemed at the beginning of this episode that it would be beneficial for my somewhat dry mouth and I helped myself to some. It was only after the action that I felt that this gum was not very chewable and on removing all three sticks from my mouth I could see that the somewhat metallic wrapping had never been removed!

'An intercom check on the two gunners in the rear brought an okay from the mid-upper but the tail-gunner said he had a head wound. I went back along the catwalk, dodged round the mid-upper's feet, and crawled to the tail. George Senior's face was covered in blood which appeared to be coming from his head. I got a field dressing and started wiping it away but could find no wound. I then noticed a great deal of blood on one of George's hands. It took a few moments to put two and two together, but what had happened was that during the action his gun had jammed and in his desperation to clear it he had, unnoticed, cut his hand on the breech mechanism. Perspiring profusely he had then wiped the sweat from his eyes with the back of the bloody hand. The anti-climax was that finding there was no battle wound we both burst into near uncontrolled laughter, probably emotional relief at surviving a very sticky situation. Eventually I started back to the front of the aircraft looking for fuselage damage as I went. As I was passing Smithy's feet in the mid-upper again I happened to notice a neat hole through the sole of one of his boots. Engine noise made normal communication impossible so to attract his attention I thumped his leg and motioned for him to come down. When he did, I could see another neat hole in the top of the same boot. He seemed puzzled so, sitting him down in the fuselage, I removed both boot and sock. I was confronted with what looked like a miniature RAF roundel on both top and bottom of his foot; a circular red wound in the centre surrounded by a blue bruise. It was apparent that during one of our sharp evasive turns a bullet had gone clean through boot and foot but Smithy hadn't felt a thing! Only after my discovery did he start to feel any pain. Although the hydraulic system had been damaged and there were 76 holes in FK123, nothing vital had been hit. Either the enemy pilots were poor shots or our evasive action was exceptionally effective.'

Beyond Italy and the Alps, over Austria and Germany or other parts of the Balkans, it was a different matter too. The battered Luftwaffe fighter force rose by night and day to meet the intrusions of the strategic bombers and the Flak at vital installations, such as oil refineries, was murderous. Wellington and Halifax squadrons, subsequently converting to Liberators, faced similar perils as the heavies operating from England. All aircrew were volunteers, yet here and there appeared the odd individual who had second thoughts about venturing into the night sky in a bomber. John Heap:

'After crewing-up at an OTU we went to the transit camp at Almaza, near Cairo. Here you knew you were getting pretty close to the war; the next step would be a squadron in Italy or India. There were a few chaps who had become detached from crews and who had been around the place for some time. The suspicion was that they were suddenly not very keen on going to war. One individual in particular was either round the bend or trying to work his ticket. From the way he carried on this appeared to be the case. At every parade he would arrive with heavy great-coat and wrapped-up as if it were freezing when the temperature was usually up in the eighties or more and the rest of us were in shorts and light shirts in the sweltering heat. We called him "Forty Below". I've no idea what they finally did with him.'

Losses were an accepted part of operational airfield life wherever the location. A newcomer's introduction to this unpleasant fact was usually the empty bed he filled. In Italy this enlightenment could be far more stark. Alan Ackerman:

'We reached No. 40 Squadron at Foggia Main in October 1944. The first thing we asked was where do we sleep and one of the chaps took us over to a tent. There were a couple of beds that were occupied and a couple of spaces. Our guide pointed to the spaces and was about to leave as we asked where our beds were. "They become available," he said, and left. So my first few nights were spent on the tent floor. But a bed did become available quite quickly. A Flight Sergeant in one of them didn't come back from a trip and I took over.'

The most harrowing experience of losses was to see an aircraft carrying a friend explode, be consumed by fire, or suffer some other form of destruction from which there could be no escape. Usually this could only be in daylight because, for the most part on night operations, darkness cloaked identities. A loss was then only felt through the absence of a crew the next morning – or the memory of last associations before the raid. William Coote:

'It was a warm evening, just before dusk, in the early spring of 1944. The aircraft of No. 70 Squadron were lined up for take-off on Tortorella airfield in Italy while the crews relaxed on the grass, waiting instructions. Presently the R/T sets left "tuned to Control" crackled into life with orders to start engines. Immediately, everyone began making for the nose ladders to enter the Wellingtons. Next in line ahead of my aircraft was Flight Sergeant Harry Pollard's and I happened to glance in that direction. Harry's rear-gunner was entering his turret from the outside, as gunners sometimes did, and he began whistling. As I mounted the ladder there came to my hearing the first few bars of the verse to *Stardust*, Hoagy Carmichael's famous composition. The piece that runs: "And now the purple shades of twilight time, steals across the meadows. . . ." Just that: then I was inside the aircraft. Five or six hours later, after de-briefing, we sat in the mess tent having our flying breakfast. The places that Harry Pollard and his crew would have occupied were vacant. As far as I am aware they were never heard from again. Strange how particular associations persist: from then on, whenever I hear the strains of that melody, the memory of Pollard's rear-gunner climbing into his turret always seems to come to mind.'

An increasing number of operations flown from Italy involved support of Resistance and undercover organizations in eastern Europe. The longest, and usually most difficult, were to Poland, begun in the autumn of 1943 and culminating with the dropping of supplies to beleaguered patriots in Warsaw a year later. Some aircrew involved, like Leon Piechocki, were Poles:

'In the winter of 1943/44 the Polish Flight of No. 138 Squadron began flying special operations to Poland out of Brindisi, Italy. The first trip for my crew was at Easter and very emotional and sentimental it was to be over our homeland again after four years. We pushed Polish traditional painted eggs, chocolate, cigarettes and other little presents into the containers. The flight took place by the full moon with snow still on the ground. The drop from the Halifax into a forest clearing was from 500 feet. As we circled after the drop we saw a light flashing V for Victory in Morse. They were doing it by opening and shutting the door of a little cottage near the drop place. You can imagine our feelings.'

Most air aid went to Resistance movements in the Balkans, in particular Yugoslavia where Tito's peasant army made life increasingly difficult for the occupiers of their country. In June 1944 an RAF Balkan Air Force was established, using RAF, SAAF and Allied units, with the purpose of rendering assistance to the Yugoslav partisans and harassing enemy communications in that theatre of war. To co-ordinate operations, close liaison was essential, with the result that now and again RAF personnel found themselves in very strange situations. Fred Pawsey tells of one of his adventures:

'One day in July 1944, Group Captain Boyd sent for me and, after offering a glass of gin, asked whether I would go to Yugoslavia to observe and advise on the discipline and signalling necessary for successful air support. Apparently the partisans were to make an attack on a small town occupied by Germans and the Ustachi [fascist Croatians] and my squadron would give air support. "You will only need a tooth brush and a revolver," he said, "as you will only be away for about 48 hours." That night I flew in a Dakota from Brindisi across the Adriatic to an airstrip in Croatia. I sat on a sack of flour surrounded by weapons and ammunition. We landed in a remote valley, guided down by a flare path of bonfires. The speed with which the flour, ammunition and myself were off-loaded was remarkable. With equal speed wounded partisans were put into the aircraft which did not stop engines and was soon on its way back to Brindisi. Before dawn I was guided to a hillside overlooking the town to be attacked. It all looked very peaceful until the time came and the battle was fought and won with my Spitfire squadron giving air support. There were no mistakes and the jubilant partisans captured the place and took some prisoners.

'After some discussion of the battle it was time to get back to the airstrip. I was asked by my escort if I could ride a horse. My experience was limited mainly to cart-horses, but pride demanded that I say yes. Shortly afterwards three magnificent, lunging and snorting horses were brought up; none had saddles. As I stood frozen at the thought of trying to ride one, my two escorts leapt like Cossacks on to the backs of two of them and literally streaked off in clouds of dust along the track. I was obviously expected to do the same as my mount reared and lunged, eager to be off. I unfroze enough to show by signs and gestures to the partisans that they would have to help me up. As soon as I was astride, the horse was released and immediately streaked off after the others with me clinging on desperately – and I mean desperately. With every stride I was pitched one way and then another, fully expecting to end up in the dust at any moment. Almost without thinking I shouted "Whoa, whoa!" The horse evidently construed this as encouragement and went even faster. Puzzled by this disobedience it occurred to me that a Croatian horse was hardly likely to respond to English commands so I hollered "Stoy!" which I knew meant stop. To my great relief the animal came to an abrupt halt, ears pricked and quivering and obviously resentful of this command. Gingerly relaxing my arm grip around its neck I sat upright to take stock of the situation. Appreciating I was alone and that it would be very difficult to explain to partisans, let alone Germans or collaborators, my presence wearing RAF battledress and sitting on a wild horse in the middle of this occupied country, I decided it less perilous to continue. Very cautiously, making encouraging noises and with gentle heel kicks, the horse was made to walk and not gallop. In the hot sun I was soon aware that my sweating backside and legs were in most uncomfortable contact with the horse's hard and sweaty hide. This soreness became more acute with the animal's every movement along the rough track.

'Eventually I reached the airstrip where my two escorts had rejoined their friends and seemed quite unperturbed by my late arrival. There was much laughter when they realized they had to help me off the horse and even more when I indicated that I was too sore to sit down on the grass and enjoy some of the black bread they were eating. When more partisans arrived there was further hilarity and slapping of bottoms as it was explained why I was standing. How was it, they inferred, that a man could fly a Spitfire and was not able to ride a horse? Only the sudden shelling of the airstrip by advancing German tanks saved me from further friendly ridicule. Suffice to say that my 48-hour visit was somewhat extended as we fled into the hills. During the ensuing adventures great kindness was shown me, but everywhere I went my companions derived great pleasure out of recounting the tale of my sore rear-end with appropriate gesticulations.'

Another division of RAF air strength in the Mediterranean was the Coastal Air Force charged, primarily, with the disruption of enemy coastal shipping. It could be a very dangerous task, particularly in circumstances such as those remembered by Eric Myring:

'We hit the Italian coast west of Trieste, turned left and followed the coast around. As we approached Venice I saw two ships which were head-on to us, outside Venice harbour. They were some distance off, so I said to Tom Corlett, my navigator, "There are two merchant ships ahead, we'll go and prang them." Over the intercom came Tom's cool and steady voice, "They look like F-Boats to me!" I shouted back, "I know what bloody F-Boats look like, these are merchant ships, we are going to have a go at them."

' "I'm sure they're F-Boats," said Tom, but again I said that he was wrong and that we were going to attack. Now, to our Beaufighter crews F-Boats were the greatest hazard when carrying out shipping attacks. They were about the size of a corvette, very heavily armoured and their armament consisted almost entirely of short-range and medium-range anti-aircraft guns. Their role was simply that of a floating anti-aircraft platform, designed to protect shipping and shore installations from low flying aircraft. To us they were "Flak Ships", to be avoided at all cost in all but exceptional circumstances.

'I called our No. 2 over the RT, a new crew on their first op, and said, "Hello Nosey 32, this is Nosey 26. There are two merchant ships ahead, we are going to attack with rockets, follow me in." As the ships were head on to us, I had to pull over to my right, then make a sweeping turn to my left so that I could make the proper approach and attack the side of the ship. We were, of course, flying at "deck level", and when I estimated that we were the right distance from the ships, I pulled up to 1,200 feet in the usual way, then dived down on the nearest ship to me. This was the first time I had been able to get a proper look at the ship and to my horror all I could see was metal deck and what looked to me, in that split second, to be "hundreds" of guns pointing into the air! I had to make a split-second decision and decided the only thing to do was to continue my dive, fire my cannons, let go my rockets, then get away corkscrewing at low level as quickly as I could. As I have said, there were two ships, and both were F-Boats, and for some reason I cannot explain there was no reaction from the boat I attacked whereas the other F-Boat started firing at me with everything they had got, or so it appeared to me. Fortunately I was flying across their line of fire and was quickly out of range of their light gun fire, otherwise we would have been blown out of the sky.

'I was sweating like mad, wondering how I had got away with such a stupid error when a little voice came over the air, "Hello Nosey 26, this is Nosey 32. I forgot to switch on my rocket switch so I didn't fire them. Are we to go round again?" I was so shattered that rather than replying that we were not, I said, "Nosey 32, they are F-Boats. You can go round if you like, I'm going back to base!" This was terribly bad leadership on my part, but fortunately he followed me so my second lapse did not have any dire consequences. When we were out of range of the ack-ack fire we turned to port to see the result of our attack and saw that the F-Boat we had attacked was listing about 30 degrees to port. Tom, quite rightly, never let me forget the incident, frequently asking, "Do you know what an F-Boat looks like, Eric?" '

Not everyone was so fortunate in escaping the murderous fire put up by German escort vessels; and ditching was a precarious business in a Beaufighter. Eric Myring again:

'Late in the day four of our aircraft had been on a shipping strike in the northern Adriatic and one had been hit by enemy Flak and was staggering home. The pilot decided he could not maintain height and as it was too low to bale out he would have to ditch in the dark. We had all been well-rehearsed in the ditching procedure – this was necessary as all our operational flying was at low level. It was reckoned that the Beaufighter would stay afloat for a maximum of ten seconds, so everything had to be done "according to the book". Both the pilot and navigator opened their escape hoods, the pilot made a perfect ditching, they both got out on the wing taking their first-aid kit, emergency rations, local maps, local money, navigation record, etc., as well as their one-man dinghies which we all carried (and sat on). In addition the aircraft carried a large dinghy in the wing which inflated when the aircraft ditched, and this also went according to plan and within the ten seconds both aircrew, complete with their emergency supplies, were safely sitting in the large dinghy waiting for the aircraft to sink. Well, the ten seconds passed, then another ten seconds, then a minute, and still there was no sign of the kite going down. By this time they were a few yards away from the aircraft and the pilot said, "This is funny," (or words to that effect!) "I'll go and see what's happened." It was summer time, the sea was warm, so he decided to swim across, lowered himself out of the dinghy into the water and found he was standing on the sea bed! North of Foggia, on the coast there is a slim piece of land between the sea and a large lagoon. In the dark the pilot hadn't seen this, and instead of ditching in the sea was smack in the middle of the lagoon!'

The Back-Up Bods

ERKS AND OTHERS

Originally an erk was an aircraftman, fitter or rigger, but the term came to be used for other-rank members of ground staff, irrespective of trade. As there were seven non-flying personnel for every member of aircrew, erks provided the largest unofficial classification in RAF man and woman power. There were more than 300 different ground trades in the service to put aircrew, aircraft and ordnance into action. Many men and women never went near an aircraft or even an airfield, being confined throughout their service to clerical, domestic or driving duties at a depot, administrative centre or the like. But for the most part the term erk was, and still is, associated in the public's mind with the men who serviced and maintained aeroplanes with oil-stained overalls and greasy hands. Indeed, theirs was a vitally important job. Poor or faulty maintenance could precipitate disaster. Good ground crews were well aware of their responsibility and gave their very best. Even so, as in all tasks, experience taught many lessons. Fred Pawsey recounts one of his:

'In May 1940 I was the corporal in charge of the duty crew at Tangmere while the evacuation from France was in full swing. The airfield was packed with a variety of aircraft coming and going. A Blenheim landed and taxied up to the control tower. The only man aboard was the pilot, a Squadron Leader who, as he clambered out, asked me to hold his briefcase and maps, which he quickly reclaimed when his feet were on the ground. He said that he would only be gone a few minutes and instructed me to make sure the tanks were filled to the top. He soon returned, still clutching his briefcase, and wanted to know if the tanks were really full. Despite my assurances he told me to remove the filler caps again. He then got up on the wing and knelt down beside me – still holding the briefcase and maps. I expected confirmation that the tanks had been filled, but his reaction was a mild reprimand because they were not full to the brim and that more fuel could be put in each. Back came the bowser and under his supervision I slowly added a little more fuel to each tank. As he replaced the filler caps he told me that he had to fly the Blenheim to France to deliver some important items and that it was unlikely there would still be refuelling facilities available. In the circumstances every drop of fuel was vital if he were going to have any chance of making a return to England. I have often wondered what this so important mission was and about the nature of the documents in the briefcase he was not letting out of his sight.

Also if the topping-up of the tanks really did see him safely back. But the incident did teach me the need for attention to detail. Thereafter I always saw that an order for full tanks received really full tanks.'

Fred Pawsey was eventually accepted for aircrew training. Many ground crew men made this transition and became excellent pilots, their technical knowledge of airframe, engine and systems probably giving a more cautious approach to flying than found in the average pilot without this background. Another who served as a mechanic while awaiting pilot training was Tom Minta who recalls the qualms of a fitter's responsibilities at the Central Flying School:

'Like most hopefuls who were waiting to be called for aircrew training, I endeavoured to get as many flights as I could. I had acquired a parachute which I kept under the engine covers and when George Stainforth or Peter Salter came down to fly one of the aircraft I'd say, "Want any ballast, sir?" Usually they were willing to let you ride in a turret or some other out-of-the-way position and I had several trips this way. On one occasion I had just been involved in changing a hydraulic pump on a Hampden and got aboard when Peter Salter wanted to take the aircraft up. I was sitting happily in the after-turret looking around when there was a great whoosh of fine mist from the back of the engine nacelle I'd been working on. Hydraulic fluid! Peter Salter said that he was afraid the hydraulic pump had gone and that we would have to make an emergency landing at an airfield with a suitably long runway as he would have no flaps. We pumped the wheels down by hand and landed safely – he was a marvellous pilot. I thought I was for the high-jump, but when the pump was examined it proved to be nothing to do with me. All the same, I can tell you I was a very worried fellow for a time. Such an experience would be beneficial to any member of ground staff.'

The aforementioned failure was of material, but elsewhere human fallibility ensured that aircraft were lost through faulty workmanship. Often the precise cause of an aircraft accident or loss was not established, but many an erk was haunted by the thought that something he had or had not done might be a contributory factor. In general, no body of men could have been more conscientious than service and maintenance crews, frequently working until the assigned job was completed, while enduring whatever the weather could inflict for their discomfort. Much of this engineering work was difficult, tedious and sometimes exasperating – although in the example of the latter that follows Frank Clarke acknowledges much was of his own making:

'While sitting on my tool-box having a rest in our "C" Flight Nissen hut at Wellesbourne, our "Chiefy" [the Flight Sergeant] called out: "Who's on Y-Yorker?" I replied: "Me Chiefy." "Well, there's a large tear in the starboard wing. Get out there and repair it!" he ordered. I got all my gear together, fabric, thread, needles and dope and wandered over to the kite, one of our Wellington Mk IIIs which were all fabric surfaces over geodetic framework. It took me about an hour and a half to do the repair, sitting up on the main spare of the wing. Finally finished, I stood up to survey my handiwork. My foot slipped off the spar and went right through both top and underside fabric of the wing. With some apprehension I went back to the hut to tell the Flight Sergeant what had happened and that the aircraft would have to be grounded for another hour or so. Best not to repeat what he said. The Wellington should have been ready for a practice bombing sortie at 14.00 hours and it eventually took off at 16.30. I was not very popular at the time.'

MECHANICAL TRANSPORT

Motor transport occupied the attention of a section of every RAF station. Handling the heavy stuff was by no means a 'cushy job' with lorry, tractor and van drivers working round the clock to meet demand. Of those men and women recruited or called up, comparatively few had civilian licences to drive motor vehicles and in consequence there were MT driver shortages at many locations. Vic Holloway was quickly initiated into this situation:

'My first posting after initial training was to Montrose in Scotland. Four of us left Blackpool in the morning of 4 May 1940 and arrived at Montrose station at twenty to ten that night – it was just starting to get dark. We 'phoned for transport to pick us up at the station, only to be told they hadn't any drivers or transport available and we would have to walk. So we struggled up to the camp, which was about two miles out of town, and reported to the guard room. Transport were notified of our arrival and a sergeant appeared. "You're just what we wanted," he beamed at me. "There's a tractor and petrol bowser out there. I want you to take it to Edzell; they're night flying." Well, this was the first time I'd been to Scotland in my life and I had never even heard of Edzell. The sergeant said it was about twelve miles away, gave me rough directions and off I went. There were no signposts but somehow I finally found my way, arriving sometime after midnight. They certainly were short of drivers for from then on I was continually on the go, snatching a few hours sleep here and there. I discovered there were only eleven drivers to serve all the transport on Montrose and four satellites. I think it was five or six weeks before I had met all the other drivers, we were so busy.'

MT was a particularly important element of the tactical air forces, following the armies in North Africa, Italy and – after D-Day – in western Europe. RAF ground personnel moved on from location to location, now and again with reminders from the enemy. Vic Holloway:

'I was driving near St. Nicholas in a convoy of recovered vehicles which we were taking to our depot near Brussels. Looking ahead, I saw a house disappear in an explosion and two or three of our vehicles went off the road into a ditch. I was far enough back only to feel the blast. At first we were puzzled by the cause and then realized it was a V-2 rocket. Luckily none of our people were killed.

'One night in the winter of 1944-5 we were instructed to collect a fleet of lorries from a works just outside Brussels and drive them to a location that would be indicated by a Belgian guide. Every lorry that was a runner towed one that was not. Although they had all been painted up and looked quite good from the outside, it was obvious they were in poor mechanical condition. The only light on each lorry was on the back axle where it could only be seen by the driver of the following vehicle. We had no idea where we went, but it must have been near to the front lines. After parking the lorries as instructed, we were taken back to our depot. I had almost forgotten about this night when, on 8 May 1945, we drivers were sent out to these same lorries which were still where we had left them. It wasn't until we returned with these vehicles that evening that we learned the war was officially over.'

SIGNALS

With the tactical air forces went various mobile support units providing radio and radar facilities for aircraft control and headquarters communications. Mostly theirs was an unglamorous job of move, set up, wait and listen. An exception was the experience of Leonard Owens' outfit which suddenly found itself present at one notable event of liberation:

'The Allied liberation force that entered Paris on Friday 25 August 1944 is recorded as being composed of French and American troops. However, there was a British component, albeit small. I know for I was part of it. My outfit was 5285 'G' Mobile Signals Unit, attached to No. 148 Wing operating from Carpiquet airfield just west of Caen. In the early hours of 24 August we were instructed to close our W/T net and be ready to move at first light. The few hours of speculation were finally relieved by our CO, Flying Officer Baber, and the chief Intelligence Officer of 85 Group, who gave us the amazing news that we were bound for Paris whose liberation was imminent. Our presence was required with that of a Ground Control Interception unit to meet the threat of Luftwaffe retaliatory raids expected once the capital was taken. Our six vehicles, carrying the equipment plus seventeen men, set off on what was to be a circuitous route of some 200 miles. The direct route through Lisieux and Evreux was not possible as fighting was still going on nearby. Instead we went south to Le Mans to join forces with the GCI unit before turning east through Chartres, where we spent the night. The following morning we set off in the wake of a column of French Army trucks and half-tracks. Progress was slow but by mid-afternoon we were in the suburbs of the capital with the welcoming crowds lining our route becoming larger as we neared the city centre. By the Eiffel Tower a huge throng barred our way and insisted we join them in their liberation celebrations. Embraces and kisses were exchanged; with true British aplomb, all were welcomed, no matter what the sex of the donor! We joined the vast assembly of citizens in singing the *Marseillaise* to a background of small-arms fire and the occasional explosion, reminders of the mopping-up operations proceeding in the vicinity.

'Eventually we were again able to proceed to our designated site, the Longchamps racecourse. The previous occupants, a German heavy Flak battery, had evacuated the position only a few hours earlier. As we "set up shop" hundreds of sightseeing Parisians arrived to line the rails and study our form. Never were runners in any Longchamps classic scrutinised more closely than we were that day! With radar and wireless aerials and antennae erected in record time, we were prepared for enemy air activity that night but this was nil. The anticipated air strike did materialize the following night when some 150 Luftwaffe bombers swept low over the city and in the course of a half hour delivered the last and heaviest air raid Paris was to suffer. Of 1,200 casualties, 200 were fatal, while 600 buildings were damaged or destroyed. The meagre cover our GCI was able to provide had been swamped by the concentration of aircraft, added to which the topography of our site, a natural bowl surrounded by woods, made both radar and W/T reception difficult. On top of this our controllers had been unable to communicate with some of the night fighter pilots in our sector as they were employing different R/T frequencies. Morale was at low ebb following our apparent inability to even minimize the raid's effect. A move was made to a more suitable location south of the city, but the enemy never returned to challenge seriously the Ack-Ack defences that were soon in position. So the next few weeks provided several off-duty trips into the city until the higher command decided the unit could be better employed at its original assignment. These halcyon days came to be savoured in memory; none more so than that extraordinary day when Paris was liberated.'

Another branch of signals activity was the 'Y' Service which had a host of Field Units dotted about the UK and the various war zones. Broadly, their work was the interception, monitoring and reporting of enemy radio traffic. Personnel were signatories to the Official Secrets Act, but few, if any, in Field Units had the slightest idea what the reams of figures and lettered code messages heard and written down concerned or revealed. Only very occasionally could a connection be made with actual events. Graham Smith, an operator with No. 5 FU in Malta:

'On a particular 10pm to 3am watch in 1943, at a time when the Allied armies were closing the final locks on Rommel's Afrika Korps, a frenzied amount of "traffic" was found to be emanating from an enemy W/T station in Sicily. As the Malta Fighter Control VHF unit was situated in the same room, we were soon aware that the enemy messages intercepted related to swift action to dispatch and direct Beaufighters of the island's night fighter force. The coded intercepts indicated that the Germans were dispatching troops by towed gliders in order to effect a last-ditch stand in the Cape Bon area of Tunisia. The atmosphere in the ops room was somewhat electrifying as the Beaufighters caught and wrought havoc among the Ju 52 transports and their helpless gliders while in transit over the Med between Sicily and Tunisia. A few days later, Corporal Normington, one of our long-serving station personnel, "picked up" on his allocated station a whole string of German messages in plane language telling the world, as it were, that surrender to the Allied forces was taking place. Notice was given that it was the operator's final message; please advise his next of kin; followed by name, rank, serial number and, of course, "Heil Hitler" to round off this poignant transmission. Again, the amount of satisfaction gained from this was quite something for we "listeners" who normally had little excitement in our task.'

'K' AND 'Q'

Of the many and varied ground assignments within the RAF, there was one that invited the enemy to 'have a go' at you; manning dummy airfields. Known as 'K' and 'Q' sites, they were situated a few miles from a parent station, a real airfield. With dummy aircraft and/or flarepaths, the sites were intended to draw the attention of enemy bombers seeking the parent station. Of the two types 'K' airfields with dummy aircraft were for deception by day and 'Q' sites had lighting for deception at night, but the majority of 'K' sites eventually had 'Q' facilities and there were a dozen purely 'Q' sites. Some two dozen airmen under a senior NCO manned each site which was provided with a concrete shelter, substantial but not enough to survive a direct hit. Ray Howlett:

'While at a dummy airfield near Bury St. Edmunds we were down the shelter on one of our nightly air raid warnings. A stick of bombs landed on the site quite near the shelter. Two chaps were playing draughts. Above the crunch of the bombs and crash of shrapnel, one of the players was heard to say: "Not too much noise chaps, I can't concentrate on my game." Next morning, when we inspected the site, this air raid came to have a more sobering effect on us. The stick of bombs had struck in a straight line directly towards our shelter. Had there been one more bomb I doubt if any of us would have survived.'

RAF SOLDIERS

The ground defence of RAF stations received scant attention until 1939. What measures were taken between the wars were largely localized to meet special requirements, notably the formation of armoured car companies in the Middle East where indigenous populations were not always receptive to RAF policing activities. Airfield defence received more attention in the late nineteen-thirties, particularly the possibility of attack by low-flying aircraft. Even then, practical measures were largely confined to selected station personnel having additional duties, manning rifle-calibre machine-guns on airfield perimeters. The army was relied upon for heavier anti-aircraft weapon support.

After the outbreak of hostilities RAF personnel charged with manning light anti-aircraft guns were designated Ground Gunners and identified by a GG sleeve motif. With the 1940 invasion threat to the UK, Ground Gunners had the additional task of defending RAF installations against enemy paratroopers and by the end of the following year more than 65,000 RAF men were involved in some form of ground defence. In February 1942 the Ground Gunners became the basis of the newly created RAF Regiment, an organization which, both in the UK and Middle East, was charged with providing ground defence of airfields. Later, when Allied forces took the initiative, the RAF Regiment was responsible for recovering airfields previously held by the enemy, and various other tasks in support of tactical air force movements.

Airfield security remained the primary function of the RAF Regiment, with a constant guard placed at points of access and important installations, such as headquarters buildings and ordnance stores. Strict observance of a station's regulations on who should and who should not be allowed to pass was expected of guards even if intimidated by rank – of which there are several known instances. Steadfastness in such a situation certainly paid off for Fred Forsdyke:

'The road between the villages of Watton and Griston was part of the perimeter track of the airfield. The locals had Air Ministry passes so they could use the road unescorted, but anyone else had to be turned away. However, if military people or others we thought important wanted to come through, it was first necessary for the guard to consult with Gun Ops for permission to escort the persons along the road. An army staff car arrived one day, driven by an ATS officer and with a general or someone of very high rank in the back. He demanded to use the road, but the guard wouldn't let him and called me, the corporal in charge. I politely told the officer I'd first have to get permission, but that really upset him and he said he was not going to wait. So I simply told some of my men, who had come out of the hut when they heard the commotion, to man the guns. "Are you threatening me?" the officer barked. "No sir, I'm stopping you," I replied. Well, I got the permission, but as he'd given me so much hassle I set off in front of his car on my motor cycle at my pace – about 15–20mph. Later that day the same officer came past the camp on another road. He sent his aide-de-camp into the guardhouse with a message and 50 cigarettes for the corporal who wouldn't let him pass until the proper authority had been obtained.'

For many, the monotony of guard duty or manning a gun post characterized service in the RAF Regiment, particularly at isolated locations where the likelihood of a hostile approach was remote but could still not be ignored. In such circumstances, senior NCOs looked round for some means of sustaining morale. John Sharman had a novel solution:

'For many of us in the RAF Regiment the biggest problem was boredom. In my case manning a Bofors gun, four hours on and four or eight hours off, day after day. Nowhere was boredom worse than at Sullom Voe in the Shetland Isles. Close to our gun site was a deserted and dilapidated building which had been a small church. I obtained permission to use this as a recreational centre. In off-guard hours we repaired the roof, decorated the interior and constructed a stage and a bar. Beer only was obtained from the NAAFI and, with bread and cakes from local shops, plus eggs from friendly Shetlanders, we had quite a cosy place. One of my chaps painted some excellent nudes on the walls – but quite tasteful. Everything went along well until one day I was approached by the RAF padre on the main base who said, "Sergeant, I hear you've renovated the old kirk. I'd like to have a look round with a view to using it for services." Well, I was taken aback and tried to explain that I did not think the place was suitable as there were some rather revealing murals. The padre, a hearty Scot, persisted and asked to have a look round. He seemed a bit shaken when he saw the nudes. However, I suggested that we could drape the stage curtains over the walls when we had a service. He was delighted. The services were very popular with the men. The padre was a good old boy. "No sermons," he said. "What I like is a bloody good hymn. Something to raise the roof." We told him, "You name them – we'll sing 'em." And so we did.'

Airfield anti-aircraft gun-emplacements had to be manned night and day although more relaxed systems were introduced at many UK stations during the latter half of the war when the danger of air raids had lessened. Manning an open machine-gun or cannon post was not only tedious but frequently exposed gunners to most trying weather conditions. In the circumstance a little excitement was welcomed; sometimes it was not. Fred Forsdyke again:

'A 24-hour watch had to be kept by all gun crews whatever the weather. There was a terrible storm one night while I and another fellow were on duty at the Hispano cannon site near a hangar. It was raining cats and dogs and I had need to relieve myself. Usually we had to go over to a lav by the hangar, but with the heavy downpour I didn't think a little more water would make much difference if I just went outside our sandbagged emplacement. It was an offence not to use a toilet, but no officer was likely to be out on such a foul night. So shouted where I was going to my mate and went out of the entrance and round the blastwall. As I was standing there, out of the corner of my eye I suddenly saw a still figure watching me. If my hair could have stood on end under my steel helmet I'm sure it would have done, such was the scare I had. My first thought was that an officer had caught me out. Then, peering through the gloom, I realized the figure was the poison gas detector, a can device on top of a 5-foot pole. Relieved, I walked back round the blastwall and into the emplacement only to be knocked nearly silly with a blow to my head. It turned out the other fellow didn't hear me shout that I was just popping outside and he thought I was still in the emplacement when in the dark he saw an intruder in the entrance. He grabbed the first hefty thing available – his tin hat – and struck out with it. Not my night!'

RAF SAILORS

From its formation the RAF had need of maritime vessels to use in servicing floatplanes and flying-boats. To the more than a hundred small vessels for this and associated purposes on hand by the late nineteen-thirties were added the designs known as high-speed launches. These were specifically intended for the fast rescue of airmen who parachuted into the sea or whose aircraft had crashed into 'the drink'. Further procurements established the HSLs as a major element in the Air Sea Rescue service that evolved during the early months of hostilities, and eventually came under Coastal Command control. By 1945 the RAF world-wide had more than 900 'boats', of which some 300 were manned for ASR duties. While the remainder were chiefly employed in support of flying-boats, several marine craft were used for specialized purposes such as barrage balloon launch beds and targets for estuary ranges. The success of the Air Sea Rescue launches was significant. More than 6,000 persons had been plucked from the sea around the UK and some 3,000 from the Mediterranean by the end of the war, rescues often conducted in enemy-controlled areas. Most former HSL crewmen can relate tales of the remarkable or unusual from their service experiences. The following from Ted Shute are certainly in these categories:

'During the siege of Malta we were frequently at sea picking up both British and enemy aircrews who had baled out and landed in the drink. One lovely sunny day with a calm sea, we approached a Spitfire pilot who was sitting in his dinghy awaiting our arrival. As we came alongside, one of our deckhands put out a boathook to draw the dinghy alongside. In so doing the boathook punctured the dinghy and the survivor got a ducking. When we got him on board he greeted us with a broadside of non-technical language which made it clear to us that he was not pleased at the soaking we had given him. After a while he calmed down and then we got the explanation for his displeasure at the ducking. Unbeknown to us, some of the pilots on Malta had been putting a coin into a kitty every time they went on a sortie. The kitty was to go to the first pilot who had to bale out in combat and who managed to inflate his dinghy just before ditching so that he could land in it – dry! The pilot we had just picked up had achieved a dry ditching and was looking forward to picking up a useful reward on returning to the airfield. But – we had not taken him aboard dry and so deprived him of quite a useful sum of money.

'While based at Gibraltar I was on High-Speed Rescue Launch 2583 when we were called out to a position midway between Gibraltar and the North African coast and all ships in the area had also been alerted. A Lancaster had taken off from Gibraltar on her way to England and the controls had gone so that she could not attempt to land again and the crew would have to bale out. The aircraft was flying in a wide circle over the Straits of Gibraltar and slowly losing height. We saw a number of parachutes drop on land near Algeciras, but there was still one more man to bale out.

'When the aircraft was down to less than a thousand feet it passed close to us and we could see a man sitting in the aft hatch waving. The next time the aircraft approached us it was obvious that it was on the point of ditching. At that moment the aircrew bod doubled up into a ball and rolled out of the aircraft. He hit the sea and bounced a couple of times and stopped near to a Spanish fishing-boat which picked him up. We arrived alongside within minutes and took him on board. He was somewhat shaken up but apart from that he only appeared to have a broken ankle. Apparently he did not have a parachute and so could not bale out earlier with the rest of his colleagues.'

All Air Sea Rescue crews were close-knit, self-surviving, jealous and proud of their boats. This is very evident in Cecil Featherstone's eulogy of his beloved No. 2551.

'She was one of the "whalebacks", so named because of the resemblance of the superstructure to that mammal. She was very fast, uncomfortable in a rough sea, but so very seaworthy and a great joy to us. We had experienced many trips, good and bad, and twice volunteered to go to sea when the local lifeboat reckoned it was too rough for our boat. Once, when on patrol off the Dutch coast searching for an aircrew down somewhere in a dinghy, the sea was extremely rough and a freak wave broke over us. It cleared the deck of all gear – the Carley Float, life-belts, rubber dinghies, mast aerials, searchlights – and split the superstructure. The boat was filling quickly and temporary measures were taken to try and stop the inrush. Our engines were swamped, but our two engineers worked like beavers in most difficult and very uncomfortable conditions and managed to get them restarted, a heroic effort, and slowly but surely we got back to base. We were sometimes followed back by E-Boats, mainly because we knew the way through the minefields and also because they knew that we were not carrying any armament that would be effective against them. A signal back to base and out would come the MTBs, roaring past us to do battle outside the Scroby Sands. We made many trips, some successful, some not, some in bad weather, some when the sea was glassy calm and the thrill of full speed ahead was so completely exhilarating.

'On our last trip we were some twenty miles off the Dutch coast, late June 1944; clear sky, sea fairly calm and good visibility – too good in some senses. Instructions were radioed to us to proceed to a position to pick up an American aircrew in a dinghy. On plotting this position I made it almost inside Ijmuiden harbour. After consulting with the skipper I asked the wireless operator to call back for a check. It came back exactly the same. I couldn't believe this, so asked again. I was told in no uncertain terms to get on with the job and not to disbelieve their accuracy. So it was tin hats on and in we went. German soldiers could be seen walking along the harbour walls; why they didn't fire is a mystery, but sure enough there was the dinghy with eight Americans. Over went the crash nets and all eight were hauled aboard as quickly as possible; then with the three engines flat out we headed due west. What a sigh of relief! We'd got away with it. There had been some air cover but it would seem they were running short of fuel and left before any replacement arrived. About ten minutes later down came three German aircraft and shot us up, killing three of our chaps and setting the boat on fire. There was nothing for it, we had to take to the sea. Not much was left in the way of rubber dinghies and the Carley Float was damaged. We all had Mae Wests and salvaged what we could to help our survival. The chief engineer had his knee badly shot up but the rest of us were, surprisingly, unharmed. Back came the German fighters and strafed us again but, luckily, no one was hit. We saw a lone bomber returning to England and hoped he'd seen us so that if our Mayday signal hadn't been received someone might know where we were.

'Some hours later we heard the sound of engines and only hoped they were British. They were, and the sight of two of our own HSLs was unbelievable. Sadly, our skipper had died of exhaustion and one of the Americans drowned. HSL 2551 had sunk and we had lost our skipper and three of the crew. Those of us left now knew what it was like to be on the other side of the game. When we got back to England one of the Americans insisted that I have his flying-jacket. It became my most prized souvenir.'

While manning the seaplane servicing vessels rarely incurred the risk of enemy action, manoeuvring these vessels, particularly in rough weather, was exacting work requiring considerable skill if the comparatively fragile aircraft were not to be damaged. There were lighter moments such as that recalled by Cecil Featherstone:

'While ferrying an aircrew out to a Catalina flying-boat at Oban, I witnessed an amusing incident which also illustrated the need to keep cool in all circumstances. The perspex blisters on the sides of the fuselage gave access to the Catalina, but were very vulnerable to damage from any boat coming alongside, most especially the heavy refuellers which were not the easiest of craft to manoeuvre. Such a refuelling tender was approaching the aircraft with a regular and experienced coxswain, but with a new and raw deckhand. The deckhand leaned over the bow of the refueller, boathook in hand, to pick up the mooring buoy of the aircraft in order to drop back alongside and commence refuelling. Not being very adept he leaned too far, missed the buoy and fell overboard. Some seconds later he shot upwards out of the water, boathook erect. The coxswain, still trying to keep the boat from hitting the aircraft, looked over the side and quite quietly said, "Oh come on Neptune; come back on board and do the bloody thing right!" '

Pay-Off

THE WRONG SIDE OF THE DRINK

'God, its cold! Where the hell are the bed-clothes? What clot's pinched them? In reaching down to pull the clothes up my hand just grasped fresh air. The bed seemed much harder than usual and my pillow seemed to have gone as well, but at least the b. . . . . had left me with the sheet I was lying on. Flat on my back I opened my eyes and gradually focused. Above me was the sky, dark but clear, with the stars just a blur. Damn! This was the first time I'd ended up in a ditch. However sloshed, I'd always managed to make it back to the billet before – but then, there always has to be a first time! Everything was so quiet. Not a sound to be heard, not a light in sight. What on earth anyway, was I doing in the middle of a field? And what were these cords doing tangled up with my arms? Groping around I gradually traced the cords which seemed to be attached to the sheet, but were also attached to the harness which was still strapped on. Then realization came. I was lying on a parachute. But how did I get here? How long it took while I gathered my senses together I'll never know. I tried to read my watch but, annoyingly, was unable to focus properly. Gradually, things became clearer. Dropping through the forward escape hatch, seeing the black bulk of the aircraft above me, pulling the rip-cord, then – nothing, till I woke up on the ground. For a while I tried to reconstruct events to convince myself that we had completed our trip and I had baled out over England on our return. But the true facts eventually came to mind. We hadn't reached the target and on our run-in to Dortmund the aircraft wing had caught fire somewhere east of Aachen and I was now the wrong side of the Channel. Action now seemed to be imperative. I must hide the chute and run. But which way? I did not know on which side of the Dutch-German border I had landed, but south-west seemed the most sensible way to go. In one movement I hit the quick-release of the harness, gathered up the parachute, jumped up to run – only to fall flat on my face. I was getting short on oxygen when I had baled out and consequently was concerned to open my parachute in case I blacked-out. We had been at 19,000 feet. Failure then to follow procedure to protect my head had resulted in the heavy clips hitting me as the parachute snapped open, so knocking me out with – if one may pun – two perfect clips to the jaw.

'Being unconscious I must have landed like a sack of potatoes and my legs and back had been jarred. The knock-out had produced concussion as a result of which my vision was blurred and this was to remain so for the next two or three weeks. However, I was alive and perhaps ignorance is bliss, for I was to find out later that I was the only member of the crew to come out without a scratch. Two were killed, one blown out of the aircraft to have a leg amputated, one with a torn thigh, but who was looked after and patched up by a sympathizer; one with a broken ankle and the other with a sprain. It seemed in retrospect that I was lucky to be knocked out.'

The foregoing is No. 76 Squadron navigator Tom Wingham's account of the realization that his Halifax had been shot down and he was in a foreign land. A parachute descent in darkness was fraught with danger as, unable to see where they were going to, many men were injured and some killed. Dick Enfield admits that he was lucky after jumping from a No. 428 (RCAF) Squadron Lancaster:

'We were at about 18,000 feet when I baled out near Bremen. All I could see were fires burning, the searchlights and Flak over the city, but where I floated down it was completely dark. There was quite a strong southerly wind and as I weighed less than 10 stones my descent took about twenty minutes. I could distinguish nothing below and had no idea when or what I was going to hit until "splash" I was underwater. As I was quite unprepared and didn't even have my feet together it was fortunate I had gone into water. I came up under the canopy but as I was a good swimmer I was able to detach myself and swim free. The water was salt so I knew I was in the sea or the estuary of the Weser. There was nothing to see but the fires and searchlights so I kicked off my boots and swam in that direction. After about a half-mile I found myself in saltings. Staggering up banks and falling down into more saltings, I finally decided to wait until light. Taking off my Mae West I lay down and went to sleep. On waking I walked along the shore and finally found a little lane leading inland. Just as I reached a bend in the lane, round the corner came a German policeman on a bike and carrying a fishing-rod. He must have had a shock because I was covered from head to foot in mud and orange sea-marker dye from the tablet attached to the Mae West. But he just rode past and said "Morgen" to which I replied "Morgen" and kept on walking. A few seconds later I heard his bike go down and a voice said "Halt!" Turning round I saw he had a revolver pointed at me so the sensible thing to do was raise my hands. He took me along until we came to a small café on the main road. The people there must have been slightly sorry for this enemy because of the mess I was in. They made me a cup of ersatz coffee and treated me well, until I was collected by Luftwaffe people.'

Arrival in enemy-held territory was preceded by the traumatic experience of escape from a stricken aircraft, a situation not lost on German interrogators who hoped to gain valuable information while captured airmen were still distressed. Stan Brooks of No. 75 (New Zealand) Squadron:

'I was the wireless operator of a Wellington shot down over Froyennes, Belgium, by ack-ack on the night of 20/21 May 1940; the very first of 193 aircraft lost by the squadron during the war, which had the second highest losses in Bomber Command. My parachute had only just opened fully before I hit the ground. Shells were exploding and machine-gun and rifle fire were going on all around and I had no idea whether I was with friend or foe. I crawled to the edge of the field hoping to find a ditch in which to hide till daylight. There didn't appear to be a ditch so I continued crawling along the edge of the field. Suddenly a

brilliant light picked me out and figures ran towards me ordering "Hande Hoch!"
I knew I was very much in enemy territory. After spending the night in a cottage
cellar with German army types, at 8am I was put on the pillion of a BMW motor-
cycle combination, guard in the sidecar, and taken on a hair-raising journey of
about fifteen miles to a farm where two other members of my crew were being
held prisoner. The three of us were then conveyed another twenty miles to a
beautiful château where we were handed over to the Luftwaffe. Here the pilot
officer who had been flying as our rear-gunner was taken up the wide staircase.
After about a half-hour he returned and the Observer was taken up. The PO told
me he had been interrogated by a Flak regiment major and, when my turn came,
to give only name, rank and number. Eventually our Observer returned and I was
taken up the stairs and into a huge room.

'The interrogating officer was seated behind a desk chatting to two young
Luftwaffe pilots. As one had a bandaged leg and the other an arm in a sling, they
were obviously convalescing. Both smiled at me and said, "Good Morning" in
English before moving out to the balcony of the room which overlooked a lake.
The interrogating officer bade me sit down and then pushed a box of 50 Players
towards me. I took one and he lit it with a lighter. Then he commenced to ask me
all sorts of questions to which I would give no answers other than those laid down
by the International Red Cross Geneva Convention. This carried on for twenty
minutes with the major becoming more annoyed and exasperated. I was not
exactly pleased myself. All the time I was aware the two Luftwaffe fliers were
taking a keen interest in the proceedings and from their reactions I was fairly sure
they understood English. Suddenly, in his rage the major opened his desk
drawer, took out a Luger and pointed it at my chest saying, "If I don't get answers
to my questions I will shoot." At this point the two officers hurried in from the
balcony and one pushed the major's revolver arm tight on the desk while they
appeared to admonish him for his action. The major replaced the gun in the
drawer and the two officers returned to the balcony.

'The questioning continued with, "We know you were the pilot of the
Blenheim we shot down last night and we know the airfield you came from in
England." I was a humble AC1 at the time and I then realized that as I had no
flying brevet on my uniform they had assumed I was the pilot. As the Wellington
exploded in the air and only three men of the crew had apparently been captured,
the Germans assumed the aircraft to be a Blenheim. When I was eventually
returned to the others and we had a chance to compare notes I learned their
interrogation had been on similar lines. We hoped the pilots had managed to
escape and the 2nd pilot, who had spent his early years in Belgium, had a good
chance of going underground. Only after the war did I learn that he had been hit
by ground fire while descending by parachute. Our skipper was killed in the
aircraft.'

At a latter stage, most captured aircrew were processed by specially trained
interrogation staff at Oberursel near Frankfurt. Dick Enfield's experience was
not untypical:

'Before being sent to prison camp I went through the interrogation centre at
Oberursel. For about ten days I was kept in solitary and brought out each day or
so for an hour and asked questions. They knew more about the squadron than I

did! When I walked into the interrogation room there was a book laid on a table in front of me with the heading 428 Squadron. The questions ranged over all sorts of subjects, but aware they might try and trick me I stuck to the usual name, rank and number and nothing else. Many of the questions about the squadron I would not have been able to answer anyway. They asked the name of the CO and while I wouldn't have told them I honestly didn't know. They tried vague threats, but chiefly seemed to be trying to wear one down. They used to shut the windows and put the heat on during the day and at night open the windows and shut the heat off. This, and the most atrocious food – black bread and weak soup – must have been all part of the treatment to break your morale. There was no contact with any other Allied airmen, but one day when I was being escorted to the toilet I found the fellow from the next cell was also being taken there. He was a Wing Commander who complained bitterly that somebody in passing had whipped his good shoes – which had to be placed outside the cell each night – and left a battered old pair in their place.'

As the war progressed and Bomber Command wrought destruction in Germany on a devastating scale, so the reception awaiting any member of aircrew who landed in the enemy homeland became more hostile. If taken prisoner by Wehrmacht and Luftwaffe personnel one was usually safe; if civilians were involved there was a grave risk of lynching. John Hart had some anxious moments with a hostile crowd:

'Our No. 156 Squadron Lancaster was hit by Flak during a daylight raid in 1945. The pilot ordered the three of us in the rear to bale out, although subsequently he was able to get the aircraft back to friendly territory. At about 1630 hours on Saturday 24 March 1945 I was a wireless operator in a 156 Squadron Lancaster approaching our target at Harpenerweg when the aircraft received substantial flak damage. The aircraft commenced to burn and the pilot ordered the crew to bale out. The navigator, mid-upper gunner and myself left by the rear door, at a height of about 17,000 feet. My parachute opened shortly after leaving the aircraft. It took an estimated thirteen minutes (at a fall rate of approximately 1,200 feet per minute) to reach the ground. The time seemed interminable. I tried spilling some air out of the chute and rotating the chute, as we had been taught during training. Yet each time I looked down the ground seemed a long way off and I seemed no nearer to it, though I knew I must be getting closer. Suddenly the ground appeared to rush up to meet me. Before I had time to brace myself the parachute swung and I landed on my back uninjured. I was in a grass field near a small town.

'Almost immediately a solitary German soldier arrived from one direction, puffing from shortness of breath as he had clearly run some distance. From other directions a collection of people were arriving. The German soldier, before advancing within ten yards, asked if I had a pistol, when I indicated that I didn't have one, he told me to put up my hands, which I did. He then approached and clouted me around the left ear. He went to repeat the action but I stuck out my left elbow and he seemed to then decide that his personal heroics were over; he was middle-aged while I was a fit 20-year-old. At the time of the German soldier's intervention the mob was continuing to grow. Among the arrivals was one in a black SS uniform who promptly clouted me in the teeth with a pistol barrel, breaking one of my upper front teeth off at the gums, and another off leaving a partial stump. Someone else gave me an almighty clout on the back of the head – I had seen someone arrive with a long-handled four-tine fork, but whether I was hit with this or another object I don't know. With the situation getting uglier by the second I realized I had to act quickly if I was to escape from the mob. I picked up my parachute and started walking towards the built-up area. The mob followed me like a flock of sheep. I had no idea where I was going, but I knew that I was moving away from a very violent atmosphere. Eventually we were going through one of the streets, with me leading everybody, when an official-looking individual arrived on a motor cycle, and the procession led by him proceeded to a local building. There I was shortly joined by my navigator, who had also absorbed a lot of physical violence and we were put into a cell together.'

There were those for whom the greater part of their RAF service was spent behind barbed wire in an enemy prison camp. By the end of hostilities more than 12,000 RAF aircrew were incarcerated in prison camps and several hundred more had been repatriated or died in captivity. Treatment was generally fair although much depended upon the administrators at individual camps. Very basic welfare became bare existence during the closing months of the war when the Germans could no longer find sufficient food to meet the required rations, and transport disruptions delayed Red Cross supplies. Enduring such privation was painful, but as one air-gunner who was confined for four years commented, 'At least I was alive whereas the rest of my crew never made it, I assume.' Morale varied from camp to camp and, understandably, depended much upon the degree of deprivation suffered by the inmates. Generally there was an extraordinary resilience and any opportunity to mock the gaolers was never passed up. 'Goon Baiting' was the term for the kind of action Dick Enfield recalls:

'At Stalag Luft VII the guards in the sentry-boxes were changed at the same time every day. The relief guards always marched up along the other side of the wire singing marching songs. A whole bunch of our people would form up in threes and when the guards arrived they would march along beside them inside the wire singing *Roll Out the Barrel* and other ditties at the top of their voices. Each group tried to out-sing the other although we probably drowned them out because of greater numbers.'

The most publicised PoW camp was Stalag Luft III at Sagan, due to the Gestapo's execution of 50 men who escaped. This dreadful act apart, the Sagan camp was reckoned by many hardened PoWs to be one of the best – until the final months of hostilities. Many famous and highly decorated airmen were incarcerated there, including the first DFC of the war, Wing Commander Stanford Tuck, and Wing Commander Braham, treble DSO, treble DFC. No. 10 Squadron navigator Kevin Murphy was particularly impressed with the high morale at Stalag Luft III, exhibited through the many and varied activities:

'The most astonishing took place in the summer of '44. Of all things, a summer fête was staged on the rugger pitch. It may have had an ulterior motive unknown to me – the "Goons" certainly thought so – but most of us took it as it seemed on the surface. Cigarettes were used as cash for the sideshows which were amazingly good. The sun shone as it probably would not have done at a real English country fête and the day was a howling success. Among the many odd characters in the camp who came into their own on this occasion was a Canadian who claimed to have been a "barker" at fairs in his home province. I teamed up with a group who proposed to engage in an Indian fire walking act. Wearing pyjamas, turbans and similar eastern looking atire, our skins were browned with a mixture of old cocoa and marg'. In full view of the guards a trough was made in the sand and this was filled with newspapers, copies of the Volkiscker Beobachter, which were then set alight. When burning nicely a member of our band, dressed as a fakir, slowly walked one leg through the flames. The guards were obviously astounded by our levity and this apparently supernatural display. Unknown to most kriegie spectators too, was the fact that the fire-proof fakir – a fighter pilot, of course – had an artificial leg of steel and plastic. I presume his covering pyjama trousers had been well soaked with water beforehand.'

Not every airman ended up in a PoW camp. More than 2,000 evaded capture and escaped to neutral countries or were secreted out of occupied Europe by escape organizations. Tom Wingham was one of the fortunate befriended and returned. Like most evaders, he is forever grateful to those who sheltered him and with enduring admiration for their bravery:

'For four months I had been hiding out in the Liège area of Belgium. A standstill order was being operated by the Escape Lines due to the chaos on the French railways caused by pre- and post-invasion bombing. The Resistance had placed me on a small farm with Monsieur Schoofs, a cattle dealer, and his delightful family. I had spent an almost idyllic July and August picking cherries, apples, plums and pears in their orchard. But now life was getting a bit tricky. The farm stood on a crossroads and in September the German Army was retreating, often sleeping and resting around the farm buildings or in the orchard. At 10am one September morning a German officer arrived and announced he was commandeering M. Schoofs' study, that there would be a small advance-party of troops just after lunch, and a large contingent billeted in the barns that night. When M. Schoofs recounted this to me I suggested that perhaps it might be a good idea for me to vacate the premises and go back to my previous safe house. M. Schoofs would have none of this; everything would be okay. Although the average German did not speak French very well, there was a risk one of them might recognize my smattering for what it was. Therefore I was to become a Flemish deaf-mute and if any queries were raised about me by the Germans my presence would be explained. Whatever happened I was to remain dumb.

'Eight of us were sitting down to the midday meal, the Schoofs and their three teenage children, a farmhand, the daily help and myself, when two German trucks drove into the courtyard. The advance-party had arrived early! The family and servants left the table and went to the outer scullery door, leaving me alone sitting at the end of the table with my back to the study door. Not my usual place, but in view of what happened next a most fortuitous change. I could hear the family laying down the law to the troops who had arrived. Then two soldiers appeared outside the living-room window fixing up a telelphone line to the study. I was conscious of their two faces pressed against the glass, the attraction being the plates of hot food on the table. They were almost drooling and I doubt whether they had seen a proper meal for some days. Suddenly they straightened up and started to busy themselves again. I realized why when the next moment the door behind me was opened and hit my chair. Fortunately the chair restricted entry, but did allow for the commandeering officer to poke his head through. He was inquiring about something to do with moving the furniture. I could see his head out of the corner of my eye over my right shoulder.

'My role as deaf-mute was about to be taxed. I decided to add an element of the village idiot to my play and flicked a few peas along the table. The door was pulled back and banged against my chair and the question repeated. I chased a few more peas round my plate and shovelled some food in my mouth. Again, the door crashed against my chair and the question put at a level that brooked no denial. However deaf I was I could not evade the movement of my chair and it seemed that nineteen weeks on the run had been in vain and would probably end with all the family being shot.

'At that point Mme. Schoofs, hearing the shouting, came back into the living-room. She was a fine, bonny and buxom woman who immediately sized up the situation, planted herself firmly in the middle of the room and let fly as possibly only a Belgian woman could. The Belgians, outwardly at least, would never show fear of the Germans and she really had a very wide range of invective about dirty Boche boots in a Belgian housewife's kitchen. He may have commandeered the study, but that gave him no rights in the rest of her house and he could take his blankety blank presence back the other side of the study door. If he had any queries, come round the proper way and ask in a civilized fashion. With that she advanced on the retreating officer, slammed the door and producing a key turned the lock.

'It was a close-run thing and after a quick conference it was decided to keep me out of the way pending arrangements to get me out. I went up to my room and waited. Within a short time my escape had been organized and I was told to be dressed and ready to leave at 2 o'clock. Nobody warned me what to expect other than that someone would collect me at that time. I was called just after 2pm and came down the back stairs into the scullery, dressed in black pin-striped trousers and black coat. My documents indicated that my name was Thomas Denis and I worked at the local coal-mine. All the family were standing in the scullery doorway which went out into the courtyard. The Schoofs girls were giggling and their parents chatting to someone standing just outside. Germans were sitting around in the courtyard, some finishing their rations, all mildly interested in the activity at the house. I was pushed through the door to greet my "wife", who proved to be a gross fat peasant woman of perhaps 35 years. With me looking all my 21 years, a more unlikely couple you never saw. There was yet more to come. A child about two-and-a-half years old was playing near the Germans and as I turned to go her Mama called out: "Now come along, get into the pram or Papa won't push you." The pushchair was put into my hands, the child strapped in and we were ready to go. With my extraordinary "wife" on my arm and pushing "my baby", we started on our way. The family stood laughing and waving us goodbye. Nobody had mentioned any release from my deaf-mute pose, so as we went past a group of soldiers I was looking over my shoulder "oo-ing" and grunting in response to the many adieus. What an exit!'

Many of the prison camps for Allied airmen were in the eastern part of the Nazi empire. When the Soviet forces advanced towards Berlin, the inmates of the camps were moved west in an attempt to prevent their liberation by the Russians. In a few instances this movement brought tragedy. Stan Brooks:

'In April 1945 a column of 2,000 PoWs was marched west from Fallingbostel when the Russians were nearing our camp. At the village school in Gresse we picked up food parcels in a distribution organized by the Swedish Red Cross. We had just settled down in a country lane to partake of our first decent meal for twelve days when six aircraft appeared in the distance. Shouts along the column warned us to keep a sharp eye on them; not too soon, for the aircraft wheeled into line astern and dived towards us. At low level they opened up with machine-guns and cannon and swept the length of we helpless PoWs. Hundreds of us jumped the hedge and ran to find cover in the fields as the aircraft, Typhoons, came in for a second attack. The leader, seeing we had scattered must have ordered the line abreast pass that followed. After this third attack I again picked myself up and started running and was then aware of pain in my left arm and upper leg. I noticed some brave RAF types standing up wearing inside-out greatcoats, the white linings hopefully signalling that we were not a marching Wehrmacht column. Perhaps this did the trick for the Typhoons broke off their fourth dive and pulled away. Confusion reigned with dead and injured scattered about. Thirty PoWs had been killed and more than sixty wounded, half seriously. Eight German guards had also been killed and several wounded. The attack took place at 10.30am and it was a couple of hours before the local population organized farm carts and transported the casualties to a cottage hospital at Boizemburg, a couple of miles away. Here I was operated on that evening for the removal of shrapnel by two German Army doctors. These two worked non-stop for several hours and the rest of the staff did a wonderful job for us.

'After surviving the British army artillery bombardment prior to their crossing the Elbe, we were liberated by a patrol from the 6th Airborne Division and eventually transported to an airfield near Luneburg Heath for an air ambulance flight to the UK. While lying on our stretchers on the tarmac, a Wing Commander with a Canadian shoulder-flash walked among us and asked how we ex-PoWs had been injured. An army type informed him in no uncertain terms of the shoot-up and the casualties which occurred. Tears immediately welled up in his eyes as he quickly walked away. He told us he had been the flight leader of the six Typhoons.'

VE-DAY AND DEMOB

On 8 May 1945 the war in Europe was officially over; Victory in Europe – VE-Day – was the tag for this occasion. Much of the war in the air had finished days and weeks before as objectives were realized. Now the ordinary chap who wore air force blue seriously began to think about 'civvy street'. But first a celebration, and knowing just how effectively aircrew could celebrate some cautioning words were voiced by wary commanders to their units. As usual, cautions had little effect; this was a very special celebration. Albert Benest of No. 75 (New Zealand) Squadron:

'On the eve of VE-Day our squadron commander called all the officers together and said something like: "Now chaps, I don't want any funny business when peace is declared. There is no need to go mad. I'm relying on you all to set a good example to the other ranks. I'm expecting your best behaviour." Well, when the end came an enormous celebration party was arranged. And who broke his leg jumping over a fire? Why, our squadron commander.'

Many wartime recruits enjoyed service life and considered making it a permanent career. Those men who wanted to go back to civilian life could not get out fast enough. However, demobilization was to be a slow process. Hugh Fisher:

'When it came to being demobbed the release date was based on an age and service group number. If you had plenty of age and years of service you had a very low number. Only wartime service counted and as I had the full six years and had been aircrew, my number was fairly low – 24. Aircrew release group numbers came up quicker than those for ground duty people. When I came out in November 1945 they were still only up to group 7 for ground staff on my station.'

Former prisoners-of-war expected preferential consideration for release in view of their unpleasant confinement, but they did not always get it. Dick Enfield:

'After liberation from PoW camp I was sent home on leave and then received orders to report to Wittering where I expected I would soon be demobbed. Instead I was told I had to undergo a Rehabilitation Course to turn us from obstructionists into complying with discipline again! There would be no demob until my age and service group number came up – in my case two years later.'

When the day finally arrived, releasees were transported to demobilization centres for 'processing'. Eddie Wheeler was in a group sent to London:

'The big hall at Olympia was a hive of activity. We received our gratuity, £75 in my case, and we proceeded to the civilian clothing hall. Scenes of hysterical laughter as suits, sports jackets, raincoats and hats of varying descriptions were tried on. After six years of nothing but service uniforms, to see all these chaps in pork-pie hats, pin-stripe suits, etc., we just could not contain ourselves but finally the NCOs in charge pushed us out to make way for the constantly arriving buses loaded with "demobs". Outside, the "spivs" were waiting to offer £25 for the complete outfits. Many "demobs" were content to accept the £25 whereupon they headed for the nearest public house with their friends and probably were flat broke by the time they reached home.'

Young men relieved from the tedium and danger of war were generally not given to assessing their RAF service in 1945, being too busy making their way through the drab period of scarcities and restrictions that characterized those immediate post-war years. Only later were they given to reflection. Whether or not the views expressed a near half-century on are true of 1945 is not easily gauged. Those questioned insist the assessment unchanged, but admit that, as so often is the case, it is all much rosier with hindsight. Don Nunn:

'If I'm completely honest my RAF service was the best thing that ever happened to me. It gave a profound sense of something worthwhile. There was never a great deal of fear; I never really dwelt on the risks involved. We were all lads together having fun and at times doing foolish things; perhaps our youth cushioned us against the real nature of the dangers faced.'

List of Contributors

Alan Ackerman
George Aldridge
Muriel Anderson (Kenworthy)
D. Arthur
G. Anthony
Leonard J. Barcham, DFC
Denis Baxter
Albert G. Benest
Hugh F. Berry
James Betteridge
Maureen D. Brickett (Bowers)
Stanley Brooks
Kenneth Brotherhood
Frederick Brown
G. Roy Browne
Kenneth Campbell
Peter Catchpole
Steve Challen
E. Frank Cheesman
Frank Clarke
Cyril H. Clifford
William V. Coote
H. H. (Sid) Cottee
Rex Croger
Peter Culley
William Dickinson
James A. Donson
James C. Double
Kenneth Doughty
Alan Drake
William G. Drinkell
Bernard Dye
H. Ernest Edwards
James Eley
Arthur H. Elks
Roy Ellis-Brown

Vincent Elmer
Richard G. Enfield
John Everett
L. C. (Pop) Ewins
Reginald J. Fayers
Cecil Featherstone
Hugh Fisher
William Fleming
Frank (Fred) Forsdyke
Ian F. Glover, AFC
James Goodson
Ralph H. Harrington, DFC
John R. Hart
Gerald D. Hatt
Alan Haworth, DFC and Bar
Albert W. Heald
John Heap
Peter J. Hearne
Gerhard Heilig
Albert Herbert
J. Morgan Hewinson
Victor Holloway
Ray Howlett
Thomas Imrie
George S. Irving
William C. Japp
Desmond Jenkins
Alfred Jenner
Raymond A. E. Jones
James Kernahan
Harold Kidney
Philip Knowles
Roy Larkins
Peter Lee
Elsie Lewis
Ronald W. Liversage, MBE

Ray Lomas
G. T. Hamish Mahaddie, DSO, DFC, AFC
Martin Mason
Tom Minta
Ivan Mulley
Antoni (Tony) Murkowski
Kevin Murphy
Eric Myring, D.F.C.
Horace Nears
Donald T. Nunn
Arthur (Mick) Osborne
John Osborne
Leonard Owens
Frederick W. Pawsey, DFC
John Peak
Leon Piechocki
Joseph Pugh
Alfred Pyner
F. H. (Harry) Quick
D. A. Reid
J. A. M. (Tony) Reid, DFM
William Reid, VC
Harry Robinson
John C. Sampson, DFC
John Sharman
C. E. (Ted) Scott

F. E. (Ted) Shute
Eva Sizzey
George Smith
Graham J. Smith
Harold Southgate, DFC and Bar
A. (Tony) Spooner, DSO, DFC*
Alan Staines
Irene Storer (Forsdyke)
John Studd
Harold I. Sutton
James F. Swale
Louise Tetley (Howell)
Robert Thompson
Ernest Thorpe
Stanley Tomlinson
Hilary Upward
Stanley Ward
Derek Waterman, DFC
George Watts
Edwin Wheeler, DFC
Vernon Wilkes
Roy Wilkinson
S. (Tom) Wingham
F. A. (Mick) Wood
John B. Wray, DFC.

*A. (Tony) Spooner is the author of *Warburton's War*, the biography of Wing Commander Adrian Warburton, the legendary photographic reconnaisance pilot.

Index